THE GHOST HUNTER

Hans Holzer

FALL RIVER PRESS

New York

FALL RIVER PRESS

New York

An Imprint of Sterling Publishing
387 Park Avenue South
New York, NY 10016

FALL RIVER PRESS and the distinctive Fall River Press logo are registered
trademarks of Barnes & Noble, Inc.

Jacket design by Jo Obarowski

ISBN 978-1-4351-5102-4

For information about custom editions, special sales, and premium and
corporate purchases, please contact Sterling Special Sales at 800-805-5489
or specialsales@sterlingpublishing.com.

Manufactured in the United States of America

2 4 6 8 10 9 7 5 3 1

www.sterlingpublishing.com

Contents

The Original
Ghost Hunter

MY FATHER, THE LATE AND great professor and prolific author Dr. Hans Holzer, spent most of his life studying the paranormal. His life's casework was collected in dozens of books that have been read by hundreds of thousands of people. Today, my father's writing appeals to a broad range of people who seek out the inhabitants of a world beyond this one. Although many people will most likely remember him from his books about the Amityville haunting and his work on the groundbreaking TV show *In Search Of...*, it was *The Ghost Hunter*, published 50 years ago, that changed Hans's life forever.

Hans grew up in Vienna, Austria. As a little boy, he loved listening to his uncle Henry's tales about fairies, telling ghost stories, and thinking about the enigmas of existence. School became a place to discover who would be intrigued by his stories and who wouldn't. One teacher was disturbed enough by one of his tales to write a note home to his father, who initially scolded the precocious young Hans, but later laughed it off as he knew his son all too well. Little did Hans know that he would eventually come face to face with many of those same occult mysteries that fascinated him in his youth.

In 1938, Hans and his parents left Austria for America. His father, Leonard, ran a tailor shop in Manhattan. Hans's brother Kurt took after their father in business, but Hans's interest in ghosts and witches did not seem as promising a career path. After just a few months of working alongside his father in the shop, Hans left and started working as a journalist, honing his writing and interviewing skills for publications as varied as the *New York Times*, the *New Yorker*, and *Exploring the Unknown*. That was when his supernatural adventure began.

After a swank cocktail party in Manhattan one night, Hans ran into some women who spoke about being psychic. This intrigued him enough to start looking into strange phenomena, which did not appear to have rational explanation. Shortly thereafter, he started his investigations, enlisting the help of academics and photographers to test assertions made by people who claimed to have psychic abilities. Although he would later come to be famously identified with the supernatural, Hans was a skeptic, first and foremost. People from all walks of life started gravitating to his home to hear about his investigations and maybe even get a tarot reading.

Word spread around New York that an intriguing young writer was lurking about the city asking questions of anybody he could find who had had a ghostly encounter. Soon after, Hans was discovered by Manhattan's famed Irish medium, Eileen Garrett. He later contributed a remembrance to her autobiography, *Adventures in the Supernormal*, about how they met during a time when he was exploring other professional paths besides the paranormal:

> Eileen was always "right on" and did not mince words when it came to the quality of work she considered proper by working trance mediums, or, for that matter working researchers. Just as I was about to try my luck with a Broadway musical, she summoned me and told me I was to investigate haunted houses in the eastern United States, and turn in a report about them. One simply could not say no to

Eileen: so I did not, and went ahead and for two years investigated ghosts. When I wanted to return to my Broadway musical, she told me I was to write a book. Again, I could not refuse. The book, *The Ghost Hunter*, went to eleven printings, and changed my life forever...

In *The Ghost Hunter*, my father bridged a gap between science and mysticism by pioneering the Holzer Method, in which scientific fact and observation are used to study paranormal phenomena, instead of less rigorously applied psychic and metaphysical methods.

The book was notable at the time due to the fact that Hans talked about different ways of looking at life and death and opening one's self up to the possibility that there are more ways to "see" than with just the eyes. By talking about ghosts and apparitions in such a conversational, relatable manner, *The Ghost Hunter* also helped people around the world to start having conversations and exchanging stories about what they thought about the afterlife. Although Hans had thought that he might be a Broadway composer (and actually did compose music Off-Broadway), after the success of *The Ghost Hunter* he never went back to his musical passion. The dead were in demand. The Ghost Hunter was born.

To many peers, colleagues, admirers, and fans, this book remains their bible. Many books— not to mention TV and radio shows—have followed the trail my father bravely blazed in 1963 with *The Ghost Hunter*. But very few of those who have come after him have managed to create as pioneering, insightful, and iconic a work as this classic account of communicating with the otherworldly.

Hans Holzer left behind a strong body of work that vividly illustrates that there is something greater than us at play in this universe. Because of this pioneering research, he remains today the true father of the paranormal.

—Alexandra Holzer, 2013

Ghosts, Anyone?

AS A PROFESSIONAL GHOST HUNTER, I am forever on the lookout for likely prospects. There is no dearth of haunted houses. There is, however, a king-sized amount of shyness among witnesses to ghostly phenomena which keeps me from getting what I am after. Occasionally, this shyness prevents me from investigating a promising case.

There was a man on Long Island who was appalled at the idea of my bringing a medium to his house. Even though he did not question my integrity as a psychic investigator, he decided to discuss the matter with his bishop. Mediums and such are the work of the Devil, the cleric sternly advised the owner of the haunted house, and permission for my visit was withdrawn.

Although the "poltergeist" case of Seaford, Long Island, had been in all the papers, and even on national television, the idea of a volunteer medium trying to help solve the mystery proved too much for this owner of the house.

Then, there was the minister who carefully assured me that there couldn't be anything to the rumors I'd heard about footsteps and noises when there wasn't anyone there. What he meant, of course, was that he *preferred* it that way. Still, that was one more potential case I lost before even getting to first base. Don't get me wrong— these people understand who I am; they may respect my scientific credentials; and they know their anonymity will be carefully guarded. They know I'm not a crackpot or an amateur—amusing himself with something he does not understand. In fact, they're very much interested to hear all about these things, provided it happened in *someone else's* house.

I am a professional investigator of ghosts, haunted houses, and other "spontaneous" phenomena, to use the scientific term—that is, anything of a supernormal nature, not fully explained by orthodox happenings, and thus falling into the realm of parapsychology or psychic research.

I wasn't born a ghost hunter. I grew up to be one, from very early beginnings, though. At the age of three, in my native Vienna, my *Kindergarten* teacher threatened me with expulsion from the class for telling ghost stories to my wide-eyed classmates. These, however, were the non-evidential kind of stories I had made out of whole cloth. Still, it showed I was hot on the subject, even then!

Even in Vienna, ghost-story telling is not considered a gainful profession, so my schooling prepared me for the more orthodox profession of being a writer. I managed to major in history and archeology, knowledge I found extremely helpful in my later research work, for it taught me the methods of painstaking corroboration and gave me a kind of bloodhound approach in the search for facts. The fact that I was born under the truth-seeking sign of Aquarius made all this into a way of life for me.

I am the Austrian-born son of a "returnee" from New York; thus I grew up with an early expectation of returning to New York as soon as I was old enough to do so. Meanwhile, I lived like any other child of good family background, alternately sheltered and encouraged to express myself.

I had barely escaped from *Kindergarten* when my thoughtful parents enrolled me in a public school one year ahead of my time. It took hundreds of dollars and a special *ukase* by the Minister of

Education to get me in at that early age of five, but it was well worth it to my suffering parents.

I had hardly warmed the benches of my first-grade class when I started to build radio sets, which in those days were crystal powered. For the moment, at least, ghosts were not in evidence. But the gentle security into which I had lulled my elders was of brief duration. I had hardly turned nine when I started to write poems, dramas (all of four pages)—and, you're right—ghost stories. Only now they had more terror in them, since I had absorbed a certain amount of mayhem, thanks to the educational motion pictures we were treated to in those days and certain literary sources known as Zane Grey and Karl May.

My quaint writings earned me the reputation of being "special," without giving me any compensation of fame or fortune.

Gradually, girls began to enter my world. This fact did not shatter my imaginative faculties. It simply helped populate my ghost stories with more alluring female ghosts.

I was now about thirteen or fourteen, and I frequently visited my Uncle Henry in his native city of Bruenn. My Uncle Henry was as "special" as was I, except that his career as a businessman had restricted his unusual interests to occasional long talks and experiments. In his antique-filled room in my grandparents' house, we held weird rites which we called the "raising of the spirits," and which, for all we knew, might have raised a spirit or two. We never waited around long enough to find out, but turned the lights back on when it got too murky. Needless to say, we also indulged in candle rites and readings from my uncle's substantial collection of occult books.

I didn't think my uncle ever believed in the occult, but many years later, just before his passing, he did confess to me that he had no doubts about the reality of "the other world" and spirit communication. If I am to believe several professional and nonprofessional mediums who have since brought me messages from him, he is now in a position of proving this reality to himself, and to me.

When I was fifteen, I had become a collector of antiques and coins and was also an ardent bibliophile. One day, while digging through the stacks at a bookseller's, I came across an early account of the scientific approach to the occult, called *Occultism in This Modern Age*. It was the work of Dr. T. K. Oesterreich, a professor at the University of Tübingen in Germany. This 1928 book started me off on a serious approach to ghosts.

At first, it was idle curiosity mixed with a show-me kind of skepticism. I read other books, journals, and learned bulletins. But I didn't attend any seances or have any actual contact with the subject while a teen-ager. My training at this point veered toward the newspaper-writing profession.

I took a course in practical journalism, and started selling articles to local papers. The reportorial training added the "interview in depth" approach to my later investigations. All this time, we had dreamed of coming back to New York, of which my father had fond memories. But it wasn't until I had turned eighteen that I set foot on American soil. My first job had nothing to do with occultism, and it paid only fifteen dollars weekly in a day when that was just enough to live on uncomfortably. Falling back on my knowledge of antiquities and coins, I became an expert cataloguer and writer for one of the big importers of such things.

After a few years, I quit my job—I was then associate editor of a scientific magazine dealing with coins and antiquities—and became a free-lance writer. My old interest in the occult revived; the flame had never died but had been dormant, and now it burst forth again. More books, more lectures, more seeking out the unorthodox, the tantalizingly unsolved.

A few years after that, I was sent to Europe as an accredited foreign correspondent, with the assignment of writing articles on cultural activities, the theater, and other human interest stories. I had begun to write plays and compose music myself, a skill which I later used professionally in the New York theater. On this trip, which led me from the heel of the boot of Italy to the northern part of Sweden, I realized that much psychic research activity was going on in the countries I visited. However, the brevity of my stay in each place precluded any close contact with these bodies.

The following year I returned to Europe, again as a foreign correspondent. In this capacity, I covered the theater in London and other major cities of Europe. One evening, I was invited backstage at the Hippodrome Theatre in London, where comedian Michael Bentine was then appearing as one of the stars. Mr. Bentine offered me a homegrown tomato instead of a drink: he immediately ingratiated himself to me since I am a vegetarian. It also developed that Michael and I had birthdays on the same day, though a few years apart. A friendship grew quickly between us, especially when we discovered our common interest in the occult.

I remember Michael and I had a luncheon date in one of London's Spanish restaurants. Luncheon was served at twelve noon, conversation started at one, and at five o'clock the owner gently tip-toed over to us and whispered, "Dinner is being prepared"! When I returned home that night, I began working on a proposal for a television series based on actual hauntings.

Back in New York, I was led to a study group composed of earnest young people from various walks of life, who met regularly in the rooms belonging to the Edgar Cayce Foundation in New York. Their purpose was simply the quest for truth in the vast realm of extrasensory perception. From then on, I devoted more and more time and energies to this field.

One of the greatest of all living mediums and, at the same time, psychic researchers was Eileen Garrett, who was later president of the Parapsychology Foundation of New York, a world-wide organization that encourages and supports truly scientific investigations and studies in the realm of extrasensory perception. The Foundation also publishes magazines, and has helped the publication of important books on psychic subjects.

I had met Mrs. Garrett briefly years before without realizing that she was the same person whose psychic reputation had long awed me. The contact with her became stronger after my return from Europe, when I discussed my work and ideas on psychic research with her.

Eileen Garrett had no patience with guesswork or make-believe. She taught me to be cautious and painstaking, so that the results of my research would not be open to question. My friendship with Eileen Garrett helped me a great deal. Since she was both a great medium and researcher, I adopted her severe approach. I neither believed nor disbelieved; I looked only for facts, no matter what the implications.

At the Edgar Cayce Foundation on 16th Street and elsewhere, I also met the handful of nonprofessional mediums who helped me so much in my investigations. My method frequently calls for the presence of a sensitive person to pick up clairvoyantly, or through trance, tangible material about a haunted house, that could then later be examined for veracity. I don't hold with the ghost hunter who spends a night alone in a haunted house, and then has nothing more to show for his bravery than a stiff back.

To me, the purpose of investigation is twofold: one, to establish the observed facts of the phenomena, and two, to make contact with the alleged ghost. The chances of seeing an apparition, if you're not sensitive yourself, are nil, and I don't like to waste time.

"Ghosts" are people, or part of people, anyway, and thus governed by emotional stimuli; they do not perform like trained circus animals, just to please a group of skeptics or sensation seekers. Then too, one should remember that an apparition is really a re-enactment of an earlier emotional experience, and rather a personal matter. A sympathetic visitor would encourage it; a hostile onlooker inhibit it.

Sometimes an "ordinary" person does manage to see or hear a ghost in an allegedly haunted location, be it a building or open space. Such a person is of course sensitive or mediumistic, without knowing it, and this is less unusual than one might think.

Even though I am an artistic, and therefore sensitive, person, I do not profess to mediumship, and certainly would not be satisfied with the meager impressions I might gather myself, psychically. A more advanced psychic talent is very necessary to get results. So, I take my "sensitive" with me. If I also see or hear some unearthly things, well and good—that's a bonus. But I don't like unfinished cases. And rarely indeed have I come home empty-handed when I set out in the company of a good medium.

Are good mediums hard to find? They are! That is why I spent a considerable portion of my efforts in this field in search for good new mediums. These are people with the extrasensory gift, whose interest is scientific, not financial. Natural talents in this field, just as in any other, can be trained. There are strict methods and conditions, and when you work in a field that is still on the fringes of recognized science, the more stringent your conditions are, the better.

Today, my methods are well thought out. When I hear of a likely case or prospect, I call the owners or tenants of the building, or if an open area, the nearest neighbor or potential witness, and introduce myself. I get as much information as I can on witnesses and type of phenomena observed, then call the witnesses and interview them. Only after this preliminary work has been done do I call in one of my sensitive-collaborators. I tell them only that a case has come up, and when I will need them.

I discuss everything *but the case* with them on our way to the location, and when we get there, the hosts have been informed not to volunteer any information, either.

A good medium like Mrs. Ethel Meyers will immediately get "impressions" upon arriving, and sometimes even on the way toward our goal. A little later, she will lapse into a trance, and in this condition, the alleged ghost can operate her vocal cords, and speak to me directly.

Sometimes there is another sitter present, and sometimes not. I take notes or use a tape recorder, or both. And sometimes, too, there is an infrared camera present, just in case.

After the trance is over, the medium awakens without remembering anything that has just come through her mouth or vocal cords while under the control of an alleged ghost. Sometimes, though not often, the medium recalls all or part of the information thus received because the trance had been light. This does not mean the medium is faking, or that the material obtained is less reliable; it only means that the medium's trance faculties are not in full operating condition, and perhaps hypnosis is in order to get her "down deeper" into the unconscious condition. Generally speaking, the medium remembers nothing of what went on during her trance state.

Now I allow the hosts and other sitters to discuss the case freely and comment upon what they have just heard or witnessed. Often enough, corroboration takes place right then and there, but more often I have to dig it up in the public library, special libraries, or other sources to which I have access. The research always takes place after the investigation is closed. The Sensitive is never kept abreast of the progress of the corroboration until the case is ready for publication or filing.

There is always drama, and sometimes comedy, involved. Ghosts are people, haunted by unhappy memories, and incapable of escaping by themselves from the vicious net of emotional entanglements. It's not a good idea for a ghost hunter to be afraid of *anything*, because fear attracts undesirables even among the Unseen.

An authoritative and positive position is quite essential with both medium and ghost. Sometimes, these "entities" or visitors in temporary control of the medium's speech mechanism like their newly found voice so much, they don't want to leave. That's when the firm orders of the Investigator alone send them out of the medium's body.

There are dangers involved in this work, but only for the *amateur*. For a good psychic researcher does know how to rid the medium of unwanted entities. If all this sounds like a medieval text to you, hold your judgment. You may not have seen a "visitor" take over a Sensitive's body, and "operate" it the way you might operate a car! But I have, and other researchers have, and when the memories are those of the alleged ghost, and certainly not those of the medium, then you can't dismiss such things as fantastic!

Too much disbelieving is just as unscientific as too much believing. Even though the lady in T. S. Eliot's *Confidential Clerk* says blandly, "I don't believe in facts," I do. Facts—come to think of it—are the only things I really *do* believe in.

The Bank Street Ghost

ONE MORNING, MANY YEARS AGO, I picked up a copy of *The New York Times,* that most unghostly of all newspapers, and was reading Meyer Berger's column, "About New York." That column wasn't about houses or people this particular day. It was about ghosts.

Specifically, Mr. Berger gave a vivid description of a house at 11 Bank Street, in Greenwich Village, where a "rather friendly" ghost had apparently settled to share the appointments with the flesh-and-blood occupants. The latter were Dr. Harvey Slatin, an engineer, and his wife, Yeffe Kimball, who was of Osage Indian descent and well known as a painter.

The house in which they lived was then 125 years old, made of red brick, and still in excellent condition. Digging into the past of their home, the Slatins established that a Mrs. Maccario had run the house as a nineteen-room boarding establishment for years before selling it to them. However, Mrs. Maccario wasn't of much help when questioned. She knew nothing of her predecessors.

After the Slatins had acquired the house, and the other tenants had finally left, they did the house over. The downstairs became one long living room, extending from front to back, and adorned by a fireplace and a number of good paintings and ceramics. In the back part of this room, the Slatins placed a heavy wooden table.

The rear door led to a small garden, and a narrow staircase led to the second floor.

The Slatins were essentially "uptown" people, far removed from any Bohemian notions or connotations. What attracted them about Greenwich Village was essentially its quiet charm and artistic environment. They gathered around them friends of similar inclinations, and many an evening was spent "just sitting around," enjoying the tranquil mood of the house.

During these quiet moments, they often thought they heard a woman's footsteps on the staircase, sometimes crossing the upper floors, sometimes a sound like a light hammering. Strangely enough, the sounds were heard more often in the daytime than at night, a habit most unbecoming a traditional haunt. The Slatins were never frightened by this. They simply went to investigate what might have caused the noises, but never found any visible evidence. There was no "rational" explanation for them, either. One Sunday in January, they decided to clock the noises, and found that the ghostly goings-on lasted all day; during these hours, they would run upstairs to trap the trespasser—only to find empty rooms and corridors. Calling out to the Unseen brought no reply, either. An English carpenter by the name of Arthur Brodie was as well adjusted to reality as are the Slatins, but he also heard the footsteps. His explanation that "one hears all sorts of noises in old houses" did not help matters any. Sadie, the maid, heard the noises too, and after an initial period of panic, got accustomed to them as if they were part of the house's routine—which indeed they were!

On a chilly morning in February, Arthur Brodie was working in a room on the top floor, hammering away at the ceiling. He was standing on a stepladder that allowed him to just about touch the ceiling. Suddenly, plaster and dust showered down on his head, and something heavy fell and hit the floor below. Mrs. Slatin in her first-floor bedroom heard the thump. Before she could investigate the source of the loud noise, there was Brodie at her door, saying: "It's me, Ma'am, Brodie. I'm leaving the job! I've found the body!" But he was being facetious. What he actually found was a black-painted metal container about twice the size of a coffee can. On it there was a partially faded label, reading: "*The last remains of Elizabeth Bullock, deceased. Cremated January 21, 1931.*" The label also bore the imprint of the United States Crematory Company, Ltd., Middle Village, Borough of Queens, New York, and stamped on the top of the can was the number—37251.

Mrs. Slatin, whose Native American forebears made her accept the supernatural without undue alarm or even amazement, quietly took the find, and called her husband at his office. Together with Brodie, Dr. Slatin searched the hole in the ceiling, but found only dusty rafters.

Curiously, the ceiling that had hidden the container dated back at least to 1880, which was long before Elizabeth Bullock had died. One day, the frail woman crossed Hudson Street, a few blocks from the Slatin residence. A motorist going at full speed saw her too late, and she was run over. Helpful hands carried her to a nearby drugstore, while other by-standers called for an ambulance. But help arrived too late for Mrs. Bullock. She died at the drugstore before any medical help arrived. But strangely enough, when Dr. Slatin looked through the records, he found that Mrs. Bullock had never lived at 11 Bank Street at all!

Still, Mrs. Bullock's ashes were found in that house. How to explain that? In the crematory's books, her home address was listed at 113 Perry Street. Dr. Slatin tried to call on Charles Dominick, the undertaker in the case. His place of business had been on West 11th Street, not far from Bank Street. Unfortunately, Mr. Dominick had since died.

The Slatins then tried to locate the woman's relatives, if any. The trail led nowhere. It was as if the ghost of the deceased wanted to protect her secret. When the search seemed hopeless, the Slatins put the container with Mrs. Bullock's ashes on the piano in the large living room, feeling somehow that Mrs. Bullock's ghost might prefer that place of honor to being cooped up in the attic. They got so used to it that even Sadie, the maid, saw nothing extraordinary in dusting it right along with the rest of the furniture and bric-a-brac.

Still, the Slatins hoped that someone would claim the ashes sooner or later. Meanwhile, they considered themselves the custodians of Mrs. Bullock's last remains. And apparently they had done right by Elizabeth, for the footsteps and disturbing noises stopped abruptly when the can was found and placed on the piano in the living room.

One more strange touch was told by Yeffe Kimball to Meyer Berger. It seems that several weeks before the ashes of Mrs. Bullock were discovered, someone rang the doorbell and inquired about rooms. Mrs. Slatin recalls that it was a well-dressed young man, and that she told him they would not be ready for some time, but that she would take his name in order to notify him when they were. The young man left a card, and Mrs. Slatin still recalls vividly the name on it. It was E. C. Bullock. Incidentally, the young man never did return.

It seems odd that Mrs. Slatin was not more nonplussed by the strange coincidence of the Bullock name on the container and card, but, as I have already stated, Mrs. Slatin is quite familiar with the incursions from the Nether World that are far more common than most of us would like to think. To her, it seemed something odd, yes, but also something that no doubt would "work itself out." She was neither disturbed nor elated over the continued presence in her living room of Mrs. Bullock's ashes. Mrs. Slatin is gifted with psychic talents, and therefore not afraid of the Invisible. She takes the Unseen visitors as casually as the flesh-and-blood ones, and that is perhaps the natural way to look at it, after all.

Greenwich Village has so many haunted or allegedly haunted houses that a case like the Slatins' does not necessarily attract too much attention from the local people. Until Meyer Berger's interview appeared in the *Times,* not many people outside of the Slatins' immediate circle of friends knew about the situation.

Mr. Berger, who was an expert on Manhattan folklore, knew the Slatins, and also knew about ghosts. He approached the subject sympathetically, and the Slatins were pleased. They had settled down to living comfortably in their ghost house, and since the noises had stopped, they gave the matter no further thought.

I came across the story in the *New York Times,* and immediately decided to follow up on it. I didn't know whether my friend and medium, Mrs. Ethel Meyers, also read the article; it is possible that she did. At any rate, I told her nothing more than that a haunted house existed in the Village and she agreed to come with me to investigate it. I then called the Slatins and, after some delay, managed to arrange for a seance to take place on July 17th at 9:30 P.M. Present were two friends of the Slatins, Mr. and Mrs. Anderson, Meyer Berger, the Slatins, Mrs. Meyers, and myself.

Immediately upon entering the house and sitting down at the table, around which we had grouped ourselves, Mrs. Meyers went into trance. Just as she "went under" and was still in that borderline condition where clairvoyance touches true trance, she described the presence of a little woman who walked slowly, being paralyzed on one side, and had a heart condition. "She's Betty," Mrs. Meyers murmured, as she "went under." Now the personality of "Betty" started to use the vocal apparatus of the medium.

Our medium continued in her trance state: "He didn't want me in the family plot—my brother—I wasn't even married in their eyes. . . . But I was married before God . . . Edward Bullock. . . . I want a Christian burial in the shades of the Cross—any place where the cross is—*but not with them!*" This was said with so much hatred and emotion that I tried to persuade the departed Betty to desist, or at least to explain her reasons for not wishing to join her family in the cemetery.

"I didn't marry in the faith," she said, and mentioned that her brother was Eddie, that they came from Pleasantville, New York, and that her mother's maiden name was Elizabeth McCuller. "I'm at rest now," she added in a quieter mood.

How did her ashes come to be found in the attic of a house that she never even lived in?

"I went with Eddie," Betty replied. "There was a family fight . . . my husband went with Eddie . . . steal the ashes . . . pay for no burial . . . he came back and took them from Eddie . . . hide ashes . . . Charles knew it . . . made a roof over the house . . . ashes came through the roof . . . so Eddie can't find them . . ."

I asked, were there any children?

"Eddie and Gracie. Gracie died as a baby, and Eddie now lives in California. Charlie protects me!" she added, referring to her husband.

At this point I asked the departed what was the point of staying on in this house now? Why not go on into the Great World Beyond, where she belonged? But evidently the ghost didn't feel that way at all! "I want a cross over my head . . . have two lives to live now . . . and I like being with you!" she said, bowing toward Mrs. Slatin. Mrs. Slatin smiled. She didn't mind in the least having a ghost as a boarder. "What about burial in your family plot?" That would seem the best, I suggested. The ghost became vehement.

"Ma never forgave me. I can never go with her and rest. I don't care much. When she's forgiven me, maybe it'll be all right . . . only where there's a green tree cross—and where there's no more fighting over the bones . . . I want only to be set free, and there should be peace. . . . I never had anything to do with them. . . . Just because I loved a man out of the faith, and so they took my bones and fought over them, and then they put them up in this place, and let them

smoulder up there, so nobody could touch them . . . foolish me!
When they're mixed up with the Papal State. . . ."

Did her husband hide the ashes all by himself?

"There was a Peabody, too. He helped him."

Who cremated her?

"It was Charles' wish, and it wasn't Eddie's and therefore, they
quarreled. Charlie was a Presbyterian . . . and he would have put me
in his Church, but I could not offend them all. They put it beyond my
reach through the roof; still hot . . . they stole it from the crematory."

Where was your home before, I asked.

"Lived close by," she answered, and as if to impress upon us
again her identity, added—"Bullock!"

Throughout the seance, the ghost had spoken with a strong Irish
brogue. The medium's background is not Irish, and I have a fine ear
for authenticity of language, perhaps because I speak seven of them,
and can recognize many more. This was not the kind of brogue a
clever actor puts on. This was a real one.

As the entranced medium served the cause of Mrs. Bullock,
I was reminded of the time I first heard the tape recordings of what
became later known as Bridie Murphy. I remember the evening when
the author of *The Search for Bridie Murphy,* Morey Bernstein, let
me and a small group of fellow researchers in on an exciting case he
had recently been working on. The voice on the tape, too, had an
authentic Irish brogue, and a flavor no actor, no matter how brilliant,
could fully imitate!

Now the medium seemed limp—as the ghost of Elizabeth
Bullock withdrew. A moment later, Mrs. Meyers awoke, none the
worse for having been the link between two worlds.

After the seance, I suggested to Mrs. Slatin that the can containing the ashes be buried in her garden, beneath the tree I saw through
the back window. But Mrs. Slatin wasn't sure. She felt that her ghost
was just as happy to stay on the piano.

I then turned my attention to Mrs. Slatin herself, since she admitted to being psychic. A gifted painter, Yeffe Kimball *knew* that Mrs. Meyers had made the right contact when she heard her describe the little lady with the limp at the beginning of the seance; she herself had often "seen" the ghost with her "psychic eye," and had developed a friendship for her. It was not an unhappy ghost, she contended, and particularly now that her secret was out—why deprive Elizabeth Bullock of "her family"? Why indeed?

The house is still there on Bank Street, and the can of ashes may still grace the piano. Whether the E. C. Bullock who called on the Slatins years ago was the Eddie whom the ghost claimed as her son, I can't tell. My efforts to locate him in California proved as fruitless as the earlier attempts to locate any other kin.

So the Slatins continued to live happily in their lovely, quiet house in the Village, with Elizabeth Bullock as their star boarder. Though I doubt the census taker will want to register her.

The Whistling Ghost

O NE OF MY DEAR FRIENDS was the celebrated clairvoyant Florence Sternfels of Edgewater, New Jersey, a lady who assisted many a police department in the apprehension of criminals or lost persons. Her real ambition, however, was to assist serious scientists to find out what makes her "different," where that power she had—"the forces," as she called them—came from. Many times she volunteered her time to sit with investigators, something few professional mediums will do.

I had not seen Florence in over a year when one day the telephone rang, and her slightly creaky voice wished me a cheery hello. It seemed that a highly respected psychiatrist in nearby Croton, New York, had decided to experiment with Florence's psychic powers. Would I come along? She wanted me there to make sure "everything was on the up-and-up." I agreed to come, and the following day Dr. Kahn himself called me, and arrangements were made for a young couple, the Hendersons, to pick me up in their car and drive me out to Croton.

When we arrived at the sumptuous Kahn house overlooking the Hudson River, some thirty persons, mostly neighbors and friends of the doctor's, had already assembled. None of them was known to Florence, of course, and few knew anything about the purpose of her visit. But the doctor was such a well-known community leader and teacher that they had come in great expectations.

The house was a remodeled older house, with an upstairs, and a large garden going all the way down to the river.

Florence did not disappoint the good doctor. Seated at the head of an oval, next to me, she rapidly called out facts and names about people in the room, their relatives and friends, deceased or otherwise, and found quick response and acknowledgment. Startling information, like "a five-year-old child has died, and the mother, who is paralyzed in the legs, is present." She certainly was. "Anyone here lost a collie dog?" Yes, someone had, three weeks before. Florence was a big success.

When it was all over, the crowd broke up and I had a chance to talk to our hostess, the doctor's young wife. She seemed deeply interested in psychic matters, just as was her husband; but while it was strictly a scientific curiosity with Dr. Kahn, his wife seemed to be intuitive and was given to "impressions" herself.

"You know, I think we've got a ghost," she said, looking at me as if she had just said the most ordinary thing in the world.

We walked over to a quiet corner, and I asked her what were her reasons for this extraordinary statement—unusual for the wife of a prominent psychiatrist. She assured me it was no hallucination.

"He's a whistling ghost," she confided, "always whistling the same song, about four bars of it—a happy tune. I guess he must be a happy ghost!"

"When did all this start?" I asked.

"During the past five years I've heard him about twenty times," Mrs. Kahn replied. "Always the same tune."

"And your husband, does he hear it, too?"

She shook her head.

"But he hears raps. Usually in our bedroom, and late at night. They always come in threes. My husband hears it, gets up, and asks who is it, but of course there is nobody there, so he gets no answer.

"Last winter, around three in the morning, we were awakened by a heavy knocking sound on the front door. When we got to the door and opened it, there was no one in sight. The path leading up to the road was empty, too, and believe me, no one could have come down that path and not be still visible by the time we got to the door!"

"And the whistling—where do you hear it usually?"

"Always in the living room—here," Mrs. Kahn replied, pointing at the high-ceilinged, wood-paneled room, with its glass wall facing the garden.

"You see, this living room used to be a stage . . . the house was once a summer theater, and we reconverted the stage area into this room. Come to think of it, I also heard that whistling in the bedroom that was used by the former owner of the house, the man who built both the theater and the house."

"What about this man? Who was he?"

"Clifford Harmon. He was murdered by the Nazis during World War II, when he got trapped in France. The house is quite old, has many secret passageways—as a matter of fact, only three weeks ago, I dreamed I should enter one of the passages!"

"You dreamed this?" I said. "Did anything ever come of it, though?"

Mrs. Kahn nodded. "The next morning, I decided to do just what I had done in my dream during the night. I entered the passage I had seen myself enter in the dream, and then I came across some musty old photographs."

I looked at the pictures. They showed various actors of both sexes, in the costumes of an earlier period. Who knows what personal tragedy or joy the people in these photographs had experienced in this very room? I returned the stack of pictures to Mrs. Kahn.

"Are you mediumistic?" I asked Mrs. Kahn. It seemed to me that she was the catalyst in this house.

"Well, perhaps a little. I am certainly clairvoyant. Some time ago, I wrote to my parents in Miami, and for some unknown reason, addressed the letter to 3251 South 23rd Lane. There was no such address as far as I knew, and the letter was returned to me in a few days. Later, my parents wrote to me telling me they had just bought a property at 3251 South 23rd Lane."

At this point, the doctor joined the conversation, and we talked about Harmon.

"He's left much unfinished business over here, I'm sure," the doctor said. "He had big plans for building and improvements of his property, and, of course, there were a number of girls he was interested in."

I had heard enough. The classic pattern of the haunted house was all there. The ghost, the unfinished business, the willing owners. I offered to hold a "rescue circle" type of seance, to make contact with the "whistling ghost."

We decided to hold the seance in August, and that I would bring along Mrs. Meyers, since this called for a trance medium, while Florence, who had originally brought me to this house, was a clairvoyant and psychometrist. A psychometrist gets "impressions" by holding objects that belong to a certain person.

Again, the transportation was provided by Mrs. Henderson, whose husband could not come along this time. On this occasion there was no curious crowd in the large living room when we arrived. Only the house guests of the Kahns, consisting of a Mr. and Mrs. Bower and their daughter, augmented the circle we formed as soon as the doctor had arrived from a late call. As always, before sliding into trance, Mrs. Meyers gave us her psychic impressions; before going into the full trance it is necessary to make the desired contact.

"Some names," said Mrs. Meyers, "a Robert, a Delia, a Harold and the name Banks ... Oh ... and then a Hart." She seemed unsure of the proper spelling.

At this very moment, both Mrs. Kahn and I distinctly heard the sound of heavy breathing. It seemed to emanate from somewhere above and behind the sitters. "Melish and Goldfarb!" Mrs. Meyers mumbled, getting more and more into a somnambulant state. "That's strange!" Dr. Kahn interjected. "There was a man named Elish here, some fifteen years ago . . . and a Mr. Goldwag, recently!"

"Mary . . . something—Ann," the medium now said. Later, after the seance, Dr. Kahn told me that Harmon's private secretary, who had had full charge of the big estate, was a woman named—Mary Brasnahan. . . .

Now Mrs. Meyers described a broad-shouldered man with iron-gray hair, who, she said, became gray at a very early age. "He wears a double-breasted, dark blue coat, and has a tiny mustache. His initials are R. H." Then she added, "I see handwriting . . . papers . . . signatures . . . and there is another, younger man, smaller, with light brown hair—and he is concerned with some papers that belong in files. His initials are J. B. I think the first man is the boss, this one is the clerk." Then she added suddenly, "Deborah!"

At this point Mrs. Meyers herself pulled back, and said: "I feel a twitch in my arm; apparently this isn't for publication!" But she continued and described other people whom she "felt" around the house; a Gertrude, for instance, and a bald-headed man with a reddish complexion, rather stout, whom she called B. B. "He has to do with the settlements on Deborah and the other girls."

Mrs. Meyers knew of course nothing about Harmon's alleged reputation as a bit of a ladies' man.

"That's funny," she suddenly commented, "I see two women dressed in very old-fashioned clothes, much earlier than their own period."

I had not mentioned a word to Mrs. Meyers about the theatrical usage which the house had once been put to. Evidently she received the impressions of two actresses.

"Bob . . . he's being called by a woman."

At this point, full trance set in, and the medium's own personality vanished, to allow the ghost to speak to us directly, if he so chose. After a moment Albert, the medium's control, came and announced that the ghost would speak to us. Then he withdrew, and within seconds a strange face replaced the usual benign expression of Mrs. Meyer's face. This was a shrewd, yet dignified man. His voice, at first faint, grew in strength as the seconds ticked off.

"So . . . so it goes . . . Sing a Song of Sixpence . . . all over now. . . ."

Excitedly Mrs. Kahn grabbed my arm and whispered into my ear: "That's the name of the song he always whistled . . . I couldn't think of it before." Through my mind went the words of the old nursery rhyme—

> Sing a Song of Sixpence,
> A pocket full of rye,
> Four and Twenty Blackbirds,
> Baked in a pie.
> When the pie was opened,
> The birds began to sing
> Isn't that a dainty dish
> To set before the King?

Like a secret password, our ghost had identified himself through the medium.

Why did Harmon pick this song as his tune? Perhaps the melodic lilt, the carefree air that goes with it, perhaps a sentimental reason. Mrs. Kahn was aglow with excitement.

The communicator then continued to speak: "All right, he won't come anymore. She isn't here . . . when you're dead, you're alive."

I thought it was time to ask a few questions of my own. "Why are you here?"

"Pleasant and unpleasant memories. My own thoughts keep me . . . happy, loved her. One happiness—*he* stands in the way. She didn't get what was hers. Jimmy may get it for her. *He* stands in the way!"

"Why do you come to this house?"

"To meet with her. It was our meeting place in the flesh. We still commune in spirit though she's still with you, and I return. We can meet. It is my house. My thought-child."

What he was trying to say, I thought, is that in her dream state, she has contact with him. Most unusual, even for a ghost! I began to wonder who "she" was. It was worth a try.

"Is her name Deborah?" I ventured. But the reaction was so violent our ghost slipped away. Albert took over the medium and requested that no more painfully personal questions be asked of the ghost. He also explained that our friend was indeed the owner of the house, the other man seen by the medium, his secretary, but the raps the doctor had heard had been caused by another person, the man who is after the owner's lady love.

Presently the ghost returned, and confirmed this.

"I whistle to call her. He does the rappings, to rob. . . ."

"Is there any unfinished business you want to tell us about?" That should not be too personal, I figured.

"None worth returning for, only love."

"Is there anything under the house?" I wondered. . . .

"There is a small tunnel, but it is depleted now." At this, I looked searchingly toward the doctor, who nodded, and later told me that such a tunnel did indeed exist.

"What is your name?"

"Bob. I only whistle and sing for happiness."

Before I could question him further, the gentleman slipped out again, and once more Albert, the control, took over:

"This man died violently at the hands of a firing squad," he commented, "near a place he thinks is Austerlitz . . . but is not sure. As for the estate, the other woman had the larger share."

There was nothing more after that, so I requested that the seance be concluded.

After the medium had returned to her own body, we discussed the experience, and Dr. Kahn remarked that he was not sure about the name Harmon had used among his friends. It seemed absurd to think that Clifford, his official first name, would not be followed by something more familiar—like, for instance, Bob. But there was no certainty.

"Did the Nazis really kill him?" I asked. There was total silence in the big room now. You could have heard a pin drop, and the Bowers, who had never been to any seances before, just sat there with their hands at their chins, wide-eyed and full of excitement. Albert, through his "instrument," as he called his medium, took his time to answer me.

"I'm afraid so. But I don't think it was a firing squad that killed him. He was beaten to death!" I looked with horror at Dr. Kahn, trying to get confirmation, but he only shrugged his shoulders.

Actually, nobody knows exactly how Harmon died, he revealed later. The fact is that the Nazis murdered him during the war. Could he have meant *Auschwitz* instead of Austerlitz?

I didn't feel like pursuing the subject any further. With Albert's assistance, we ended the seance, bringing the medium out of her trance state as quickly as possible.

The lights, which had been subdued during the sitting, were now allowed to be turned back on again. Mrs. Meyers recalled very little of what had transpired, mostly events and phrases at the onset and very end of her trance condition, but nothing that happened in the middle portion, when her trance state was at its deepest.

It was now midnight, and time to return to New York. As I said good night to my mediumistic friend, I expressed my hope that all would now be quiet at Croton.

This was wishful thinking.

The following morning, Mrs. Kahn telephoned me. Far from being quiet—the manifestations had increased around the house.

"What exactly happened?" I inquired. Mrs. Kahn bubbled over with excitement.

"We went to bed shortly after you left," she replied, "and all seemed so peaceful. Then, at 3 A.M., suddenly the bedroom lights went on by themselves. There is only one switch. Neither my husband nor I had gotten out of bed to turn on that switch. Nevertheless, when I took a look at the switch, it was *turned on,* as if by human hands!"

"Amazing," I conceded.

"Oh, but that isn't all," she continued. "Exactly one hour later, at four o'clock, the same thing happened again. By the way, do you remember the drapery covering the bedroom wall? There isn't a door or window nearby. Besides, the windows were all shut. No possible air current could have moved those draperies. All the same, I saw the draperies move by their own accord, plainly and visibly."

"I suppose he wants to let you know he's still there!" I said, rather meekly. Ghosts can be persistent at times. But Mrs. Kahn had more to tell me.

"Our house guest, Mrs. Bower, has the room that used to be Harmon's bedroom. Well, this morning she was dressing in front of the big closet. Suddenly she saw the door to the room open slowly, and then, with enormous force, pin her into the closet! There was nobody outside the room, of course."

"Anything else?" I asked quietly.

"Not really. Only, I had a dream last night. It was about a man in a blue suit. You remember Mrs. Meyers saw a man in a blue suit, too. Only with me, he said, 'Miller.' Said it several times, to make sure I got it. I also dreamed of a woman in a blue dress, with two small children, who was in danger somehow. But Miller stood out the strongest."

I thanked Mrs. Kahn for her report, and made her promise me to call the instant there were any further disturbances.

I woke up the following morning, sure the phone would ring and Mrs. Kahn would have more to tell me. But I was wrong. All remained quiet. All remained peaceful the next morning, too. It was not until four days later that Mrs. Kahn called again.

I prepared myself for some more of the ghost's shenanigans. But, to my relief, Mrs. Kahn called to tell me no further manifestations had occurred. However, she had done a bit of investigating. Since the name "Miller" was totally unknown to her and the doctor, she inquired around the neighborhood. Finally, one of the neighbors did recall a Miller. He was Harmon's personal physician.

"One thing I forgot to mention while you were here," she added. "Harmon's bed was stored away for many years. I decided one day to use it again. One night my husband discovered nails similar to carpet tacks under the pillow. We were greatly puzzled—but for lack of an explanation, we just forgot the incident. Another time I found something similar to crushed glass in the bed, and again, although greatly puzzled—forgot the incident. I don't know whether or not these seemingly unexplainable incidents mean anything."

Could it be that Harmon objected to anyone else using his bed? Ghosts are known to be quite possessive of their earthly goods, and resentful of "intruders."

All seemed quiet at the Kahns, until I received another call from Mrs. Kahn in the last days of October.

The "Whistling Ghost" was back.

This was quite a blow to my prestige as a ghost hunter, but on the other hand, Harmon's wraith apparently was a happy spirit and liked being earthbound. To paraphrase a well-known expression, you can lead a ghost to the spirit world, but you can't make him stay—if he doesn't want to. Next morning a note came from Mrs. Kahn.

"As I told you via phone earlier this evening, we again heard our whistler last night about 1 A.M., and it was the loudest I have ever heard. I didn't have to strain for it. My husband heard it too, but he thought it was the wind in the chimney. Then, as it continued, he agreed that it was some sort of phenomena. I got out of bed and went toward the sound of the whistle. I reached the den, from where I could see into the living room. Light was coming through a window behind me and was reflected upon the ceiling of the living room ... *I saw a small white mist,* floating, but motionless, in front of the table in the living room. I called to my husband. He looked, but saw nothing. He said he would put the light on and I watched him *walk right through the mist*—he turned the lamp on and everything returned to normal."

I lost touch with the Kahns after this time.

Is the whistling ghost still around? If he is, nobody seems to mind. That's how it is sometimes with happy ghosts. They get to be one of the family.

The Metuchen Ghost

ONE DAY IN THE SPRING, while the snow was still on the ground and the chill in the air, my good friend Bernard Axelrod, with whom I shared many a ghostly experience, called to say that he knew of a haunted house in New Jersey, and was I still interested.

I was, and Bernard disclosed that in the little town of Metuchen, there were a number of structures dating back to Colonial days. A few streets down from where he and his family lived in a modern, up-to-date brick building, there stood one wooden house in particular which had the reputation of being haunted, Bernard explained. No particulars were known to him beyond that. Ever since the Rockland County Ghost in the late Danton Walker's colonial house had acquainted me with the specters from George Washington's days, I have been eager to enlarge this knowledge. So it was with great anticipation that I gathered a group of helpers to pay a visit to whoever might be haunting the house in Metuchen. Bernard, who is a very persuasive fellow, managed to get permission from the owner of the house, Mr. Kane, an advertising executive. My group included Mrs. Meyers, as medium, and two associates of hers who would operate the tape recorder and take notes, Rosemarie de Simone and Pearl Winder. Miss de Simone is a teacher and Mrs. Winder is the wife of a dentist.

It was a midafternoon in March, when we rolled into the sleepy town of Metuchen. Bernard Axelrod was expecting us, and took us across town to the colonial house we were to inspect.

Any mention of the history or background of the house was studiously avoided en route. The owners, Mr. and Mrs. Kane, had a guest, a Mr. David, and the eight of us sat down in a circle in the downstairs living room of the beautifully preserved old house. It is a jewel of a colonial country house, with an upper story, a staircase and very few structural changes. No doubt about it, the Kanes had good taste, and their house reflected it. The furniture was all in the style of the period, which I took to be about the turn of the eighteenth century, perhaps earlier. There were several cats smoothly moving about, which helped me greatly to relax, for I have always felt that no house is wholly bad where there are cats, and conversely, where there are several cats, a house is bound to be wonderfully charming. For the occasion, however, the entire feline menagerie was put out of reach into the kitchen, and the tape recorder turned on as we took our seats in a semicircle around the fireplace. The light was the subdued light of a late winter afternoon, and the quiet was that of a country house far away from the bustling city. It was a perfect setting for a ghost to have his say.

As Mrs. Meyers eased herself into her comfortable chair, she remarked that certain clairvoyant impressions had come to her almost the instant she set foot into the house.

"I met a woman upstairs—in spirit, that is—with a long face, thick cheeks, perhaps forty years old or more, with ash-brown hair that may once have been blond. Somehow I get the name Mathilda. She wears a dress of striped material down to her knees, then wide plain material to her ankles. She puts out a hand, and I see a heavy wedding band on her finger, *but it has a cut in it,* and she insists on calling my attention to the cut. Then there is a man, with a prominent nose, tan coat and black trousers, standing in the back of the room looking as if he were sorry about something . . . he has very piercing eyes . . . I think she'd like to find something she has lost, and he blames her for it."

We were listening attentively. No one spoke, for that would perhaps give Mrs. Meyers an unconscious lead, something a good researcher will avoid.

"That sounds very interesting," I heard Bernard say, in his usual noncommittal way. "Do you see anything else?"

"Oh, yes," Mrs. Meyers nodded, "quite a bit—for one thing, there are *other* people here who don't belong to *them* at all . . . they come with the place, but in a different period . . . funny, halfway between upstairs and downstairs, I see one or two people *hanging*."

At this remark, the Kanes exchanged quick glances. Evidently my medium had hit pay dirt. Later, Mr. Kane told us a man committed suicide in the house around 1850 or 1860. He confirmed also that there was once a floor in between the two floors, but that this later addition had since been removed, when the house was restored to its original colonial condition.

Built in 1740, the house had replaced an earlier structure, for objects inscribed "1738" have been unearthed here.

"Legend has always had it that a revolutionary soldier haunts the house," Mr. Kane explained after the seance. "The previous owners told us they did hear *peculiar noises* from time to time, and that they had been told of such goings-on also by the owner who preceded *them*. Perhaps this story has been handed down from owner to owner, but we have never spoken to anyone in our generation who has heard or seen anything unusual about the place."

"What about you and your wife?" I inquired.

"Oh, we were a bit luckier—or unluckier—depending on how you look at it. One day back in 1956, the front door knocker banged away very loudly. My wife, who was all alone in the house at the time, went to see who it was. There was nobody there. It was winter, and deep snow surrounded the house. *There were no tracks in the snow.*"

"How interesting," Bernard said. All this was new to him, too, despite his friendship with the family.

Mr. Kane slowly lit a pipe, blew the smoke toward the low ceiling of the room, and continued.

"The previous owners had a dog. Big, strapping fellow. Just the same, now and again he would hear some strange noises and absolutely panic. In the middle of the night he would jump into bed with them, crazed with fear. But it wasn't just the dog who heard things. They, too, heard the walking—steps of someone walking around the second floor, and in their bedroom, on the south side of the house—at times of the day when they *knew* for sure there was nobody there."

"And after you moved in, did you actually *see* anything?" I asked. Did they have any idea what the ghost looked like?

"Well, yes," Mr. Kane said. "About a year ago, Mrs. Kane was sleeping in the Green Room upstairs. *Three nights in a row, she was awakened in the middle of the night, at the same time, by the feeling of a presence.* Looking up, she noticed a white form standing beside her bed. Thinking it was me, at first, she was not frightened. But when she spoke to it, it just disappeared into air. She is sure it was a man."

Although nothing unusual had occurred since, the uncanny feeling persisted, and when Bernard Axelrod mentioned his interest in ghosts, and offered to have me come to the house with a qualified medium, the offer was gladly accepted. So there we were, with Mrs. Meyers slowly gliding into trance. Gradually, her description of what she saw or heard blended into the personalities themselves, as her own personality vanished temporarily. It was a very gradual transition, and well controlled.

"She is being blamed by him," Mrs. Meyers mumbled. "Now I see a table, she took four mugs, four large mugs, and one small one. Does she mean to say, four older people and a small one? I get a name,

Jake, John, no, *Jonathan!* Then there are four Indians, and they want to make peace. *They've done something they should not have,* and they want to make peace." Her visions continued.

"Now instead of the four mugs on the table, there's a whole line of them, fifteen altogether, but I don't see the small mug now. There are many individuals standing around the table, with their backs toward me—then someone is calling and screaming, and someone says 'Off above the knees.' "

I later established through research that during the Revolutionary War the house was right in the middle of many small skirmishes; the injured may well have been brought here for treatment.

Mrs. Meyers continued her narrative with increasing excitement in her voice.

"Now there are other men, all standing there with long-tailed coats, white stockings, and talking. Someone says 'Dan Dayridge' or 'Bainbridge,' I can't make it out clearly; he's someone with one of these three-cornered hats, a white wig, tied black hair, a very thin man with a high, small nose, not particularly young, with a fluffy collar and large eyes. Something took place here in which he was a participant. He is one of the men standing there with those fifteen mugs. It is night, and there are two candles on either side of the table, food on the table—*smells like chicken*—and then there is a paper with red seals and gold ribbon. But something goes wrong with this, and now there are only four mugs on the table . . . I think it means, only four men return. *Not the small one.* This man is one of the four, and somehow the little mug is pushed aside, I see it put away on the shelf. I see now a small boy, he has disappeared, he is gone . . . but always trying *to come back.* The name *Allen* . . . he followed the man, but the Indians got him and he never came back. They're looking for him, trying to find him. . . ."

Mrs. Meyers now seemed totally entranced. Her features assumed the face of a woman in great mental anguish, and her voice quivered;

the words came haltingly and with much prodding from me. For all practical purposes, the medium had now been taken over by a troubled spirit. We listened quietly, as the story unfolded.

"*Allen's* coming back one day . . . call him back . . . my son, do you hear him? They put those Indians in the tree, do you hear them as they moan?"

"Who took your boy?" I asked gently.

"They did . . . he went with them, with the men. With his father, *Jon*."

"What Indians took him?"

"Look there in the tree. They didn't do it. I know they didn't do it."

"Where did they go?"

"To the *river*. My boy, did you hear him?"

Mrs. Meyers could not have possibly known that there was a river not far from the house. I wanted to fix the period of our story, as I always do in such cases, so I interrupted the narrative and asked what day this was. There was a brief pause, as if she were collecting her thoughts. Then the faltering voice was heard again.

"December One. . . ."

December One! The old-fashioned way of saying December First.

"What year is this?" I continued.

This time the voice seemed puzzled as to why I would ask such an obvious thing, but she obliged.

"Seventeen . . . seventy . . . six."

"What does your husband do?"

"Jonathan . . . ?"

"Does he own property?"

"The field. . . ."

But then the memory of her son returned. "Allen, my son Allen. He is calling me. . . ."

"Where was he born?"

"Here."

"What is the name of this town?"

"Bayridge."

Subsequently, I found that the section of Metuchen we were in had been known in colonial times as *Woodbridge,* although it is not inconceivable that there also was a Bayridge.

The woman wanted to pour her heart out now. "Oh, look," she continued, "they didn't do it, they're in the tree . . . those Indians, dead ones. They didn't do it, I can see their souls and they were innocent of this . . . in the cherry tree."

Suddenly she interrupted herself and said—"Where am I? Why am I so sad?"

It isn't uncommon for a newly liberated or newly contacted "ghost" to be confused about his or her own status. Only an emotionally disturbed personality becomes an earthbound "ghost."

I continued the questioning.

Between sobs and cries for her son, Allen, she let the name "Mary Dugan" slip from her lips, or rather the lips of the entranced medium, who now was fully under the unhappy one's control.

"Who is Mary Dugan?" I immediately interrupted.

"He married her, Jonathan."

"Second wife?"

"Yes . . . I am under the tree."

"Where were you born? What was your maiden name?"

"Bayridge . . . Swift . . . my heart is so hurt, so cold, so cold."

"Do you have any other children?"

"Allen . . . Mary Anne . . . Georgia. They're calling me, do you hear them? Allen, he knows I am alone waiting here. He thought he was a *man!*"

"How old was your boy at the time?" I said. The disappearance of her son was the one thing foremost in her mind.

"My boy . . . eleven . . . December One, 1776, is his birthday. That was his birthday all right."

I asked her if Allen had another name, and she said, Peter. Her own maiden name? She could not remember.

"Why don't I know? They threw me out. . . it was Mary took the house."

"What did your husband do?"

"He was a *potter*. He also was paid for harness. His shop . . . the road to the south. Bayridge. In the tree orchard we took from two neighbors."

The neighborhood is known for its clay deposits and potters, but this was as unknown to the medium as it was to me until after the seance, when Bernard told us about it.

In *Boyhood Days in Old Metuchen,* a rare work, Dr. David Marshall says: "Just south of Metuchen there are extensive clay banks."

But our visitor had enough of the questioning. Her sorrow returned and suddenly she burst into tears, the medium's tears, to be sure, crying—"I want Allen! Why is it I look for him? I hear him calling me, I hear his step . . . I know he is here . . . why am I searching for him?"

I then explained that Allen was on "her side of the veil," too, that she would be reunited with her boy by merely "standing still" and letting him find her; it was her frantic activity that made it impossible for them to be reunited, but if she were to becalm herself, all would be well.

After a quiet moment of reflection, her sobs became weaker and her voice firmer.

"Can you see your son now?"

"Yes, I see him." And with that, she slipped away quietly.

A moment later, the medium returned to her own body, as it were, and rubbed her sleepy eyes. Fully awakened a moment later, she remembered nothing of the trance. Now *for the first time* did we talk about the house, and its ghostly visitors.

"How much of this can be proved?" I asked impatiently.

Mr. Kane lit another pipe, and then answered me slowly.

"Well, there is quite a lot," he finally said. "For one thing, this house used to be a tavern during revolutionary days, known as the Allen House!"

Bernard Axelrod, a few weeks later, discovered an 1870 history of the town of Metuchen. In it, there was a remark about the house, which an early map showed at its present site in 1799:

"In the house . . . lived a Mrs. Allen, and on it was a sign 'Allentown Cake and Beer Sold Here.' Between the long Prayer Meetings which according to New England custom were held mornings and afternoons, with half hour or an hour intermission, it was not unusual for the young men to get ginger cake and a glass of beer at this famous restaurant. . . ."

"What about all those Indians she mentioned?" I asked Mr. Kane.

"There were Indians in this region all right," he confirmed.

"Arrowheads have been found right here, near the pond in back of the house. Many Indian battles were fought around here, and incidentally, during the War for Independence, both sides came to this house and had their ale in the evening. This was a kind of no-man's land between the Americans and the British. During the day, they would kill each other, but at night, *they ignored each other over a beer at Mrs. Allen's tavern!*"

"How did you get this information?" I asked Mr. Kane.

"There was a local historian, a Mr. Welsh, who owned this house for some thirty years. He also talked of a revolutionary soldier whose ghost was seen plainly 'walking' through the house about a foot off the ground."

Many times have I heard a ghostly apparition described in just such terms. The motion of walking is really unnecessary, it seems, for the spirit form *glides* about a place.

There were interesting accounts in the rare old books about the town of Metuchen in the local library. These stories spoke of battles between the British and Americans, and of "carts loaded with dead bodies, after a battle between British soldiers and Continentals, up around Oak Tree on June 26th, 1777."

No doubt, the Allen House saw many of them brought in along with the wounded and dying.

I was particularly interested in finding proof of Jonathan Allen's existence, and details of his life. So far I had only ascertained that Mrs. Allen existed. Her husband was my next goal.

After much work, going through old wills and land documents, I discovered a number of Allens in the area. I found the will of his father, Henry, leaving his "son, Jonathan, the land where he lives" on April 4th, 1783.

A 1799 map shows a substantial amount of land marked "Land of Allen," and Jonathan Allen's name occurs in many a document of the period as a witness or seller of land.

The Jonathan Allen I wanted had to be from Middlesex County, in which Metuchen was located. I recalled that he was an able-bodied man, and consequently may have seen some service. Sure enough, in the *Official Register of the Officers and Men of New Jersey in the Revolutionary War,* I found my man—"Allen, Jonathan—Middlesex."

It is good to know that the troubled spirit of Mrs. Allen can now rest close to her son's; and perhaps the other restless one, her husband, will be accused of negligence in the boy's death no more.

The Stranger at
the Door

I HAVE FOUND THAT THERE ARE GHOSTS in all sorts of places, in ancient castles, modern apartment houses, farms and ships—but it is somewhat of a jolt to find out you've lived in a house for a few years and didn't even know it was haunted. But that is exactly what happened to me.

For three years I was a resident of a beautiful twenty-nine-story apartment building on New York's Riverside Drive. I lived on the nineteenth floor, and seldom worried about what transpired below me. But I was aware of the existence of a theater and a museum on the ground floor of the building. I was also keenly aware of numerous inspired paintings, some Tibetan, some Occidental, adorning the corridors of this building. The museum was known as the Riverside Museum, and the paintings were largely the work of the great Rohrach, a painter who sought his inspirations mainly in the mysticism of Tibet, where he spent many years. On his return from the East, his many admirers decided to chip in a few millions and build him a monument worthy of his name. Thus, in 1930, was raised the Rohrach building as a center of the then flourishing cult of Eastern mysticism, of which Rohrach was the high priest. After his death, a schism appeared among his followers, and an exodus took place.

A new "Rohrach Museum" was established by Seena Fosdick a few blocks away from the imposing twenty-nine-story structure originally known by that name. In turn, the building where I lived changed its name to that of the Master Institute, a combination apartment building and school, and, of course, art gallery.

It was a February afternoon when I met at a tea party—yes, there were such things in that day and age—a young actress and producer, Mrs. Roland, who had an interesting experience at "my" building some years ago. She was not sure what year it was, but she was quite sure that it happened exactly the way she told it to me that winter afternoon in the apartment of famed author Claudia de Lys.

A lecture-meeting dealing with Eastern philosophy had drawn her to the Rohrach building. Ralph Huston, the eminent philosopher, presided over the affair, and a full turnout it was. As the speaker held the attention of the crowd, Mrs. Roland's eyes wandered off to the rear of the room. Her interest was invited by a tall stranger standing near the door, listening quietly and with rapt attention. Mrs. Roland didn't know too many of the active members, and the stranger, whom she had never seen before, fascinated her. His dress, for one thing, was most peculiar. He wore a gray cotton robe with a high-necked collar, the kind one sees in Asian paintings, and on his head he had a round black cap. He appeared to be a fairly young man, certainly in the prime of life, and his very dark eyes in particular attracted her.

For a moment she turned her attention to the speaker; when she returned to the door, the young man was gone.

"Peculiar," she thought; "why should he leave in the middle of the lecture? He seemed so interested in it all."

As the devotees of mysticism slowly filed out of the room, the actress sauntered over to Mrs. Fosdick whom she knew to be the "boss lady" of the group.

"Tell me," she inquired, "who was that handsome dark-eyed young man at the door?"

Mrs. Fosdick was puzzled. She did not recall any such person. The actress then described the stranger in every detail. When she had finished, Mrs. Fosdick seemed a bit pale.

But this was an esoteric forum, so she did not hesitate to tell Mrs. Roland that she had apparently seen an apparition. What was more, the description fitted the great Rohrach—in his earlier years—to a T. Mrs. Roland had never seen Rohrach in the flesh.

At this point, Mrs. Roland confessed that she had psychic abilities, and was often given to "hunches." There was much head shaking, followed by some hand shaking, and then the matter was forgotten.

I was of course interested, for what would be nicer than to have a house ghost, so to speak?

The next morning, I contacted Mrs. Fosdick. Unfortunately, this was one of the occasions when truth did not conquer. When I had finished telling her what I wanted her to confirm, she tightened up, especially when she found out I was living at the "enemy camp," so to speak. Emphatically, Mrs. Fosdick denied the incident, but admitted knowing Mrs. Roland.

With this, I returned to my informant, who reaffirmed the entire matter. Again I approached Mrs. Fosdick with the courage of an unwelcome suitor advancing on the castle of his beloved, fully aware of the dragons lurking in the moat.

While I explained my scientific reasons for wanting her to remember the incident, she launched into a tirade concerning her withdrawal from the "original" Rohrach group, which was fascinating, but not to me.

I have no reason to doubt Mrs. Roland's account, especially as I found her extremely well poised, balanced, and indeed, psychic.

I only wondered if Mr. Rohrach would sometime honor me with a visit, or vice versa, now that we were neighbors?

A Greenwich Village Ghost

B ACK IN THE EARLY DAYS of my career, when I spent much of my time writing and editing material of a most mundane nature, always, of course, with a weather eye cocked for a good case of hunting, I picked up a copy of *Park East* and found to my amazement some very palatable grist for my psychic mills. "The Ghost of Tenth Street," by Elizabeth Archer, was a well-documented report of the hauntings on that celebrated Greenwich Village street where artists made their headquarters, and many buildings date back to the eighteenth century. Miss Archer's story was later reprinted by *Tomorrow* magazine, upon my suggestion. In *Park East*, some very good illustrations accompany the text, for which there was no room in *Tomorrow*.

Up to 1956, the ancient studio building at 51 West 10th Street was a landmark known to many connoisseurs of old New York, but it was demolished to make way for one of those nondescript, modern apartment buildings that were gradually taking away the charm of Greenwich Village, and give us doubtful comforts in its stead.

Until the very last, reports of an apparition, allegedly the ghost of artist John La Farge, who died in 1910, continued to come in. A few houses down the street is the Church of the Ascension; the altar painting, "The Ascension," is the work of John La Farge. Actually, the artist did the work on the huge painting at his studio, Number 22, in 51 West 10th Street. He finished it, however, in the church itself, "in place." Having just returned from the Orient, La Farge used a new technique involving the use of several coats of paint, thus making the painting heavier than expected. The painting was hung, but the chassis collapsed; La Farge built a stronger chassis and the painting stayed in place this time. Years went by. Oliver La Farge, the great novelist and grandson of the painter, had spent much of his youth with his celebrated grandfather. One day, while working across the street, he was told the painting had fallen again. Dashing across the street, he found that the painting had indeed fallen, and that his grandfather had died *that very instant!*

The fall of the heavy painting was no trifling matter to La Farge, who was equally as well known as an architect as he was a painter. Many buildings in New York for which he drew the plans over one hundred years ago are still standing. But the construction of the chassis of the altar painting may have been faulty. And therein lies the cause for La Farge's ghostly visitations, it would seem. The artists at No. 51 insisted always that La Farge could not find rest until he had corrected his calculations, searching for the original plans of the chassis to find out what was wrong. An obsession to redeem himself as an artist and craftsman, then, would be the underlying cause for the persistence with which La Farge's ghost returned to his old haunts.

The first such return was reported in 1944, when a painter by the name of Feodor Rimsky and his wife lived in No. 22. Late one evening, they returned from the opera. On approaching their studio, they noticed that a light was on and the door open, although they distinctly remembered having *left it shut*. Rimsky walked into the studio, pushed aside the heavy draperies at the entrance to the studio itself, and stopped in amazement. In the middle of the room, a single lamp plainly revealed a stranger behind the large chair in what Rimsky called his library corner; the man wore a tall black hat and a dark, billowing velvet coat. Rimsky quickly told his wife to wait, and rushed across the room to get a closer look at the intruder. But the man *just vanished* as the painter reached the chair.

Later, Rimsky told of his experience to a former owner of the building, who happened to be an amateur historian. He showed Rimsky some pictures of former tenants of his building. In two of them, Rimsky easily recognized his visitor, wearing exactly the same clothes Rimsky had seen him in. Having come from Europe but recently, Rimsky knew nothing of La Farge and had never seen a picture of him. The ball dress worn by the ghost had not been common at the turn of the century, but La Farge was known to affect such strange attire.

Three years later, the Rimskys were entertaining some guests at their studio, including an advertising man named William Weber, who was known to have had psychic experiences in the past. But Weber never wanted to discuss this "special talent" of his, for fear of being ridiculed. As the conversation flowed among Weber, Mrs. Weber, and two other guests, the advertising man's wife noticed her husband's sudden stare at a cabinet on the other side of the room, where paintings were stored. She saw nothing, but Weber asked her in an excited tone of voice—"Do you see that man in the cloak and top hat over there?"

Weber knew nothing of the ghostly tradition of the studio or of John La Farge; no stranger could have gotten by the door without being noticed, and none had been expected at this hour. The studio was locked from the *inside*.

After that, the ghost of John La Farge was heard many times by a variety of tenants at No. 51, opening windows or pushing draperies aside, but not until 1948 was he *seen* again.

Up a flight of stairs from Studio 22, but connected to it—artists like to visit each other—was the studio of illustrator John Alan Maxwell. Connecting stairs and a "secret rest room" used by La Farge had long been walled up in the many structural changes in the old building. Only the window of the walled-up room was still visible from the outside. It was in this area that Rimsky felt that the restless spirit of John La Farge was trapped. As Miss Archer puts it in her narrative, "walled in like the Golem, sleeping through the day and close to the premises for roaming through the night."

After many an unsuccessful search of Rimsky's studio, apparently the ghost started to look in Maxwell's studio. In the spring of 1948, the ghost of La Farge made his initial appearance in the illustrator's studio.

It was a warm night, and Maxwell had gone to bed naked, pulling the covers over himself. Suddenly he awakened. From the amount of light coming in through the skylight, he judged the time to be about one or two in the morning. *He had the uncanny feeling of not being alone in the room.* As his eyes got used to the darkness, he clearly distinguished the figure of a tall woman, bending over his bed, lifting and straightening his sheets several times over. Behind her, there was a man staring at a wooden filing cabinet at the foot of the couch. Then he opened a drawer, looked in it, and closed it again. Getting hold of himself, Maxwell noticed that the woman wore a light red dress of the kind worn in the nineteenth century, and the man a white shirt and dark cravat of the same period. It never occurred to the illustrator that they were anything but *people*; probably, he thought, models in costume working for one of the artists in the building.

The woman then turned to her companion as if to say something, but did not, and walked off toward the dark room at the other end of the studio. The man then went back to the cabinet and leaned on it, head in hand. By now Maxwell had regained his wits and thought the intruders must be burglars, although he could not figure out how they had entered his place, since he had locked it from the *inside* before going to bed! Making a fist, he struck at the stranger, yelling, "Put your hands up!"

His voice could be heard clearly along the empty corridors. *But his fist went through the man and into the filing cabinet.* Nursing his injured wrist, he realized that his visitors had dissolved into thin air. There was no one in the dark room. The door was still securely locked. The skylight, 150 feet above ground, could not very well have served as an escape route *to anyone human.* By now Maxwell knew that La Farge and his wife had paid him a social call.

Other visitors to No. 51 complained about strange winds and sudden chills when passing La Farge's walled-up room. One night, one of Maxwell's lady visitors returned, shortly after leaving his studio, in great agitation, yelling, "That man! That man!" The inner court of the building was glass-enclosed, so that one could see clearly across to the corridors on the other side of the building. Maxwell and his remaining guests saw nothing there.

But the woman insisted that she saw a strange man under one of the old gaslights in the building; he seemed to lean against the wall of the corridor, dressed in old-fashioned clothes and possessed of a face so cadaverous and death-mask-like, that it set her ascreaming!

This was the first time the face of the ghost had been observed clearly by anyone. The sight was enough to make her run back to Maxwell's studio. Nobody could have left without being seen through the glass-enclosed corridors and no one had seen a stranger in the building that evening. As usual, he had vanished into thin air.

So much for Miss Archer's account of the La Farge ghost. My own investigation was sparked by her narrative, and I telephoned her at her Long Island home, inviting her to come along if and when we held a seance at No. 51.

I was then working with a group of parapsychology students meeting at the rooms of the Association for Research and Enlightenment (Cayce Foundation) on West Sixteenth Street. The director of this group was a phototechnician of the *Daily News*, Bernard Axelrod, who was the only one of the group who knew the purpose of the meeting; the others, notably the medium, Mrs. Meyers, knew nothing whatever of our plans.

We met in front of Bigelow's drugstore that cold February evening, and proceeded to 51 West Tenth Street, where the then occupant of the La Farge studio, an artist named Leon Smith, welcomed us. In addition, there were also present the late *New York Daily News* columnist, Danton Walker, Henry Belk, the noted playwright Bernays, Marguerite Haymes, and two or three others considered students of psychic phenomena. Unfortunately, Mrs. Belk also brought along her pet chihuahua, which proved to be somewhat of a problem.

All in all, there were fifteen people present in the high-ceilinged, chilly studio. Dim light crept through the tall windows that looked onto the courtyard, and one wished that the fireplace occupying the center of the back wall had been working.

We formed a circle around it, with the medium occupying a comfortable chair directly opposite it, and the sitters filling out the circle on both sides; my own chair was next to the medium's.

The artificial light was dimmed. Mrs. Meyers started to enter the trance state almost immediately and only the loud ticking of the clock in the rear of the room was heard for a while, as her breathing became heavier. At the threshold of passing into trance, the medium suddenly said—"Someone says very distinctly, *Take another step and I go out this window!* The body of a woman . . . closefitting hat and a plume . . . closefitting bodice and a thick skirt . . . lands right on face . . . I see a man, dark curly hair, *hooked nose, an odd, mean face* . . . cleft in chin . . . light tan coat, lighter britches, boots, whip in hand, cruel, mean. . . ."

There was silence as she described *what I recognized as the face of La Farge.*

A moment later she continued: "I know the face is not to be looked at anymore. It is horrible. It should have hurt but I didn't remember. Not long. I just want to scream and scream."

The power of the woman who went through the window was strong. "I have a strange feeling," Mrs. Meyers said, "I *have to go out that window* if I go into trance." With a worried look, she turned to me and asked, "If I stand up and start to move, *hold me*." I nodded assurance and the seance continued. A humming sound came from her lips, gradually assuming human-voice characteristics.

The next personality to manifest itself was apparently a woman in great fear. "They're in the courtyard. . . . He is coming . . . they'll find me and whip me again. I'll die first. Let me go. I shouldn't talk so loud. Margaret! Please don't let him come. See the child. My child. Barbara. Oh, the steps, I can't take it. Take Bobby, raise her, I can't take it. He is coming . . . *let me go!* I am free!"

With this, the medium broke out of trance and complained of facial stiffness, as well as pain in the shoulder.

Was the frantic woman someone who had been mistreated by an early inhabitant of No. 22? Was she a runaway slave, many of whom had found refuge in the old houses and alleys of the Village?

I requested of the medium's "control" that the most prominent person connected with the studio be allowed to speak to us. But Albert, the control, assured me that the woman, whom he called Elizabeth, was connected with that man. "He will come only if he is of a mind to. He entered the room a while ago."

I asked Albert to describe this man.

"Sharp features, from what I can see. You are closer to him. Clothes . . . nineties, early 1900's."

After a while, the medium's lips started to move, and a gruff man's voice was heard: "*Get out* . . . get out of my house."

Somewhat taken aback by this greeting, I started to explain to our visitor that we were his friends and here to help him. But he didn't mellow.

"I don't know who you are . . . who is everybody here. Don't have friends."

"I am here to help you," I said, and tried to calm the ghost's suspicions. But our visitor was not impressed.

"I want help, but not from you . . . *I'll find it!*"

He wouldn't tell us what he was looking for. There were additional requests for us to get out of his house. Finally, the ghost pointed the medium's arm toward the stove and intoned—"I put it there!" A sudden thought inspired me, and I said, lightly—"We found it already."

Rage took hold of the ghost in an instant. "You took it . . . you betrayed me . . . it is mine . . . I was a good man."

I tried in vain to pry his full name from him.

He moaned. "I am sick all over now. Worry, worry, worry. Give it to me."

I promised to return "it," if he would cooperate with us.

In a milder tone he said, "I wanted to make it so pretty. *It won't move.*"

I remembered how concerned La Farge had been with his beautiful altar painting, and that it should not fall *again*. I wondered if he knew how much time had passed.

"Who is President of the United States now?" I asked.

Our friend was petulant. "I don't know. I am sick. William McKinley." But then he volunteered—"I knew him. Met him. In Boston. Last year. Many years ago. Who are you? I don't know any friends. *I am in my house.*"

"What is your full name?"

"Why is that so hard? I know William and I don't know my *own* name."

I have seen this happen before. A disturbed spirit sometimes cannot recall his own name or address.

"Do you know you have passed over?"

"I live here," he said, quietly now. "Times changed. I know I am not what I used to be. *It is there!*"

When I asked what he was looking for, he changed the subject to Bertha, without explaining who Bertha was.

But as he insisted on finding "it," I finally said, "You are welcome to get up and look for it."

"I am bound in this chair and can't move."

"Then tell us where to look for it."

After a moment's hesitation, he spoke. "On the chimney, in back . . . it was over there. I will find it, but I can't move now . . . *I made a mistake* . . . I can't talk like this."

And suddenly he was gone.

As it was getting on to half past ten, the medium was awakened. The conversation among the guests then turned to any feelings they might have had during the seance. Miss Archer was asked about the building.

"It was put up in 1856," she replied, "and is a copy of a similar studio building in Paris."

"Has there ever been any record of a murder committed in this studio?" I asked.

"Yes . . . between 1870 and 1900, *a young girl went through one of these windows*. But I did not mention this in my article, as it *apparently* was unconnected with the La Farge story."

"What about Elizabeth? And Margaret?"

"That was remarkable of the medium," Miss Archer nodded. "You see, Elizabeth was La Farge's wife . . . and Margaret, well, she also fits in with his story."

For the first time, the name La Farge had been mentioned in the presence of the medium. But it meant nothing to her in her conscious state.

Unfortunately, the ghost could not be convinced that his search for the plans was unnecessary, for La Farge's genius as an architect and painter has long since belonged to time.

A few weeks after this seance, I talked to an advertising man named Douglas Baker. To my amazement, he, too, had at one time occupied Studio 22. Although aware of the stories surrounding the building, he had scoffed at the idea of a ghost. But one night he was roused from deep sleep by the noise of someone opening and closing drawers. Sitting up in bed, he saw a man in Victorian opera clothes in his room, which was dimly lit by the skylight and windows. Getting out of bed to fence off the intruder, he found himself alone, just as others had before him.

No longer a scoffer, he talked to others in the building, and was able to add one more episode to the La Farge case. It seems a lady was passing No. 51 one bleak afternoon when she noticed an odd-looking gentleman in opera clothes standing in front of the building. For no reason at all, the woman exclaimed, "My, you're a funny-looking man!"

The gentleman in the opera cloak looked at her in rage. "Madam—how dare you!"

And with that, *he went directly through the building—the wall of the building, that is!*

Passers-by revived the lady.

Now there is a modern apartment building at 51 West 10th Street. Is John La Farge still roaming its modern corridors? Not long ago, I went into the Church of the Ascension, gazed at the marvelous altar painting, and prayed a little that he shouldn't *have to.*

The Hauntings at
Seven Oaks

E LEANOR SMALL WAS A CHARMING WOMAN in her late
forties who dabbled in real estate and business. She came
from a very good family which once had considerable wealth,
and was what was loosely termed "society." She wasn't the kind of
person one would suspect of having any interest in the supernatural.

One evening, as we were discussing other matters, the conversation got around to ghosts. To my amazement, Eleanor was fascinated
by the topic; so much so, that I could not help asking her if by chance
she knew of a haunted house somewhere for me to investigate!

"Indeed I do," was the reply, and this is how I first heard about
Seven Oaks. In Mamaroneck, New York, up in posh Westchester
County, there stood until recently a magnificent colonial mansion
known as Seven Oaks. Situated near the edge of Long Island Sound,
it was one of the show places of the East. Just as did so many fine
old mansions, this one gave way to a "development," and now there
are a number of small, insignificant, ugly modern houses dotting the
grounds of the large estate.

During the Battle of Orient Point, one of the bloodier engage-
ments of the Revolutionary War, the mansion was British-held, and

American soldiers, especially the wounded, were often smuggled out to Long Island Sound via an "underground railway," passing through the mansion.

"When I was a young girl," Eleanor said, "I spent many years with my mother and my stepfather at Seven Oaks, which we then owned. I was always fascinated by the many secret passageways which honeycombed the house."

The entrance was from the library; some books would slide back, and a slender wooden staircase appeared. Gaslight jets had been installed in the nineteenth century to light these old passages. A butler working for Eleanor's parents stumbled onto them by chance.

"When did you first hear about ghosts?" I asked.

"We moved into the house about June 1932. Right away, a neighbor by the name of Mabel Merker told us that the place was *haunted. Of course*, we paid no attention to her."

"Of course." I nodded wryly.

"But it wasn't too long before Mother changed her mind about that."

"You mean she saw the ghost?"

Eleanor nodded. "Regularly, *practically every night.*" Eleanor's mother had described the ghost as a woman of about forty-five, with long blond hair and a sweet expression on her face. One of these apparitions had its comic aspects, too.

"Mother had her private bathroom, which connected directly with her bedroom. One night, after all doors had been locked and Mother knew there was no one about any more, she retired for the night. Entering the bathroom from her bedroom, she left the connecting door open in the knowledge that her privacy could not possibly be disturbed! Suddenly, looking up, *she saw, back in her room, the ghost standing and beckoning to her in the bathroom,* as if she wanted to tell her something of utmost urgency. There was such an expression of sadness and frustration on the wraith's face, Mother could never forget it."

"But what did she *do?*" I asked.

"She approached the apparition, but when she got halfway across the room, the ghost just evaporated into thin air."

"And this was in good light, and the apparition was not shadowy or vaporous?"

"Oh no, it looked just like someone of flesh and blood—until that last moment when she *dissolved before Mother's eyes.*"

"Was your mother very upset?"

"Only at first. Later she got used to the idea of having a ghost around. Once she saw her up on the second floor, in the master bedroom. There she was standing in front of the two beds. Mother wondered what she could do to help her, but the ghost again vanished."

"Did she ever hear her talk or make any kind of noise?" I asked.

"Not talk, but noise—well, at the time Mother moved into the house, the previous owner, Mrs. Warren, still maintained a few things of her own in a closet in the house, and she was in the habit of returning there occasionally to pick some of them up, a few at a time. One evening Mother heard some footsteps, but thought them to be Mrs. Warren's.

"The next day, however, she found out that no one had been to the house. Our family dog frequently barked loudly and strongly before the fireplace, at *something* or *someone* we could not see, but evidently he *could.*"

"Did anyone else see the ghost?"

"The servants, especially the men, constantly complained of *being pulled from their beds,* in the servants' quarters, by unseen hands. It was as if someone wanted their attention, but there never was anyone there when the lights were turned on."

"She probably wanted to talk to someone, as ghosts often do!" I said. Communication and inability to be heard or seen by the people of flesh and blood is the main agony of a wraith.

"That must be so," Eleanor nodded, "because there was another incident some years later that seems to confirm it. My stepfather's son and his seventeen-year-old bride came to live at Seven Oaks. The young girl was extremely sensitive. They were given a room on the top floor of the old mansion, with a double bed in the center.

"One night they retired early, and the son was already in bed, while his wife stood nearby in the room. Suddenly, as she looked on with horror, she saw her *husband bodily pulled out of bed by unseen hands.*

"The next morning, the young couple left Seven Oaks, never to return."

The Central Park West Ghost

MRS. M. DALY HOPKINS WAS a lady of impeccable taste, and gracious surroundings meant a great deal to her and her husband. Consequently, when they decided to look for a new apartment, they directed their steps toward Central Park West, which had become one of New York's more desirable residential areas.

As they were walking up the tree-lined street, they noticed a man in working overalls hanging up a sign on a building, reading "Apartment for Rent." The man turned out to be the superintendent of one of three identical gray five-story buildings on the corner of 107th Street and Central Park West.

Mrs. Hopkins, who later reported her uncanny experiences in a story entitled "Ten Years with a Ghost," was overjoyed. The location was perfect; now if only the apartment suited them! With hearts beating a trifle faster, the Hopkinses approached the building.

The apartment for rent was on the top floor, that is, it occupied the southeast corner of the fifth floor of the building, and it contained a total of eight rooms. This seemed ideal to the Hopkinses, who needed plenty of space for themselves, their small son, and his nurse.

It seemed the former tenants had just moved out, after living in the apartment for many years. Most of the people in the building, the superintendent added, had been there a long time. The tenants of this particular apartment had been just husband and wife. By November of the same year, the Hopkins family was settled in the new apartment.

Nothing unusual happened during the first few weeks of their stay, except that on a number of occasions Mrs. Hopkins heard her housekeeper cry out, as if surprised by someone or something!

Finally, the middle-aged woman came to Mrs. Hopkins, and said: "Something's strange about this place. I often feel someone standing behind me, and yet, when I turn around, there is nobody there!"

Mrs. Hopkins, naturally, tried to talk her out of her apprehensions, but to no avail. For two years Annie, the housekeeper, tolerated the "unseen visitor." Then she quit. She just could not go on like this, she explained. "*Somebody keeps turning my doorknob*. I am not a superstitious person, but I do believe you have a *ghost* here."

Mrs. Hopkins wondered why no one else in the apartment noticed anything unusual. After Annie left, Josephine was hired, and slept in the apartment. Before long, Josephine, too, kept exclaiming in surprise, just as Annie had done for so long.

Finally, Josephine came to see Mrs. Hopkins and asked if she could talk to her. Mrs. Hopkins sat back to listen.

"This apartment is haunted," Josephine said.

Mrs. Hopkins was not surprised. She admitted openly now that there was an "unseen guest" at the apartment, but she loved the apartment too much to give it up. "We'll just have to live with that ghost!" she replied. Josephine laughed, and said it was all right with her, too.

She felt the ghost was female, and from that day on, for seven and a half years, Josephine would speak aloud to the ghost on many occasions, addressing her always as "Miss Flossie" and asking the unquiet spirit to tell her what was troubling her so much. Finally, one morning, Josephine came into Mrs. Hopkins' room and told her that she knew why "Miss Flossie" could not find rest.

"Miss Flossie killed herself, Ma'am," she said quietly.

Josephine never actually *saw* the ghost, for "no matter how quickly I turn, the ghost is even quicker" to disappear. But as is the case so often with children, the Hopkinses' small son *did see* her. The boy was then just four years old.

He had been asleep for several hours that particular night, when Mrs. Hopkins heard him call out for her. Mrs. Hopkins rushed to his side. The boy said a "lady visitor waked me up when she kissed me." Mrs. Hopkins insisted that she and her husband were the only ones at home. The boy insisted that he had seen this woman, and that she looked like "one of those dolls little girls play with."

Mrs. Hopkins calmed her boy, and after he had returned to sleep, she went to her husband and brought him up to date on this entire ghost business. He didn't like it at all. But somehow the household settled down to routine again, and it was several years before another manifestation occurred, or was noticed, at least.

One night, while her son was in boarding school and her husband out of town on business, Mrs. Hopkins found herself all alone in the apartment. It was a quiet, rainy night, and Mrs. Hopkins did not feel unduly nervous, especially as "Miss Flossie" had not been active for so long.

Sometime after going to bed, Mrs. Hopkins was awakened by someone calling her name. "Mrs. Hop-kins! Mrs. Hop-kins!" There was a sense of urgency about the voice, which seemed to be no different from that of someone close by. Mrs. Hopkins responded immediately. "Yes, what is it?" Fully awake now, she noticed by her clock that the time was 1 A.M. Suddenly she became aware of an entirely different sound. Overhead, on the roof, there were footsteps, and somehow she knew it was a burglar. Jumping from bed, Mrs. Hopkins examined the hall door. The three locks were all off. She tried to telephone the superintendent, but found the line had been cut! Without a moment's hesitation, she retraced her steps to the bedroom, and *locked herself in the room.*

The next morning, the superintendent informed Mrs. Hopkins that the two other houses in the block had their top floor apartments burglarized during the night, but her apartment had somehow been spared! Mrs. Hopkins smiled wanly. How could she explain that a ghost had saved her that night?

One evening Mrs. Hopkins and her husband returned from the theater and found a small black kitten crying on the front doorstep of the house. She felt pity for the kitten, and took it into the apartment, locking it into the maid's room for the night. At first they thought it was a neighbor's cat, but nobody came to claim it, and in the end they kept it.

The cat behaved strangely right from the start. Dashing through the apartment with fur disarranged, she seemed terrified of something. Josephine told Mrs. Hopkins that the ghost hated the kitten, and would kill it before long.

A week later, Mrs. Hopkins sat alone in a comfortable chair, reading. It was evening, and the kitten was curled up, sleeping peacefully nearby. Suddenly the cat looked toward the doorway leading into the hall. Getting up, she seemed to see someone enter the room, pass in front of Mrs. Hopkins, and finally stand directly behind her. The cat seemed terrified. Finally, Mrs. Hopkins said, "Kitty, don't be afraid of Miss Flossie." The cat relaxed, but not Mrs. Hopkins, who felt a terrific chill.

When her husband returned, she insisted they give up the apartment. The ghost had become too much for her. No sooner said than done, and two weeks later, they were living at the other end of town.

One night at dinner Mr. Hopkins mentioned that he had just learned more about their former apartment from one of the old tenants he had met. At the time when they rented the place, the superintendent told them the previous tenants had moved out "ten minutes before." What he had neglected to tell them, however, was *how*. The Hopkinses had come there *ten minutes after the funeral*. The wife of the former tenant had committed suicide in the living room. Mrs. Hopkins' curiosity was aroused. She went to see a Mrs. Foran, who lived at the old place directly below where their apartment had been.

"What sort of woman was this lady who died here?" she asked her.

Well, it seemed that the couple had been living elsewhere before their marriage without benefit of clergy. After they got married, they moved to this place, to make a fresh start.

But the wife was still unhappy. During the three years of their tenancy, she *imagined* the neighbors were gossiping about her. Actually, the neighbors knew nothing of their past, and cared less. "But," Mrs. Foran added as an afterthought, "she didn't *belong* here."

"Why not?" wondered Mrs. Hopkins.

"Because she had bleached hair, that's why!" replied Mrs. Foran.

Mrs. Hopkins couldn't help smiling, because she realized how right Josephine had been in calling *the spook* "Miss Flossie."

During the 1960s, I decided to pay "Miss Flossie" a visit. I first located Mrs. Hopkins in Newmarket, Canada. My letter requesting information was answered by Mrs. Hopkins' sister, Helena Daly.

"Since my sister is very handicapped following a stroke," she wrote, "I shall be pleased to give you the information you wish, as I lived there with them for a short time, but did not meet the ghost.

"The location is at 471 Central Park West, northwest corner of 106th Street, a top-floor apartment with windows facing south and also east, overlooking Central Park.

"Wishing you every success, yours truly, Helen M. Daly."

I located the house all right, even though it was at 107th Street. The apartment on the top floor was locked. I located a ground-floor tenant who knew the name of the family now living in it. The name was Hernandez, but that didn't get me into the apartment by a long shot. My three letters remained unanswered. The rent collector gave me the name of the superintendent. He didn't have a key either. The entire neighborhood had changed greatly since the Hopkinses lived there. The whole area, and of course the building at 471 Central Park West, was now populated by recent arrivals from Puerto Rico.

Weeks went by. All my efforts to contact the Hernandez family proved fruitless. There was no telephone, and they never seemed to be home when I stopped by. Finally, I decided to send a letter announcing my forthcoming visit three days hence at one thirty in the afternoon, and would they please be in, as I had the permission of their landlord to see them.

I was determined to hold a seance *outside* their very doorstep, if necessary, hoping that my Sensitive, Mrs. Meyers, would somehow catch at least part of the vibratory element, and atmosphere, of the place. I also invited a Mr. Lawrence, a newspaper writer, to come along as a witness.

To my surprise, the seance on the doorstep was unnecessary. When the three of us arrived at the apartment, somewhat out of breath after climbing four flights of stairs on a hot summer day, the door was immediately opened by a nicely-dressed young man who introduced himself as Mr. Hernandez, occupant of the apartment. He led us through the large apartment into the living room at the corner of the building, the very room I was most interested in.

Mr. Hernandez explained that he was a furniture repairman employed by one of the large hotels, and that he and his family—we saw a young wife and child—lived in the apartment. They had never seen nor heard anything unusual. He did not believe in "vibrations" or the supernatural, but had no objection to our sitting down and gathering what impressions we could. I had maintained in my letters all along that "a famous literary figure" had once occupied his apartment and we wanted to visit the rooms for that reason, as I was doing an article on this person. It doesn't pay to tell the person whose apartment you want to visit that it's his ghost you're after.

Mrs. Meyers sat down on the comfortable couch near the window, and the rest of us took seats around her. Her first impressions of the room came through immediately.

"I hear a woman's voice calling Jamie or Janie. . . . There is an older woman, kind of emaciated looking, with gray hair, long nose, wide eyes, bushy eyebrows. Then there is a black cat. Something is upsetting Jamie. There's a squeaking rocking chair, a man with a booming voice, reciting lines, heavy-set, he wears a cutaway coat . . . man is heavy in the middle, has a mustache, standup collar with wings, dark tie . . . there's something wrong with his finger . . . a wedding band? A remark *about a wedding band?*"

Mrs. Meyers looked around the carefully furnished, spotlessly clean room, and continued. "A small boy, about twelve. Someone here used to live *with the dead* for a very long time, treated as if they were alive. Just stay here, never go out, if I go out, *he* is not going to come back again, so I'll remain here! I look from the window and see him coming out of the carriage. We have dinner every night." Suddenly, Mrs. Meyers started to inhale rapidly, and an expression of fear crept upon her face.

"Gas—always have one burner—gas! Somebody is still disturbed about Jamie. I get the letters M. B. or B. M. I feel lots of people around. There is a to-do in court. Now someone walks around the outside that can't be seen. Wants to come in by the window.

"It's like a nightmare, very dark, can't look out the window. I am a mess, and I'm going to fall if I let go. There's a body laid in a casket in this room, but very few flowers; the name on the silver plaque reads Stevens or Stevenson; the curtains are drawn, it's very dark, there are candles and a body in the casket."

I asked Mrs. Meyers if she felt any restless spirits about the place still.

"The restlessness is dimming," she replied. "It was there in the past, but is much dimmer now, because a religious person lives here."

Did she get any other impressions?

"The police had something to do here, they wear long coats, the coffin contains a person in black."

After we had left the apartment, I compared Mrs. Meyer's impressions to the material in the Hopkins story, which I had never shown or mentioned to her. There was a small son, and the description of the "older woman" fit Mrs. Hopkins, as did the black cat. Mrs. Meyers' statement, that "something was wrong with his finger . . . a wedding band!" recalled the fact that the couple had been living together as man and wife for years without being married, and had this fact not disturbed the ghost so much?

The gas explosion and the funeral following "Miss Flossie's" suicide were factual. M. is Mrs. Hopkins initial and "M. B." may have been "M. D.," which is M. Daly, Mrs. Hopkins' maiden name. "Someone walking on the outside" refers to the burglar episode. Police and the coffin make sense where suicide is involved.

Shortly after our seance, I received word that Mrs. Hopkins had passed on. Now perhaps she and "Miss Flossie" can become better acquainted.

The Ghost at
St. Mark's

DESPITE THE FACT THAT MOST religious faiths, and their
clergy, take a dim view of ghosts and hauntings, there are
many recorded cases of supernormal goings-on in churches
and cemeteries. One such place of worship is New York's famed old
St. Mark's-In-the-Bouwerie church, located at the corner of Second
Avenue and 10th Street.

Originally the site of a chapel erected in 1660 by Peter
Stuyvesant for the Dutch settlers of New Amsterdam, it became the
governor's burial ground in 1672. The Stuyvesant vault was per-
manently sealed in 1953, when the last member of the family died.
A century after the death of the governor, the family had adopted the
Episcopalian faith, and a grandson, also named Peter Stuyvesant,
gave the land and some cash to build on the same spot the present
church of St. Mark's. It was completed in 1799 and has been in
service continuously since. No major repairs, additions, or changes
were made in the building.

The surrounding neighborhood was then a changing one, populated by artists, students, and derelicts, although it was once one of
the most highly respected ones in the city. But even in the confines
of the Bowery, there is a legend that St. Mark's is a haunted church.

I talked to the Reverend Richard E. McEvoy, then Archdeacon of St. John's, but for many years rector of St. Mark's, about any apparitions he or others might have seen in the church. Legend, of course, has old Peter Stuyvesant rambling about now and then. The Reverend proved to be a keen observer, and quite neutral in the matter of ghosts. He himself had not seen anything unusual. But there was a man, a churchgoer, whom he had known for many years. This man always sat in a certain pew on the right side of the church.

Queried by the rector about his peculiar insistence on that seat, the man freely admitted it was because from there he could see "her"—the "her" being a female wraith who appeared in the church to listen to the sermon, and then disappeared again. At the spot he had chosen, he could always be next to her! I pressed the rector about any *personal* experiences. Finally he thought that he had seen something like a figure in white out of the corner of one eye, a figure that passed, and quickly disappeared. That was years ago.

On the rector's recommendation, I talked to Foreman Cole, the man who came to wind the clock at regular intervals, and who had been in and around St. Mark's for over twenty-six years.

Mr. Cole proved to be a ready talker. Some years ago, Cole asked his friend Ray Borc, organist at a Roman Catholic church nearby, to have a look at the church organ. The church was quite empty at the time, which was 1 A.M. Nevertheless, Cole saw "someone" in the balcony.

About fifteen years prior, Cole had another unusual experience. It was winter, and the church was closed to the public, for it was after 5 P.M. That evening it got dark early, but there was still some light left when Cole let himself into the building. Nobody was supposed to be in the church at that time, as Cole well knew, being familiar with the rector's hours.

Nevertheless, to his amazement, *he clearly saw a woman standing in the back of the church,* near the entrance door, in the center aisle. Thinking that she was a late churchgoer who had been locked in by mistake, and worried that she might stumble in the semi-darkness, he called out to her, "Wait, lady, don't move till I turn the lights on."

He took his eyes off her for a moment and quickly switched the lights on. But he found himself alone; she had vanished into thin air from her spot well within the nave of the church.

Unnerved, Cole ran to the entrance door and found it firmly locked. He then examined all the windows and found them equally well secured.

I asked Cole if there was anything peculiar about the woman's appearance. He thought for a moment, then said, "Yes, there was. She seemed to ignore me, looked right through me, and did not respond to my words."

Six weeks later, he had another supernormal experience. Again alone in the church, with all doors locked, he saw a man who looked to him like one of the Bowery derelicts outside. He wore shabby clothes, and did not seem to "belong" here. Quickly, Cole switched on the lights to examine his visitor. But he had vanished, exactly as the woman had before.

Cole had not seen any apparitions since, but some pretty strange noises had reached his ears. For one thing, there was frequent "banging" about the church, and "uncanny" feelings and chills in certain areas of the old church. On one occasion, Cole clearly heard someone coming up the stairs leading to the choir loft. Thinking it was the sexton, he decided to give him a scare, and hid to await the man at the end of the staircase. Only, nobody came. The steps were those of an *unseen man!*

Cole had no idea who the ghosts could be. He still took care of the clock, and was reluctant to discuss his experiences with ordinary people, lest they think him mad. A man who was quite healthy and realistic, Cole was sure of his memories.

Several days later, I asked Mary R. M., a singer and gifted psychic, to accompany me to the church and see if she could get any "impressions." It turned out that my friend had been to the church once before, last November, when she was rehearsing nearby. At that time, she was *sure* the place was haunted. We sat in one of the right-hand pews, and waited. We were quite alone in the church; the time was three in the afternoon, and it was quite still. Within a minute or so, Mary told me she felt "a man with a cane walking down the middle aisle behind us." Peter Stuyvesant, buried here, walked with a cane.

Then my friend pointed to the rear, and advised me that she "saw" a woman in wide skirts standing near the rear door of the church. She added: "I see a white shape floating away from that marble slab, in the rear!"

So if you ever find yourself on a visit to St. Mark's and see someone dissolve into thin air—don't be alarmed. It's only a ghost!

A Visit with Alexander Hamilton's Ghost

THERE STANDS AT NUMBER 27, JANE STREET, in New York's picturesque Greenwich Village, a mostly wooden house dating back to pre-Revolutionary days. In this house Alexander Hamilton was treated in his final moments. Actually, he died a few houses away, at 80 Jane Street, but No. 27 was the home of John Francis, his doctor, who attended him after the fatal duel with Aaron Burr.

The facts of Hamilton's untimely passing are well known; D. S. Alexander (in his *Political History of the State of New York*) reports that, because of political enmity, "Burr seems to have deliberately determined to kill him." A letter written by Hamilton calling Burr "despicable" and "not to be trusted with the reins of government" found its way into the press, and Burr demanded an explanation. Hamilton declined, and on June 11, 1804, at Weehawken, New Jersey, Burr took careful aim, and his first shot mortally wounded Hamilton. In the boat back to the city, Hamilton regained consciousness, but knew his end was near. He was taken to Dr. Francis' house and treated, but died within a few days at his own home, across the street.

Shortly after moving into 27 Jane Street, Jean Karsavina, a writer and artist, had become aware of footsteps, creaking stairs, and the opening and closing of doors; and even the unexplained flushing of a toilet. On one occasion, she found the toilet chain still swinging, when there was no one around! "I suppose a toilet that flushes would be a novelty to someone from the eighteenth century," she was quoted in a brief newspaper account.

She also had seen a blurred "shape," without being able to give details of the apparition; her upstairs tenant, however, reports that one night not so long ago, "a man in eighteenth-century clothes, with his hair in a queue" walked into her room, looked at her and walked out again.

Ms. Karsavina turned out to be a well-read and charming lady who had accepted the possibility of living with a ghost under the same roof. Mrs. Meyers and I went to see her. The medium had no idea where we were going.

At first, Mrs. Meyers, still in waking condition, noticed a "shadow" of a man, old, with a broad face and bulbous nose; a woman with a black shawl whose name she thought was Deborah, and she thought "someone had a case"; she then described an altar of white lilies, a bridal couple, and a small coffin covered with flowers; then a very old woman in a coffin that was richly adorned, with relatives including a young boy and girl looking into the open coffin. She got the name of Mrs. Patterson, and the girl's as Miss Lucy. In another "impression" of the same premises, Mrs. Meyers described "an empty coffin, people weeping, talking, milling around, *and the American Flag atop the coffin*; in the coffin a man's hat, shoes with silver buckles, gold epaulettes. . . ." She then got close to the man and thought his lungs were filling with liquid and he died with a pain in his side.

Lapsing into semitrance at this point, Mrs. Meyers described a party of men in a small boat on the water, then a man wearing white pants and a blue coat with blood spilled over the pants. "Two boats were involved, and it is dusk," she added.

Switching apparently to another period, Mrs. Meyers felt that "something is going on in the cellar, they try to keep attention from what happens downstairs; there is a woman here, being stopped by two men in uniforms with short jackets and round hats with wide brims, and pistols. There is the sound of shrieking, the woman is pushed back violently, men are marching, someone who had been harbored here has to be given up, an old man in a nightshirt and red socks is being dragged out of the house into the snow."

In still another impression, Mrs. Meyers felt herself drawn up toward the rear of the house where "someone died in childbirth"; in fact, this type of death occurred "several times" in this house. Police were involved, too, but this event or chain of events is of a later period than the initial impressions, she felt. The name Henry Oliver or Oliver Henry came to her mind.

After her return to full consciousness, Mrs. Meyers remarked that there was a chilly area near the center of the downstairs room. There was; I felt it too. Mrs. Meyers "sees" the figure of a slender man, well-formed, over average height, in white trousers, black boots, dark blue coat and tails, white lace in front; *he is associated with George Washington and Lafayette,* and their faces appear to her, too; she feels Washington may have been in this house. The man she "sees" is a *general,* she can see his epaulettes. The old woman and the children seen earlier are somehow connected with this, too. He died young, and there "was fighting in a boat." Now Mrs. Meyers gets the name "W. Lawrence." She had a warm feeling about the owner of the house; he took in numbers of people, like refugees.

A "General Mills" stored supplies here—shoes, coats, almost like a military post; food is being handed out. The name Bradley is given. Then Mrs. Meyers sees an old man playing a cornet; two men in white trousers are "seen" seated at a long table, bent over papers, with a crystal chandelier above.

After the seance, Miss Karsavina confirmed that the house belonged to Hamilton's physician, and as late as 1825 was owned by a doctor, who happened to be the doctor for the Metropolitan Opera House. The cornet player might have been one of his patients.

In pre-Revolutionary days, the house may have been used as headquarters of an "underground railroad," around 1730, when the police tried to pick up the alleged instigators of the so-called "Slave Plot," evidently being sheltered here.

"Lawrence" may refer to the portrait of Washington by Lawrence which used to hang over the fireplace in the house. On the other hand, I found a T. Lawrence, M. D., at 146 Greenwich Street, *Elliot's Improved Directory for New York* (1812); and a "Widow Patterson" is listed by Longworth (1803) at 177 William Street; a William Lawrence, druggist, at 80 John Street. According to Charles Burr Todd's *Story of New York*, two of Hamilton's pallbearers were *Oliver* Wolcott and John L. *Lawrence*. The other names mentioned could not be found. The description of the man in white trousers is of course the perfect image of Hamilton, and the goings-on at the house with its many coffins, and women dying in childbirth, are indeed understandable for a doctor's residence.

It does not seem surprising that Alexander Hamilton's shade should wish to roam about the house of the man who tried, vainly, to save his life.

The Conference House Ghost

O NLY A FEW MINUTES BY ferry boat from bustling Manhattan lies the peaceful charm of Staten Island, where many old houses and even a farm or two still exist in their original form within the boundaries of New York City.

One of these old houses, and a major sight-seeing attraction, is the so-called "Conference House," where the British Commander, Lord Howe, received the American Conference delegation consisting of Benjamin Franklin, John Adams, and Edward Rutledge, on September 11, 1776. The purpose of the meeting was to convince the Americans that a peaceful solution should be found for the difficulties between England and the Colonies. The meeting proved unsuccessful, of course, and the Revolutionary War ensued.

The house itself is a sturdy white two-story building, erected along typical English manor-house lines, in 1688, on a site known then as Bentley Manor in what is today Tottenville. There are two large rooms on the ground floor, and a staircase leading to an upper story, also divided into two rooms; a basement contains the kitchen and a vault-like enclosure. The original owner of the house was Captain Billopp of the British Navy, and his descendants lived in the house until the close of the Revolutionary period.

Local legends have had the house "haunted" for many years. The story was that Billopp, a hard man, jilted his fiancee, and that she died of a broken heart in this very house. For several generations back, reports of noises, murmurs, sighs, moans, and pleas have been received and the old Staten Island *Transcript,* a local newspaper, had mentioned these strange goings-on over the years. When the house was being rebuilt, after having been taken over as a museum by the City of New York, the workmen are said to have heard the strange noises, too.

It was against this background that I decided to investigate the house in the company of Mrs. Meyers, who was to be our Sensitive, and two friends, Rose de Simone and Pearl Winder, who were to be the "sitters," or assistants to the medium.

After we had reached Staten Island, and were about half an hour's drive from the house, Mrs. Meyers volunteered her impressions of the house which she was yet to see! She spoke of it as being white, the ground floor divided into two rooms, a brown table and eight chairs in the east room; the room on the west side of the house is the larger one, and lighter colored than the other room, and some silverware was on display in the room to the left.

Upon arriving at the house, I checked these statements; they were correct, except that the number of chairs was now only seven, not eight, and the silver display had been removed from its spot eight years before!

Mrs. Meyers' very first impression was the name "Butler"; later I found that the estate next door belonged to the Butler family, unknown, of course, to the medium.

We ascended the stairs; Mrs. Meyers sat down on the floor of the second-story room to the left. She described a woman named Jane, stout, white-haired, wearing a dark green dress and a fringed shawl, then mentioned the name *Howe.* It must be understood that the connection of Lord Howe with the house was totally unknown to all of us until *after* checking up on the history of the Conference House, later on.

Next Mrs. Meyers described a man with white hair, or a wig, wearing a dark coat with embroidery at the neck, tan breeches, dark shoes, and possessed of a wide, square face, a thick nose, and looking "Dutch." "The man died in this room," she added.

She then spoke of the presence of a small boy, about six, dressed in pantaloons and with his hair in bangs. The child born in this room was specially honored later, Mrs. Meyers felt. This might apply to Christopher Billopp, born at the house in 1737, who later became Richmond County representative in the Colonial Assembly. Also, Mrs. Meyers felt the "presence" of a big man in a fur hat, rather fat, wearing a skin coat and high boots, brass-buckle belt and black trousers; around him she felt boats, nets, sailing boats, and she heard a foreign, broad accent, also saw him in a four-masted ship of the square-rigger type. The initial T was given. Later, I learned that the Billopp family were prominent Tory leaders up to and during the Revolution.

This man, Mrs. Meyers felt, had a loud voice, broad forehead, high cheekbones, was a vigorous man, tall, with shaggy hair, and possibly Dutch. His name was Van B., she thought. She did not know that Billopp (or Van Billopp) was the builder of the house.

"I feel as if I'm being dragged somewhere by Indians," Mrs. Meyers suddenly said. "There is violence, somebody dies on a pyre of wood, two men, one white, one Indian; and on two sticks nearby are their scalps."

Later, I ascertained that attacks by the Native Americans were frequent here during the seventeenth and eighteenth centuries and that, in fact, a tunnel once existed as an escape route to the nearby waterfront, in case of hostile sieges. Large numbers of arrowheads had been unearthed around the house.

Down in the cellar, Mrs. Meyers felt sure six people had been buried near the front wall during the Revolutionary War, all British soldiers; she thought eight more were buried elsewhere on the grounds and sensed the basement full of wounded "like a hospital." On investigation, I found that some members of Billopp's family were indeed buried on the grounds near the road; as for the British soldiers, there were frequent skirmishes around the house between Americans infiltrating from the nearby New Jersey shore, and the British, who held Staten Island since July 4, 1776. At one time, Captain Billopp, a British subject, was kidnapped by armed bands in his own house, and taken to New Jersey as a prisoner of the Americans!

We returned to the upper part of the house once more. Suddenly, Mrs. Meyers felt impelled to turn her attention to the winding staircase. I followed with mounting excitement.

Descending the stairs, our medium suddenly halted her steps and pointed to a spot near the landing of the second story. "Someone was killed here with a crooked knife, a woman!" she said. There was horror on her face as if she were reliving the murder. On questioning the custodian, Mrs. Early, I discovered that Captain Billopp, in a rage, had indeed killed a female servant on that very spot!

The Clinton Court
Ghosts

WHILE CASUALLY LEAFING THROUGH THE PAGES of *Tomorrow* magazine, a long defunct periodical devoted to psychical research in which my byline appeared on occasion, I noticed a short piece by Wainwright Evans, called "Ghost in Crinoline." The article told of a spectral inhabitant at number 422? West 46th Street, in New York City. It seemed that Ruth Shaw, an artist who had for years lived in the rear section of the old building, which she had turned into a studio for herself, had spoken to Mr. Evans about her experiences. He had come to see her at Clinton Court, as the building was called. There was a charming iron gate through which you pass by the main house into a court. Beyond the court rose an arcaded rear section, three stories high and possessed of an outdoor staircase leading to the top. This portion dates back to 1809, or perhaps even before, and was at one time used as the coach house of Governor DeWitt Clinton.

Miss Shaw informed Evans about the legends around the place, and in her painstaking manner told him of her conversations with ninety-year-old Mr. Oates, a neighborhood druggist. An English coachman, with a Danish wife, once lived in the rooms above the stables. The first ghost ever to be seen at Clinton Court was that of

"Old Moor," a sailor hanged for mutiny at the Battery, and buried in Potter's Field, which was located only a short block away from the house. Today, this cemetery has disappeared beneath the tenement houses of the middle Westside, Hell's Kitchen's outer approaches. But "Old Moor," as it were, did not have far to go to haunt anyone. Clinton Court was the first big house in his path. The coachman's wife saw the apparition, and while running away from "Old Moor," fell down the stairs. This was the more unfortunate as she was expecting a child at the time. She died of the fall, but the child survived.

The irony of it was that soon the mother's ghost was seen around the Court, too, usually hanging around the baby. Thus, Ghost Number 2 joined the cast at the Governor's old house.

One of the grandchildren of the Clinton family, who had been told these stories, used to play "ghost" the way children nowadays play cops and robbers. This girl, named Margaret, used to put on old-fashioned clothes and run up and down the big stairs. One fine day, she tripped and fell down the stairs, making the game grim reality. Many since have seen the pale little girl; Miss Shaw was among them. She described her as wearing a white blouse, full sleeves, and a crinoline. On one occasion, she saw the girl ghost skipping down the stairs *in plain daylight*—skipping is the right word, for a ghost need not actually "walk," but often floats just a little bit above ground, not quite touching it.

I thought it would be a good idea to give Miss Shaw a ring, but discovered there was no telephone at the address. Miss Shaw had moved away and even the local police sergeant could not tell me where the house was. The police assured me *there was no such number* as 422? West 46th Street. Fortunately, I had my own opinion, so my search continued. Perhaps a dozen times I walked by numbers 424 and 420 West 46th Street before I discovered the strange archway at Number 420. I walked through it, somehow driven on by an inner feeling that I was on the right track. I was, for before me opened

Clinton Court. It simply was tucked away in back of 420 and the new owners had neglected to put the 422? number anywhere within sight. Now an expensive, remodeled apartment house, the original walls and arrangements were still intact.

On the wall facing the court, Number 420 proudly displayed a bronze plaque inscribed "Clinton Court—ca. 1840—Restored by the American Society for Preservation of Future Antiquities"! The rear building, where Miss Shaw's studio used to be, was then empty. Apparently the carpenters had just finished fixing the floors, and the apartment was up for rent. I thought that fortunate, for it meant we could get into the place without worrying about a tenant. But there was still the matter of finding out who the landlord was, and getting permission. It took me several weeks and much conversation, until I finally got permission to enter the place one warm August evening.

Meanwhile I had been told by the superintendent that an old crony by the name of Mrs. Butram lived next door, at Number 424, and that she might know something of interest. I found Mrs. Butram without difficulty. Having been warned that she kept a large number of pets, my nose led me to her door. For twenty-five years, she assured me, she had lived here, and had heard many a story about the ghost next door. She had never seen anything herself, but when I pressed her for details, she finally said—

"Well, they say it's a young girl of about sixteen. . . . One of the horses they used to keep back there broke loose and frightened her. Ran down the stairs, and fell to her death. That's what they say!"

I thanked Mrs. Butram, and went home. I called my good friend Mrs. Ethel Meyers, and asked her to accompany me to a haunted house, without telling her any more than that. To my surprise, Mrs. Meyers told me on the phone that she thought she could see the place clairvoyantly that very instant.

"There is a pair of stairs outside of a house, and a woman in white, in a kind of backyard."

This conversation took place a week before Mrs. Meyers knew anything about the location or nature of our "case."

About a week later, we arrived together at Clinton Court, and proceeded immediately into the ground-floor studio apartment of the former coach house. In subdued light, we sat quietly on the shabby, used-up furniture.

"Let me look around and see what I get," Mrs. Meyers said, and rose. Slowly I followed her around the apartment, which lay in ghostly silence. Across the yard, the windows of the front section were ablaze with light and the yard itself was lit up by floodlights. But it was a quiet night. The sounds of Hell's Kitchen did not intrude into our atmosphere, as if someone bent on granting us privacy for a little while were muffling them.

"I feel funny in the head, bloated . . . you understand I am *her* now . . . there are wooden steps from the right on the outside of the place—"

Mrs. Meyers pointed at the wall. "There, where the wall now is; they took them down, I'm sure." On close inspection, I noticed traces of something that had probably been a staircase.

"A woman in white, young, teen-ager, she's a bride, she's fallen down those steps on her wedding night, her head is battered in—"

Horror came over Mrs. Meyers' face. Then she continued. "It is cold, the dress is so flimsy, flowing; she is disappointed, for someone has disappointed *her*."

Deep in thought, Mrs. Meyers sat down in one of the chairs in a little room off the big, sunken living room that formed the main section of the studio apartment now, as the new owners had linked two apartments to make one bigger one.

"She has dark hair, blue eyes, light complexion, I'd say she's in her middle teens and wears a pretty dress, almost like a nightgown, the kind they used to have seventy-five or a hundred years ago. But now I see her in a gingham or checkered dress with high neck, long sleeves, a white hat, she's ready for a trip, only someone doesn't come. There is crying, disappointment. Then there is a seafaring man also, with a blue hat with shiny visor, a blue coat. He's a heavy-set man."

I thought of "Old Moor." Mrs. Meyers was getting her impressions all at the same time. Of course, she knew nothing of either the young girl ghost nor the sailor.

Now the medium told a lively tale of a young girl ready to marry a young man, but pursued by another, older man. "I can hear her scream!" She grabbed her own throat, and violently suppressed a scream, the kind of sound that might have invited an unwelcome audience to our seance!

"Avoiding the man, she rushes up the stairs, it is a slippery and cold day around Christmas. She's carrying something heavy, maybe wood and coal, and it's the eve of her marriage, but she's pushed off the roof. There are two women, the older one had been berating the girl, and pushed her out against the fence, and over she went. It was cold and slippery and nobody's fault. But instead of a wedding, there is a funeral."

The medium was now in full trance. Again, a scream is suppressed, then the voice changes and another personality speaks through Mrs. Meyers.

"Who are you?" I said, as I always do on such occasions. Identification is a must when you communicate with ghosts.

Instead, the stranger said anxiously—"Mathew!"

"Who is Mathew?" I said.

"Why won't he come, where is he? Why?"

"Who are you?"

"Bernice."

"How old are you?"

"Seventeen."

"What year is this?"

"Eighty."

But then the anguish came to the fore again.

"Where is he, he has the ring . . . my head . . . Mathew, Mathew . . . she pushed me, she is in hell. I'm ready to go, I'm dressed, we're going to father. I'm dressed. . . ."

As she repeated her pleas, the voice gradually faded out. Then, just as suddenly as she had given way to the stranger, Mrs. Meyers' own personality returned.

As we walked out of the gloomy studio apartment, I mused about the story that had come from Mrs. Meyers' lips. Probably servant girls, I thought, and impossible to trace. Still, she got the young girl, her falling off the stairs, the stairs themselves, and the ghostly sailor. Clinton Court was still haunted all right!

I looked up at the reassuringly lighted modern apartments around the yard, and wondered if the ghosts knew the difference. If you ever happen to be in New York's "Hell's Kitchen," step through the archway at 420 West 46th Street into the yard, and if you're real, real quiet, and a bit lucky, perhaps you will meet the teen-age ghost in her white dress or crinoline—but beware of "Old Moor" and his language—you know what sailors are like!

The House Ghost
of Bergenville

ABOUT TWENTY YEARS AGO, Mrs. Ethel Meyers, who frequently accompanied me on ghost-hunting expeditions, heard from friends living in Bergen County, New Jersey, about some unusual happenings at their very old house. They were busy people of considerable prominence in the theater, but eventually the "safari for ghost" was organized, and Mr. B., the master of the house, picked us up in his car and drove us to Bergen County. The house turned out to be a beautifully preserved pre-Revolutionary house set within an enclosure of tall trees and lawns.

The building had been started in 1704, I later learned, and the oldest portion was the right wing; the central portion was added in the latter part of the eighteenth century, and the final, frontal portion was built from old materials about seventy-five years ago, carefully preserving the original style of the house. The then owners had acquired it from a family who had been in possession for several generations. The house was then empty, and the B.'s refurbished it completely in excellent taste with antiques of the period.

After they moved into the house, they slept for a few days on a mattress on the enclosed porch, which skirted the west wing of the house. Their furniture had not yet arrived, and they didn't mind roughing it for a short while. It was summer, and not too cool.

In the middle of the night, Mrs. B. suddenly awoke with the uncanny feeling that there was *someone else* in the house, besides her husband and herself. She got up and walked toward the corridor-like extension of the enclosed porch running along the back of the house. There she clearly distinguished the figure of a man, seemingly white, with a beard, wearing what she described as "something ruffly white." She had the odd sensation that this man belonged to a much earlier period than the present. The light was good enough to see the man clearly for about five minutes, in which she was torn between fear of the intruder and curiosity. Finally, she approached him, and saw him *literally dissolve before her very eyes!* At the same time, she had the odd sensation that the stranger came to look *them* over, wondering what they were doing in *his* house! Mrs. B., a celebrated actress and choreographer, was not a scoffer, nor was she easily susceptible. Ghosts to her were something one can discuss intelligently. Since her husband shared this view, they inquired of the former owner about any possible hauntings.

"I've never heard of any or seen any," Mr. S. told them, "but my daughter-in-law has never been able to sleep in the oldest part of the house. Said there was too much going on there. Also, one of the neighbors claims he saw something."

Mr. S. wasn't going to endanger his recent real-estate transaction with too many ghostly tales. The B.'s thanked him and settled down to life in their colonial house.

But they soon learned that theirs was a busy place indeed. Both are artistic and very intuitive, and they soon became aware of the presence of unseen forces.

One night Mrs. B. was alone at home, spending the evening in the upper story of the house. There was nobody downstairs.

Suddenly she heard the downstairs front door open and shut. There was no mistaking the very characteristic and complex sound of the opening of this ancient lock! Next, she heard footsteps, and sighed with relief. Apparently her husband had returned much earlier than expected. Quickly, she rushed down the stairs to welcome him. There was nobody there. There was no one in front of the door. All she found was the cat in a strangely excited state!

Sometime after, Mr. B. came home. For his wife these were anxious hours of waiting. He calmed her as best he could, having reservations about the whole incident. Soon these doubts were to be dispelled completely.

This time Mrs. B. was away and Mr. B. was alone in the downstairs part of the house. The maid was asleep in her room, the B.'s child fast asleep upstairs. It was a peaceful evening, and Mr. B. decided to have a snack. He found himself in the kitchen, which is located at the western end of the downstairs part of the house, when he suddenly heard a car drive up. Next, there were the distinct sounds of the front door opening and closing again. As he rushed to the front door, he heard the dog bark furiously. But again, there was no one either inside or outside the house!

Mr. B., a star and director, and as rational a man as could be, wondered if he had imagined these things. But he knew he had not. What he had heard were clearly the noises of an arrival. While he was still trying to sort out the meaning of all this, another strange thing happened.

A few evenings later, he found himself alone in the downstairs living room, when he heard carriage wheels outside grind to a halt. He turned his head toward the door, wondering who it might be at this hour. The light was subdued, but good enough to read by. He didn't have to wait long. A short, husky man walked into the room *through* the closed door; then, without paying attention to Mr.

B., turned and walked out into the oldest part of the house, again *through a closed door!*

"What did he look like to you?" I asked.

"He seemed dotted, as if he were made of thick, solid dots, and he wore a long coat, the kind they used to wear around 1800. He probably was the same man my wife encountered."

"You think he is connected with the oldest part of the house?"

"Yes, I think so. About a year ago I played some very old lute music, the kind popular in the eighteenth century, in there—and something happened to the atmosphere in the room. As if someone were listening quietly and peacefully."

But it wasn't always as peaceful in there. A day before our arrival, Mrs. B. had lain down, trying to relax. But she could not stay in the old room. "There was someone there," she said simply.

The B.'s weren't the only ones to hear and see ghosts. Last summer, two friends of the B.'s were visiting them, and everybody was seated in the living room, when in plain view of all, the screen door to the porch opened and closed again *by its own volition!* Needless to add, the friends didn't stay long.

Only a day before our visit, another friend had tried to use the small washroom in the oldest part of the house. Suddenly, he felt chills coming on and rushed out of the room, telling Mrs. B. that "someone was looking at him."

At this point, dinner was ready, and a most delicious repast it was. Afterwards we accompanied the B.'s into the oldest part of their house, a low-ceilinged room dating back to the year 1704. Two candles provided the only light. Mrs. Meyers got into a comfortable chair, and gradually drifted into trance.

"Marie . . . Catherine . . . who calls?" she mumbled.

"Who is it?" I inquired.

"Pop . . . live peacefully . . . love. . . ."

"What is your name?" I wanted to know.

"Achabrunn. . . ."

I didn't realize it at the time, but a German family named Achenbach had built the house and owned it for several generations. Much later still, I found out that one of the children of the builder had been called Marian.

I continued my interrogation.

"Who rules this country?"

"The Anglish. George."

"What year is this?"

"56. 1756."

"When did you stay here?"

"Always. Pop. My house. *You* stay with *me*."

Then the ghost spoke haltingly of his family, his children, of which he had nine, three of whom had gone away.

"What can we do for you?" I said, hoping to find the reason for the many disturbances.

"Yonder over side hill, hillock, three buried . . . flowers there."

"Do you mean," I said, "that we should put flowers on these graves?"

The medium seemed excited.

"Ach Gott, ja, machs gut." With this the medium crossed herself.

"What is your name?" I asked again.

"Oterich . . . Oblich. . . ." The medium seemed hesitant as if the ghost were searching his memory for his own name. Later, I found that the name given was pretty close to that of another family having a homestead next door.

The ghost continued.

"She lady . . . I not good. I very stout heart, I look up to good-blood lady, I make her good . . . Kathrish, holy lady, I worship lady . . . they rest on hill too, with three. . . ."

After the seance, I found a book entitled *Pre-Revolutionary Dutch Houses in Northern New Jersey and New York*. It was here that I discovered the tradition that a poor shepherd from Saxony married a woman above his station, and built this very house. The year 1756 was correct.

But back to my interrogation. "Why don't you rest on the hillock?"

"I take care of . . . four. . . hillock . . . Petrish. Ladian, Annia, Kathrish. . . ."

Then, as if taking cognizance of us, he added—"To care for you, that's all I want."

Mrs. B. nodded and said softly, "You're always welcome here."

Afterward, I found that there were indeed some graves on the hill beyond the house. The medium now pointed toward the rear of the house, and said, "Gate . . . we put intruders there, he won't get up any more. Gray Fox made trouble, Indian man, I keep him right there."

"Are there any passages?"

"Yeah. Go dig through. When Indian come, they no find."

"Where?"

"North hillock, still stone floor there, ends here."

From Mr. B. I learned that underground passages are known to exist between this house and the so-called "Slave House," across the road.

The ghost then revealed that his wife's father, an Englishman, had built the passage, and that stores were kept in it along with bones of Native Americans.

"Where were you born?" I inquired.

"Here. Bergenville."

Bergenville proved to be the old name of the township.

I then delicately told him that this was the twentieth century. He seemed puzzled, to say the least.

"In 1756 I was sixty-five years old. I am not 200 years older?"

At this point, the ghost recognized the women's clothing the medium was wearing, and tore at them. I explained how we were able to "talk" to him. He seemed pacified.

"You'll accept my maize, my wine, my whiskey. . . ."

I discovered that maize and wine staples were the mainstays of the area at that period. I also found that Indian wars on a small scale were still common in this area in the middle 1700's. Moreover, the ghost referred to the "gate" as being in the *rear* of the house. This proved to be correct, for what is now the back of the house was then its front, facing the road.

Suddenly the ghost withdrew and after a moment another person, a woman, took over the medium. She complained bitterly that the Indians had taken one of her children, whose names she kept rattling off. Then she too withdrew, and Mrs. Meyers returned to her own body, none the worse for her experiences, none of which, incidentally, she remembered.

Shortly afterward, we returned to New York. It was as if we had just come from another world. Leaving the poplar-lined road behind us, we gradually re-entered the world of gasoline and soot that is the modern city.

Nothing further has been reported from the house in Bergen County, but I am sure the ghost, whom Mrs. B. had asked to stay as long as he wished, is still there. There is of course now no further need to bang doors, to call attention to his lonely self. *They know he is there with them.*

The Fifth Avenue
Ghost

Some cases of haunted houses require but a single visit to obtain information and evidence, others require two or three. But very few cases in the annals of psychic research can equal or better the record set by the case I shall call The Fifth Avenue Ghost. Seventeen sessions, stretching over a period of five months, were needed to complete this most unusual case. I am presenting it here just as it unfolded for us. I am quoting from our transcripts, our records taken during each and every session; and because so much evidence was obtained in this instance that could only be obtained from the person these events actually happened to, it is to my mind a very strong case for the truth about the nature of hauntings.

It isn't very often that one finds a haunted apartment listed in the leading evening paper. Occasionally, an enterprising real-estate agent will add the epithet "looks haunted" to a cottage in the country to attract the romanticist from the big city.

But the haunted apartment I found listed in the New York *Daily News* one day was the real McCoy. Danton Walker, the late Broadway columnist, had this item—

"One for the books: an explorer, advertising his
Fifth Avenue Studio for sub-let, includes among
the attractions 'attic dark room with ghost.' . . ."

The enterprising gentleman thus advertising his apartment
for rent turned out to be Captain Davis, a celebrated explorer and
author of many books, including, here and there, some ghost lore.
Captain Davis was no skeptic. To the contrary, I found him sincere
and well aware of the existence of psychical research. Within hours,
I had discussed the case with the *study group* which met weekly at
the headquarters of the Association for Research and Enlightenment,
the Edgar Cayce Foundation. A team was organized, consisting of
Bernard Axelrod, Nelson Welsh, Stanley Goldberg and myself, and,
of course, Mrs. Meyers as the medium. Bernard Axelrod and I knew
that there was some kind of "ghost" at the Fifth Avenue address, but
little more. The medium knew nothing whatever. Two days *after* the
initial session, a somewhat fictional piece appeared in the *New York
Times* by Meyer Berger, who had evidently interviewed the *host,* but
not the *ghost.* Mr. Berger quoted Captain Davis as saying there was
a green ghost who had hanged himself from the studio gallery, and
allegedly sticks an equally green hand out of the attic window now
and then.

Captain Davis had no idea who the ghost was. This piece, it must
be re-emphasized, appeared two days *after* the initial sitting at the
Fifth Avenue house, and its contents were of course unknown to all
concerned at the time.

In order to shake hands with the good Captain, we had to climb
six flights of stairs to the very top of 226 Fifth Avenue. The building
itself is one of those big old town houses popular in the mid-Victorian
age, somber, sturdy, and well up to keeping its dark secrets behind its
thickset stone walls. Captain Davis volunteered the information that
previous tenants had included Richard Harding Davis, actor Richard

Mansfield, and a lady magazine editor. Only the lady was still around and, when interviewed, was found to be totally ignorant of the entire ghost tradition, nor had she ever been disturbed. Captain Davis also told of guests in the house having seen the ghost at various times, though he himself had not. His home was one of those fantastic and colorful apartments only an explorer or collector would own—a mixture of comfortable studio and museum, full of excitement and personality, and offering more than a touch of the Unseen. Two wild jungle cats completed the atmospheric picture, somewhat anticlimaxed by the host's tape recorder set up on the floor. The apartment was a kind of duplex, with a gallery or balcony jutting out into the main room. In the middle of this balcony was the window referred to in the *Times* interview. Present were the host, Captain Davis, Mr. and Mrs. Bertram Long, the Countess de Sales, all friends of the host's, and the group of researchers previously mentioned—a total of eight people, and, if you wish, two cats. As with most sittings, tape recordings were made of the proceedings from beginning to end, in addition to which written notes were taken.

Meeting a ghost

Like a well-rehearsed television thriller, the big clock in the tower across the square struck nine, and the lights were doused, except for one medium-bright electric lamp. This was sufficient light, however, to distinguish the outlines of most of the sitters, and particularly the center of the room around the medium.

A comfortable chair was placed under the gallery, in which the medium took her place; around her, forming a circle, sat the others, with the host operating the recorder and facing the medium. It was very still, and the atmosphere seemed tense. The medium had hardly touched the chair when she grabbed her own neck in the unmistakable manner of someone being choked to death, and nervously told of being "hung by the neck until dead." She then sat in the chair and Bernard Axelrod, an experienced hypnotist, conditioned her into her usual trance condition, which came within a few minutes.

With bated breath, we awaited the arrival of whatever personality might be the "ghost" referred to. We expected some violence and, as will be seen shortly, we got it. This is quite normal with such cases, especially at the first contact. It appears that a "disturbed personality" continuously relives his or her "passing condition," or cause of death, and it is this last agony that so frequently makes ghostly visitations matters of horror. If emotional anxiety is the cause of death, or was present at death, then the "disturbed personality," or entity, will keep reliving that final agony, much like a phonograph needle stuck in the last groove of a record. But here is what happened on that first occasion.

A Sitting on July 11 at 226 Fifth Avenue

The Medium, now possessed by unknown entity, has difficulty in speaking. Entity breaks into mad laughter full of hatred.

Entity:	. . . curry the horse. . . they're coming. . . curry the horse! Where is Mignon? WHERE IS SHE?
Question:	We wish to help you. Who is Mignon?
Entity:	She should be here . . . where is she . . . you've got her! Where is she? Where is the baby?
Question:	What baby?
Entity:	What did they do with her?
Question:	We're your friends.
Entity:	(in tears) Oh, an enemy . . . an enemy. . . .
Question:	What is your name?
Entity:	Guychone . . . Guychone. . . . (expresses pain at the neck; hands feeling around are apparently puzzled by finding a woman's body)

Question: You are using someone else's body. (Entity clutches throat.) Does it hurt you there?

Entity: Not any more . . . it's whole again . . . I can't see. . . . All is so different, all is very strange . . . nothing is the same.

I asked how he died. This excited him immediately.

Entity: (hysterical) I didn't do it . . . I tell you I didn't do it, no . . . Mignon, Mignon . . . where is she? They took the baby . . . she put me away . . . they took her. . . . (Why did she put you away?) So no one could find me (Where?) I stay there (meaning upstairs) all the time.

At this point, tapes were changed. *Entity,* asked where he came from, says Charleston, and that he lived in a white house.

Question: Do you find it difficult to use this body?

Entity: WHAT?? WHAT?? I'm HERE . . . I'm here. . . . This is my house . . . what are YOU doing here?

Question: Tell me about the little room upstairs.

Entity: (crying) Can I go . . . away . . . from the room?

At this point, the entity left, and the medium's *control,* Albert, took over her body.

Albert: There is a very strong force here, and it has been a little difficult. This individual here suffered violence at the hands of several people. He was a Confederate and he was given up, hidden here, while they made their escape.

Question: What rank did he hold?

Albert: I believe that he had some rank. It is a little dubious as to what he was.

Question: What was his name?

Albert: It is not as he says. That is an assumed name, that he likes to take. He is not as yet willing to give full particulars. He is a violent soul underneath when he has opportunity to come, but he hasn't done damage to anyone, and we are going to work with him, if possible, from this side.

Question: What about Mignon and the baby?

Albert: Well, they of course are a long time *on this side,* but he never knew that, what became of them. They were separated cruelly. She did *not* do anything to him.

Question: How did he leave this world?

Albert: By violence. (Was he hanged?) Yes. (In the little room?) Yes. (Was it suicide or murder?) He says it was murder.

The *control* then suggests to end the trance, and try for results in "open" sitting. We slowly awaken the medium.

While the medium is resting, sitter Stanley Goldberg remarks that he has the impression that Guychone's father came from Scotland.

Captain Davis observes that at the exact moment of "frequency change" in the medium, that is, when Guychone left and Albert took over, the control light of the recording apparatus suddenly blazed up *of its own accord,* and had to be turned down by him.

A standing circle was then formed by all present, holding hands, and taking the center of the room. Soon the medium started swinging forward and back like a suspended body. She remarked feeling very stiff "from hanging and surprised to find that I'm whole, having been cut open in the middle."

Both Axelrod and I observed a luminescent white and *greenish* glow covering the medium, creating the impression of an older man without hair, with high cheekbones and thin arms. This was during the period when Guychone was speaking through the medium.

The seance ended at twelve-thirty. The medium reported feeling exhausted, with continued discomfort in the throat and stomach.

The Investigation Continues

Captain Davis, unfortunately, left on a worldwide trip the same week, and the new tenant was uncooperative. I felt we should continue the investigation. Once you pry a ghost loose from his place of unhappy memories, he can sometimes be contacted elsewhere.

Thus, a second sitting took place at the headquarters of the study group, on West 16th Street. This was a small, normally-furnished room free of any particular atmosphere, and throughout this and all following sittings, subdued light was used, bright enough to see all facial expressions quite clearly. There was smoking and occasional talking in low voices, none of which ever disturbed the work. Before the second sitting, Mrs. Meyers remarked that Guychone had "followed her home" from the Fifth Avenue place, and twice appeared to her at night in a kind of "whitish halo," with an expression of frantic appeal in his eyes. Upon her admonition to be patient until the sitting, the apparition had vanished.

A Later Sitting, at 125 West 16th Street—July 14th

Question: Do you know what year this is?

Guychone: 1873.

Question: No, it is not. Over one hundred years have gone by. You are no longer alive. Do you understand?

Guychone: One hundred years? I'm not a hundred-ten years?

Question: No, you're not. You're forever young. Mignon is on your side, too. We have come to help you understand yourself. What happened in 1873?

Guychone: Nobody's goddamn business . . . mine . . . mine!

Question: All right, keep your secret then, but don't you want to see Mignon? Don't you want justice done? (mad, bitter laughter) Don't you believe in God? (more laughter) The fact you are here and are able to speak, doesn't that prove that there is hope for you? What happened in 1873? Remember the house on Fifth Avenue, the room upstairs, the horse to be curried?

Guychone: Riding, riding . . . find her . . . they took her away.

Question: Who took her away?

Guychone: YOU! (threatens to strike interrogator)

Question: No, we're your friends. Where can we find a record of your Army service? Is it true you were on a dangerous mission?

Guychone: Yes.

Question: In what capacity?

Guychone: That is my affair! I do not divulge my secrets. I am a gentleman, and my secrets die with me.

Question: Give us your rank.

Guychone: I was a Colonel.

Question: In what regiment?

Guychone: Two hundred and sixth.

Question: Were you infantry or cavalry?

Guychone: Cavalry.

Question: In the War Between the States?

Guychone: Yes.

Question: Where did you make your home before you came to New York?

Guychone: Charleston . . . Elm Street.

Question: What is your family name, Colonel?

Guychone: (crying) As a gentleman, I am yet not ready to give you that information . . . it's no use, I won't name it.

Question: You make it hard for us, but we will abide by your wishes.

Guychone: (relieved) I am very much obliged to you . . . for giving me the information that it is ONE HUNDRED YEARS. One hundred years!

I explain about the house on Fifth Avenue, and that Guychone's "presence" had been felt from time to time. Again, I ask for his name.

Apparently fumbling for paper, he is given paper and fountain pen; the latter seems to puzzle him at first, but he then writes in the artistic, stylized manner of the mid-Victorian age—"Edouard Guychone."

Question: Is your family of French extraction?
Guychone: Yes.
Question: Are you yourself French or were you born in this country?
Guychone: In this country . . . Charleston.
Question: Do you speak French?
Guychone: No.
Question: Is there anything you want us to do for you? Any unfinished business?
Guychone: One hundred years makes a difference . . . I am a broken man . . . God bless you . . . Mignon . . . it is so dark, so dark. . . .

I explain the reason for his finding himself temporarily in a woman's body, and how his hatred had brought him back to the house on Fifth Avenue, instead of passing over to the "other side."

Guychone: (calmer) There IS a God?

I ask when was he born.

Guychone: (unsure) 1840 . . . 42 years old. . . .

This was the most dramatic of the sittings. The transcript cannot fully convey the tense situation existing between a violent, hate-inspired and God-denying personality fresh from the abyss of perennial darkness, and an interrogator trying calmly to bring light into a disturbed mind. Toward the end of the session, Guychone understood about God, and began to realize that much time had passed since his personal tragedy had befallen him. Actually, the method of "liberating" a ghost is no different from that used by a psychiatrist to free a flesh-and-blood person from obsessions or other personality disturbances. Both deal with the mind.

It became clear to me that many more sessions would be needed to clear up the case, since the entity was reluctant to tell all. This is not the case with most ghosts, who generally welcome a chance to "spill" emotions pent up for long years of personal hell. Here, however, the return of reason also brought back the critical faculty of reasoning, and evaluating information. We had begun to liberate Guychone's soul, but we had not yet penetrated to his conscience. Much hatred, fear, and pride remained, and had to be removed, before the true personality could emerge.

A Still Later Sitting, July 21st

Albert, the medium's control, spoke first.

Question: Have you found any information about his wife and child?

Albert: You understand that this is our moral code, that that which comes from the individual within voluntarily is his sacred development. That which he wishes to divulge makes his soul what it should eventually be.

I asked that he describe Guychone's appearance to us.

Albert: At the moment he is little developed from the moment of passing. He is still like his latter moments in life. But his figure was of slight build, tall . . . five feet nine or ten . . . his face is round, narrow at the chin, high at the cheekbones, the nose is rather prominent, the mouth rather wide . . . the forehead high, at the moment of death and for many years previous very little hair. The eyes set close to the nose.

Question: Have you learned his *real* name?

Albert: It is not his wish as yet. He will tell you, he will develop his soul through his confession. Here he is!

Guychone: (at first grimacing in pain) It is nice to come, but it is hell . . . I have seen the light. It was so dark.

Question: Your name, sir?

Guychone: I was a gentleman . . . my name was defiled. I cannot see it, I cannot hear it, let me take it, when it is going to be right. I have had to pay for it; she has paid her price. I have been so happy. I have moved about. I have learned to right wrongs. I have seen the light.

Question: I am going to open your eyes now.

Guychone: (pointing at the tape recorder in motion) Wagon wheels!

Question: Give us the name of one of your fellow officers in the war. Write it down.

Guychone: I am a poor soul. . . . (writes: Mignon my wife . . . Guychone) Oh, my feet, oh my feet they hurt me so now . . . they bleed . . . I have to always go backwards, backwards. What shall I do with my feet? They had no shoes . . . we walked over burning weed . . . they burned the weed. . . . (Who?) The Damyankees . . . I wake up, I see the burning weed. . . . (Where? When?) I have to reach out, I have so much to reach for, have patience with me, I can only reach so far—I'll forget. I will tell you everything. . . . (Where?) Georgia! Georgia! (Did you fight under General Lee?) I fell under him. (Did you die under him?) No, no.

Question: Who was with you in the regiment?

Guychone: Johnny Greenly . . . it is like another world . . . Jerome Harvey. (Who was the surgeon?) I did not see him. Horse doctors. (Who was your orderly?) Walter . . . my boy . . . I can't tell the truth, and I try so hard. . . . I will come with the truth when it comes, you see the burning weeds came to me . . . I will think of happier things to tell . . . I'd like to tell you about the house in Charleston, on Elm Street. I think it is 320, I was born in it.

Question: Any others in the family?

Guychone: Two brothers. They died. They were in the war with me. I was the eldest. William, and Paul. (And you're Edward?) Yes. (Your mother?) Mary. (Your father?) Frederick. (Where was he born?) Charleston. (Your mother's maiden name?) Ah. . . ! (Where did you go to college?) William . . . William and . . . a white house with green grass. (When did you graduate?) Fifty-three . . . OVER ONE HUNDRED YEARS. . . . It is hard to get into those corners where I can't think any more.

"I never had my eyes open before, in trance," observed Mrs. Meyers afterwards. "While I could look at you and you looked like yourself, I could almost look through you. That never happened before. I could only see what I focused on. This machine . . . it seemed the wheels were going much, much *faster* than they are going now."

A week later, a "planchette" session was held at the home of Mrs. Meyers, with herself and the Mrs. Zoe Britton present, during which Guychone made himself known, and stated that he had a living son, eighty-nine years old, now living in a place called Seymour, West Virginia.

Evidential material begins to pile up

By now we knew we had an unusual case. I went through all the available material on this period (and there is a lot), without turning up anyone named Guychone.

These were extremely hot afternoons, but the quest went on. Rarely has any psychic researcher undertaken a similarly protracted project to hunt down psychic evidence.

Another Sitting, One Week Later (July 28th)

Finding a St. Michael's medal around my neck, Guychone says it reminds him of a medal of St. Anne, which his "Huguenot mother," Marie Guychone, had given him.

Question: Do you remember the name of your college?
Guychone: Two colleges. St. Anne's in Charleston, South Carolina. . . . Only one thought around another, that's all I had—curry the horses. Why? I know now. I remember. I want to say my mother is here, I saw her, she says God bless you. I understand more now. Thank you. Pray for me.

Next Sitting—August 4th

This sitting repeated previous information and consisted in a cat-and-mouse game between Guychone and myself. However, toward the end, Guychone began to speak of his son Gregory, naming him for the first time. He asked us to find him. We asked, "What name does Gregory use?" Guychone casually answered: "I don't know . . . Guychone . . . maybe McGowan. . . ." The name McGowan came very quietly, but sufficiently distinct to be heard by all present. At the time, we were not overwhelmed. Only when research started to yield results did we realize that it was his real name at last. But I was not immediately successful in locating McGowan on the regimental rosters, far from it! I was misled by his statement of having served in the cavalry, and naturally gave the cavalry rosters my special attention, but he wasn't in them. Late in August I went through the city records of Charleston, West Virginia, on a futile search for the Guychone family, assuming still that they were his in-laws. Here I found mention of a "McGowan's Brigade."

Sitting of August 18th

Question: Please identify yourself, Colonel.

McGowan: Yes . . . Edward . . . I can stay? I can stay?

Question: Why do you want so much to stay? Are you not happy where you are?

McGowan: Oh yes. But I like to talk very much . . . how happy I am.

Question: What was your mother's name?

McGowan: Marie Guychone.

Question: What is your own name?

McGowan: Guychone.

Question: Yes; that is the name you *used*, but you really are . . .

McGowan: Edward Mac . . . Mac . . . curry the horses! (excited, is calmed by me) Yes, I see Mac . . . McGowan! I remember more now, but I can only tell what I know . . . it is like a wall . . . I remember a dark night, I was crazy . . . war on one hand, fighting, bullets . . . and then, flying away, chasing, chasing, chasing . . .

Question: What regiment were you with?

McGowan: Six . . . two . . . sometimes horse . . . oh, in that fire. . . .

Question: Who was your commanding general?

McGowan: But—Butler.

He then speaks of his service in two regiments, one of which was the Sixth South Carolina Regiment, and he mentions a stand on a hill, which was hell, with the Damyankees on all sides. He says it was at Chattanooga.

Question: The house on Fifth Avenue, New York do you remember the name of your landlord?
McGowan: A woman ... Elsie (or L. C.) ... stout....

Actually, he says, a man collected the rent, which he had trouble paying at times. He knew a man named Pat Duffy in New York. He was the man who worked for his landlady, collecting the rent, coming to his door.

During the interrogation about his landlord, McGowan suddenly returns to his war experiences. "There was a Griffin," he says, referring to an officer he knew.

Sitting of August 25th

"The Colonel," as we now called him, came through very clearly. He introduced himself by his true name. Asked again about the landlady in New York, he now adds that she was a *widow.* Again, he speaks of "Griff... Griff...." Asked what school he went to, he says "St. Anne's College in Charleston, South Carolina, and also William and Mary College in Virginia, the latter in 1850, 51, 52, 53, 54." What was his birthday? He says "February 10, 1830." Did he write any official letters during the war? He says, "I wrote to General Robert E. Lee." What about? When? "January, 1864. Atlanta. . . . I needed horses, horses, wheels to run the things on." Did you get them? "No." What regiment was he with then? "The Sixth from South Carolina." But wasn't he from West Virginia? Amazed, McGowan says, "No, from South Carolina."

I then inquired about his family in New York. McGowan explained that his mother did live with him there, and died there, but after his own death "they" went away, including his sister-in-law Gertrude and brother William. Again, he asks that we tell his son Gregory "that his father did *not* do away with himself."

I asked, "Where is there a true picture of you?" McGowan replied, "There is one in the courthouse in Charleston, South Carolina." What kind of a picture? "Etch . . . etch . . . *tintype!*"

All through these sittings it was clear that McGowan's memory was best when "pictures" or scenes were asked for, and worst when precise names or dates were being requested. He was never sure when he gave a figure, but was very sure of his facts when he spoke of situations or relationships. Thus, he gave varying dates for his own birthday, making it clear that he was hazy about it, not even aware of having given discrepant information within a brief period.

But then, if a living person undergoes a severe shock, is he not extremely hazy about such familiar details as his name or address? Yet, most shock victims can *describe* their house, or their loved ones. The human memory, apparently, is more reliable in terms of associations, when under stress, than in terms of factual information, like names and figures.

By now research was in full swing, and it is fortunate for the sake of the Survival View that so much prima-facie evidence was obtained *before* the disclosure of McGowan's true name started the material flowing. Thus, the old and somewhat tiring argument of "mental telepathy" being responsible for some of the information, can only be applied, if at all, to a part of the sittings. No one can read facts in a mind *before* they get into that mind!

The sittings continued in weekly sessions, with Colonel McGowan rapidly becoming our "star" visitor.

Sitting of September 1st

Question: What was your rank at the end of the war?

McGowan: That was on paper . . . made to serve.

Question: Did you become a general?

McGowan: Naw . . . honors . . . I take empty honors. . . .

Question: When you went to school, what did you study?

McGowan: The law of the land.

Question: What happened at Manassas?

McGowan: Oh . . . defeat. Defeat.

Question: What happened to you personally at Manassas?

McGowan: Ah, cut, cut. Bayonets. Ah. Blood, blood.

Question: What happened at Malvern Hill?

McGowan: Success. We took the house. Low brick building. We wait. They come up and we see right in the mouth of a cannon. 1864. They burned the house around our ears. But we didn't move.

Question: What was under your command at that time?

McGowan: Two divisions.

Question: How many regiments?

McGowan: Four . . . forty . . . (Four?) TEEN!

Question: What did you command?

McGowan: My commander was shot down, I take over. (Who for?) John . . . Major. . .

Question: Listen, Colonel, your name is not Edward. Is there any other first or middle name you used? (Silence) Did anyone of high rank serve from South Carolina? (My brother William) Anyone else? (Paul)

McGowan: Do you think of Charles McGowan? That was no relation of mine. He was on the waterfront. He was . . . exporter.

McGowan: Were you at Gettysburg, Colonel? (Yes.) What regiments were under your command then?

McGowan: I had a wound at Gettysburg. I was very torn. (Where did you get the wound?) Atlanta . . . change of rank. Empty honors (About his son Gregory) Seymour . . . many years Lowell, Massachusetts, and then he went back down South, Seymour, South Carolina, and sometimes West Virginia . . . he was in a store, he left and then he came into property, mother also had property, down there near Charleston in West Virginia . . . that is where he is, yes.

Question: You say your father was Frederick? (Yes.) Who was William. (My brother.) Who was Samuel? (Long pause, *stunned,* then: *I* wrote that name!) Why didn't you tell us? (Crying: I didn't want to tell. . . .) Tell us your true rank, too. (I don't care what it was.) Please don't evade us. What was your rank? (Brigadier . . . General.) Then you are General Samuel McGowan?

McGowan: You made me very unhappy . . . such a name (crying) . . . blood, empty honors. . . .

Question: Who was James Johnson? (My commander.) What happened to him? (Indicates he was shot.) Who took over for Johnson? (I did.) What regiment was it?

McGowan: I don't know the figures . . . I don't know.

Question: Your relative in New York, what was his name?

McGowan: Peter Paul.

Question: What was his profession?

McGowan: A doctor. (Any particular kind of doctor?) Cuts. (What kind?) (McGowan points to face.) (Nose doctor?) (McGowan points to mouth and shakes head.) (Mouth doctor?) (McGowan violently grabs his teeth and shakes them.) (Oh, teeth? A dentist.) (McGowan nods assent.)

Question: I will name some regiments, tell me if any of them mean anything to you. The 10th . . . the 34th . . . the 14th. . . .

(McGowan reacts.) The 14th? Does it mean anything to you?

McGowan: I don't know, figures don't mean anything on this side . . .

Some interesting facts brought out by research

In the sitting of August 18th, McGowan stated his landlord was a woman and that her name was "Elsie" or L. C. *The Hall of Records of New York City* lists the owner of 226 Fifth Avenue as "Isabella S. Clarke, from 1853 to (at least) March 1, 1871." In the same sitting, McGowan stated that Pat Duffy was the man who actually came to collect the rent, working for the landlady. Several days *after* this information was *voluntarily* received from the entity, I found in *Trow's New York Directory for 1869/70:*

Page 195: "Clark, Isabella, wid. Constantine h. (house) 45 Cherry."

Page 309: "Duffy, Patrick, laborer, 45 Cherry."

This could be known only to someone who actually *knew* these people, years ago; it proved our ghost was *there* in 1873!

The sitting of September 1st also proved fruitful.

A "Peter McGowan, dentist, 253 W. 13 St." appears in *Trow's New York City Directory for 1870/71.*

J. F. J. Caldwell, in his *"History of a Brigade of South Carolinians known first as Gregg's, and subsequently as McGowan's Brigade."* (Philadelphia, 1866) reports:

Page 10: "The 14th Regiment South Carolina Volunteers selected for field officers . . . Col. James Jones, *Lt. Col. Samuel McGowan* . . . (1861)."

Page 12: "Colonel Samuel McGowan commands the 14th Regiment."

Page 18: "McGowan arrives from the Chickahominy river (under Lee)."

Page 24: "Conspicuous gallantry in the battle of Malvern Hill."

Page 37:   ". . . of the 11 field officers of our brigade, seven were wounded: Col. McGowan, etc. (in the 2nd battle of Manassas)."

Page 53:   "Col. Samuel McGowan of the 14th Regiment (at Fredericksburg)."

Page 60:   "The 13th and 14th regiments under McGowan. . . ."

Page 61:   "Gen. Gregg's death Dec. 14, 1862. McGowan succeeds to command."

Page 66:   "Biography: Born Laurens district, S.C. 1820. Graduated 1841 South Carolina College, Law; in Mexican War, then settled as lawyer in Abbeville, S.C. Became a Brig. Gen. January 20, 1863, assists in taking Ft. Sumter April 1861; but lapsing commission as General in State Militia, he becomes Lt. Col. in the Confederate Army, takes part at Bull Run, Manassas Plains, under Gen. Bonham. Then elected Lt. Col. of 14th Regiment, S.C.; Spring 1862, made full Col. *succeeding Col. Jones who was killed.* McGowan is *wounded* in battle of Manassas." Biographer Caldwell, who was McGowan's aide as a lieutenant, says (in 1866) "he still lives."

Page 79:   "April 29, 1863, McGowan's *Brigade* gets orders to be ready to march. Gen. McGowan commands the brigade."

Page 80:   "Wounded again (Fredericksburg)."

Page 89:   "Gen. Lee reviews troops including McGowan's. Brigade now consists of 1st, 12th, 13th, 14th Regiments and Orr's Rifles. Also known as 'McGowan's Sharpshooters.'"

Page 91:   "McGowan takes part in battle of Chancellorsville."

Page 96:   "Battle of Gettysburg: McGowan commands 13th, 12th, 14th, and 1st."

Page 110:   "McGowan near Culpepper Courthouse."

Page 122:   "Gen. McGowan returned to us in February (1864). He had not sufficiently recovered from the wound received at

Chancellorsville to walk well, but remained with us and discharged all the duties of his office."

Page 125: *About Butler:* "Butler to lead column (against McGowan) from the Eastern coast." Another Butler (Col.) commanded the Confederate 1st Regt. (Battle of Chickamauga)

Page 126: "Battle of Spottsylvania, May 1864."

Page 133: "Gen. Lee and Gen. Hill were there (defeat)."

Page 142: "McGowan wounded by a 'minie ball,' in the right arm, quits field."

But to continue with our sittings, and with McGowan's personal recollections—

Sitting of September 8th

McGowan: (speaking again of his death) It was in the forties . . . they killed me on the top floor. They dragged me up, that 'man of color' named Walter. He was a giant of a man. She was a virtuous woman, I tell you she was. But they would not believe it.

I wanted to get his reaction to a name I had found in the records, so I asked, "Have you ever met a McWilliams?"

McGowan: You have the knowledge of the devil with you. *Her* family name.

Question: Did you stay in New York until your passing?

McGowan: 1869, 1873. Back and forth. I have written to Lee, Jackson, James, and Beaufort. 1862-63, March.

Question: What did you do at the end of the war?

McGowan: Back and forth, always on the go. Property was gone, ruined. Plantations burned. I did not work. I could not. Three or four bad years. I quit. My wits, my wits. My uncle. The house was burned in Charleston. Sometimes Columbia. (Then, of Mignon, his wife, he says) She died in 1892 . . . Francois Guychone . . . he was so good to little boys, he made excursions in the Bay of Charleston—we sailed in boats. He was my uncle.

Sitting of September 15th

I asked, what did he look like in his prime.

McGowan: I wasn't too bad to look at, very good brow, face to the long, and at one time I indulged in the whiskers . . . not so long, for the chin . . . colonial . . . I liked to see my chin a good deal, sometimes I cover (indicates mustache). . . .

Question: What can you tell us about the cemetery in Abbeville?

McGowan: There is a monument, the family cemetery . . . nobody cared . . . my father was born the fifth of January. . . . (What was on your tombstone?) Samuel Edward McGowan, born 32? . . . died 1883? 1873? 1—8—7 hard to read, so dirty . . . age 40 . . . 41 . . . gray-brown stars battered. . . . I go between the bushes, I look at the monument, it's defaced. . . .

Question: What news did your family give out of your death?

McGowan: Foul play. (What happened to the body?) Cremated I guess, I think in this city. The remains were destroyed: not in the grave, a monument to a memory. . . . (What did they tell the public?) Lost forever . . . I could have been at sea . . . house was destroyed by fire. . . . (Do you mean there is no official record of your death?) No. *Not identical to passing,* they never told the exact month or day . . . I see . . . *1879* . . . very blurred . . . September 4th. . . .

Question: Were you ever injured in an argument?

McGowan: I spent much time on my back because of a wound . . .
on my head. (An argument?) Yes. (With whom?) A man.
Hand to hand. Rapier. . . . Glen, Glen. . . Ardmore.

Sitting of September 22nd

"Mother" Marie Guychone spoke briefly in French and was followed
by McGowan. He said he was at one time "An Associate Justice" in
the city of Columbia.

Here again do I wish to report some more research information
bearing on this part of the investigation. Evans, in his *Confederate
Military History,* 1899 has a picture of the General which became
available to us *after* the September 22nd sitting. His biography,
on page 414, mentions the fact that "he was associate Justice of
the (State) Supreme Court." Curiously, this author also states that
McGowan died in "December 1893." Careful scrutiny of two major
New York dailies then existing (*Post* and *Times*) brought to light
that the author of the *Confederate Military History* made a mistake,
albeit an understandable one. A certain Ned McGowan, described
as a "notorious character, aged 80" had died in San Francisco on
December 9, 1893. This man was also a Confederate hero (*The
New York Times,* XII/9). However, the same source (*The New York
Times,* August 13, 1897) reports General McGowan's death as having occurred on the ninth of August, 1897. The obituary contains
the facts already noted in the biography quoted earlier, plus one
interesting additional detail, that McGowan *received a cut across the
scalp in a duel.*

Another good source, *The Dictionary of American Biography,*
says of our subject: "*McGowan, Samuel.* Son of William and Jeannie
McGowan, law partner of William H. Parker. Died August 9, 1897 in
Abbeville. Buried in Long Cane Cemetery in Abbeville. Born Oct. 9,
1819 in Crosshill section of Laurens district, S. C. *Mother's name was*

McWilliams. Law partner of *Perrin* in Abbeville. Representative in State House of South Carolina. Elected to Congress, *but not seated.*"

A Colonel at Gettysburg, by Varina Brown, about her late husband Colonel Brown, contains the following: "In the battle of Jericho Mills, *'Griffin's Division'* of Federals wrought havoc against McGowan's Brigade."

Correspondence with Mrs. William Gaynes, a resident of Abbeville, revealed on October 1st, 1953—"The old general was a *victim of the failing mind* but he was doctored up until the date of his death. He was attended by his cousin *Dr. F. E. Harrison.*"

Eminent & Representative Men of South Carolina by Brant & Fuller (Madison, Wisconsin, 1892) gives this picture:

"Samuel McGowan was born of Scotch Irish parents in Laurens County S. C. on October 9th 1819. Graduated with distinction from the South Carolina College in 1841. Read law at Abbeville with T. C. Perrin who offered him a partnership. He entered the service as a private and went to Mexico with the Palmetto Regiment. He was appointed on the general Quartermaster's Staff with the rank of Captain. After the war he returned to Abbeville and resumed the practice of Law with T. C. Perrin. He married Susan Caroline, eldest daughter of Judge David Lewis Wardlaw and they lived in Abbeville until some years after the death of Gen. McGowan in 1897. The home of Gen. McGowan still stands in Abbeville and was sold some time ago to the Baptist Church for 50,000 dollars ... After the war he entered law practice with William H. Parker (*1869/1879*) *in Abbeville.* He took an interest in political affairs ... member of the Convention that met in Columbia in September, 1865. Elected to Congress but not allowed to take his seat. Counted out on the second election two years later. In 1878 he was a member of the State Legislature and in 1879 he was elected Associate Justice of the State Supreme Court.

"General McGowan lived a long and honorable life in Abbeville. He was a contributing member of the Episcopal Church, Trinity, and became a member later in life. At his death the following appeared in the *Abbeville Medium,* edited by Gen. R. R. Hemphill who had served in McGowan's Brigade. 'General Samuel McGowan *died at his home in this city* at 8:35 o'clock last Monday morning August 8th. Full of years and honors he passed away surrounded by his family and friends. He had been in declining health for some time and suffered intense pain, though his final sickness was for a few days only and at the end all was Peace. Impressive services were held in *Trinity Church* Tuesday afternoon, at four o'clock, the procession starting from the residence. At the Church, the procession . . . preceded by Dr. Wm. M. Grier and Bishop Ellison Capers who read the solemn service . . . directly behind the coffin old Daddy Willis Marshall, a black man who had served him well, bore a laurel wreath. Gen. McGowan was buried at *Long Lane* cemetery and there is a handsome stone on the plot."

Mrs. William Gaynes further reports:

"Gen. McGowan had a 'fine line of profanity' and used it frequently in Court. He was engaged in a duel once with Col. John *Cunningham* and was wounded behind one ear and came near passing out. Col. Cunningham challenged Col. *Perrin who refused* the challenge on the ground that he did not approve of dueling, and Gen. McGowan took up the challenge and the duel took place at Sand Bar Ferry, near Augusta, with McGowan being wounded.

"As far as I know, there was never any difficulty between Mrs. McGowan and the old General. His father-in-law, Judge Wardlaw, married *Sarah* Rebecca Allen, and *her* mother was Mary Lucia *Garvey.*"

In other words, Judge Wardlaw married *Sarah Garvey.*

Mrs. Gaynes continues: "I have seen him frequently on his way to his law office, for he had to pass right by *our* office. If he ever was out of town for any length of time, Abbeville *did not know it.*"

The inscription on Samuel McGowan's tombstone in Long Cane Graveyard reads as follows:

"Samuel McGowan, born Laurens County 9 October 1819. Died in Abbeville 9 August 1897. Go soldier to thy honored rest, thy trust and honor valor bearing. The brave are the tenderest, the loving are the daring."

Side 2: "From humble birth he rose to the highest honor in civic and military life. A patriot and a leader of men. In peace his country called him, he waited not to her call in war. A man's strength, a woman's tenderness, a child's simplicity were his and his a heart of charity fulfilling the law of love. He did good and not evil all the days of his life and at its end his country his children and his children's children rise up and call him blessed. In Mexican War 1846–1848. A Captain in United States Army. The Confederate War 1861–1865. A Brigadier General C.S.A. Member of the Legislature 1848–1850. Elected to Congress 1866. Associate Justice of Supreme Court of South Carolina 1878–1894. A hero in two wars. Seven times wounded. A leader at the Bar, a wise law giver a righteous judge. He rests from his labors and his works do follow him."

McGowan becomes a "regular" of the weekly sittings.

General McGowan had by now become an always impatient weekly "guest" at our sittings, and he never liked the idea of leaving. Whenever it was suggested that time was running short, McGowan tried to prolong his stay by becoming suddenly very talkative.

Sitting of September 29th

A prepared list of eight names, all fictitious but one (the sixth is that of Susan Wardlaw, McGowan's wife) is read to him several times. McGowan reacts to two of the nonexistent names, but not to the one of his wife. One of the fictitious names is John D. Sumter, to which

McGowan mumbles, "Colonel." Fact is, there *was* a Colonel Sumter in the Confederate Army!

McGowan also described in detail the farm where his son Gregory now lives. Asked about the name Guychone, he says it comes from Louisiana; Mignon, on her mother's side, had it. He identifies his hometown newspapers as "Star-Press." ("*Star-Press,* paper, picture, Judge, Columbia, picture in paper. . . .")

Question: Who was Dr. Harrison?
McGowan: Family doctor.
Question: Is your home in Abbeville still standing?
McGowan: It isn't *what it was.* Strange pictures and things. (Anyone live in it?) No. Strange things, guns and cannons.

Sitting of October 14th

McGowan says he had two daughters. Trying again to read his tombstone, he says, "1887, or is it 97?" As to his birthyear, he reads, "1821. . . . 31?"

Sitting of October 20th

When the control introduces McGowan, there is for several moments intense panic and fear brought on by a metal necklace worn by the medium. When McGowan is assured that there is no longer any "rope around his neck," he calms down, and excuses himself for his regression.

Question: Who was the Susan you mentioned the last time?
McGowan: The mother of my children.
Question: What was her other name?

McGowan: Cornelia.

Question: Were you elected to Congress?

McGowan: What kind of Congress? (The U. S. Congress.) I lost. Such a business, everybody grabs, everybody steals. . . . Somebody always buys the votes and it's such a mess.

Question: Are Mignon and Susan one and the same person or not?

McGowan: I don't wish to commit myself. (I insist.) They are *not!*

Question: Let us talk about Susan. What profession did your father-in-law follow?

McGowan: Big man . . . in the law.

Question: What was your mother-in-law's first name?

McGowan: Sarah.

Question: Did she have another name?

McGowan: Garfey. . . .

Question: Coffee? Spell it.

McGowan: Not coffee. *Garvey!*

At a sitting on October 28th, at the home of Mrs. Meyers, McGowan's alleged grandson, Billy, manifested himself as follows:

"My name is William, I passed in 1949, at Charleston. I'm a grandson of General McGowan. I was born in Abbeville, January 2nd, 1894. Gregory is half-brother, son of the French woman. He (McGowan) would have married her, but he had a boss, grandfather, who held the purse strings. Susan's father of Dutch blood, hard-headed."

Sitting of October 29th

McGowan: You must find Gregory. He may be surprised about his father, but I must let him know I wanted for him, and they took for *them* . . . all. And they gave him nothing. Nothing! I had made other plans. (Was there a will?) There was . . . but I had a Judge in the family that made other plans ... THEY WERE NOT MINE! You must tell Gregory I provided. .... I tell you only the truth because I was an honest man ... I did the best for my family, for my people, for those I considered my countrymen, that what you now call posterity ... I suffer my own sins. .... For you maybe it means nothing, for me, for those who remember me, pity ... they are now aware of the truth, only now is my son unaware of the truth. Sir, you are my best friend. And I go into hell for you. I tell you always the truth, Sir, but there are things that would not concern you or anybody. But I will give you those names yet!

Question: I ask again for the name of McGowan's father-in-law.
McGowan: Wida ... Wider.

The "ghost" is freed.

One of the functions of a "rescue circle" is to make sure a disturbed entity does not return to the scene of his unhappiness. This mission was accomplished here.

Sitting of November 3rd

McGowan: I see the house where I lived, you know, where you found me. *I go there now, but I am not anymore disturbed.* I found my mother and my father. They could not touch me, but *now,* we touch hands. I live over my life, come back to many things. Herman! He was a good soul, he helped me when I was down in Atlanta. He bathed my feet, my legs were scorched, and he was good to me, and he is over here. I thank him. I thanked him then, but I was the big man, and he was nothing, but now I see he is a fine gentleman, he polished my boots, he put my uniform in order.

Sitting of November 6th

I was alone with the medium, Mrs. Meyers, at her home, when I had
a chance to question McGowan about his apparent murder, and the
"conspiracy of silence" concerning it.

McGowan: The Judge protected them, did not report my death. They
had devised the kidnapping. I was murdered downstairs,
strangled by the kidnapper Walter. He took her (Mignon)
all the way to Boston. I wore the uniform of Damyankees
(during the war), rode a horse *every night* to Boston . . .
no, I made a mistake. I came to my Uncle Peter Paul in
New York, I had a letter from Marie Guychone, she was
in New York. Begged me to find Mignon and Gregory.
I come to New York. I can't find her, she was in Boston
then, but I didn't know that until later. Marie Guychone
remained with my uncle, and I gave up the chase, and like
a thief crawled back to Confederate grounds. That was
in 1863. After the war, there was a struggle, property was
worthless, finally the Union granted that we withdraw our
holdings, and with that I came to New York. My mother
and father came also, until rehabilitation was sufficient for
their return.

I continued to live with my wife, Susan, and the children, and I found Mignon. She had escaped, and came to
her mother in New York. I made a place for them to live
with my uncle and when my wife returned to stay with her
father (the Judge), I had Mignon, but she was pregnant
and she didn't know it, and there was a black child—there
was unpleasantness between us, I didn't know if it were
mine and Mignon was black, but it was not so, it was his
child (Walter's), and he came for it and for her, he traced
her to my house (on Fifth Avenue); my father-in-law (the

Judge) was the informer, and he (Walter) strangled me, he was a big man.

And when I was not dead yet, he dragged me up the stairs. Mignon was not present, not guilty. I think . . . it was in January 1874. But I may be mistaken about time. Gregory had two sons, William and Edward. William died on a boat in the English Channel in 1918. Gregory used the name *Fogarty,* not McGowan. The little black boy died, they say. It was just as well for him.

McGowan then left peacefully, promising more information about the time lag between his given date and that officially recorded. I told him the difference was "about twenty years." For the first time, McGowan had stated his story reasonably, although some details of it would be hard to check. No murder or suicide was reported in the newspapers of the period, similar to this case. But of course anyone planning a crime like this might have succeeded in keeping it out of the public eye.

We decided to continue our sittings.

Sitting of November 10th

McGowan talked about the duel he fought, which cost him his hair, due to a wound on the left side, back and top of his head. It was over a woman and against a certain Colonel C., something like "Collins," but a longer name. He said that Perry or Perrin *did so* make a stand, as if someone had doubted it!

More proof turns up!

Leading away from personal subjects, the questioning now proceeded toward matters of general interest about New York at the time of McGowan's residence here. The advantage of this line of questioning is its neutral value for research purposes; and as *no research* was undertaken until after the sittings of November 17th, mental telepathy must be excluded as an alternate explanation!

Sitting of November 17th

McGowan: You don't have a beard. They called them *milksops* in my
        days, the beardless boys!

Question: What did they call a man who was a nice dresser and
        liked ladies?

McGowan: A Beau Brummel.

Question: What did they call a gentleman who dressed too well,
        too fancifully?

McGowan: A fop.

Question: What was your favorite sport?

McGowan: Billiards. (He explains he was good at it, and the balls
        were *made of cloth.*)

Question: What was the favorite game of your day?

McGowan: They played a *Cricket* kind of game. . . .

Question: Who was mayor of New York?

McGowan: Oh . . . Grace. Grace . . . *Edmond* . . . Grace . . . something
        like it.

William R. Grace was mayor of New York, 1881–1882, and Franklin Edson (not Edmond) followed, 1883–1884. Also, plastic billiard balls as we know them today are a comparatively recent invention, and billiard balls in the Victorian era were indeed made of cloth. The cricket kind of game must be baseball. Beau Brummel, fop, milksop are all authentic Victorian expressions.

Sitting of November 26th

I asked the General about trains in New York in his time.

McGowan: They were smoke stacks, up in the air, smoke got in your eyes, they went down to the Globe Building near City Hall. The *Globe* building was near Broadway and Nassau. The train went up to Harlem. It was a *nice* neighborhood. I took many strolls in the park.

Question: Where was the Hotel Waldorf-Astoria?

McGowan: Near Fifth Avenue and 33rd, near my house . . . and the Hotel Prince George. Restaurants were Ye Olde Southern, Hotel Brevoort. You crack my brain, you are worse than that boss in the Big House, Mr. Tammany and Mr. Tweed. (I discussed his house, and he mentioned doing business with—) Somebody named *Costi* . . . I paid $128.50 a month for the entire house. A suit of clothes cost $100.00.

Question: Who lived next door to you?

McGowan: Herman . . . *was a carriage smith.* He had a business where he made carriages. He lived next door, but his business was not there, the shop was on Third Avenue, Third Street, near the river.

Question: Any other neighbors?

McGowan: Corrigan Brown, *a lawyer* . . . lived three houses down. The editor of the *Globe* was White . . . Stone . . . White . . . the editor of the *Globe* was not good friends with the man in the Big House. They broke his house down when he lived on Fifth Avenue. *He was a neighbor.* Herman the carriage maker made good carriages. I bought one with fringes and two seats, a cabrio. . . .

Question: Did you have a janitor?

McGowan: There was a man named Ted, mainly black servants, we had a gardener, white, named Patrick. He collects the rent, he lives with the Old Crow on Cherry Street. Herman lives next door. He had a long mustache and square beard. He wore a frock coat, a diamond tie pin, and spectacles. I never called him Herman ... (trying to remember his true name) Gray ... I never called him Herman. He had a wife named Birdie. His wife had a sister named Finny who lived there too ... Mrs. Finny ... she was a young widow with two children ... she was a good friend to my Susan.

McGowan then reluctantly signs his name as requested.

Research, undertaken *after* the sitting, again excluded mental telepathy. The facts were of a kind not likely to be found in the records, *unless* one were specifically looking for them!

The *New York Globe* building, which McGowan remembers "near Broadway and Nassau," was then (1873) at 7 Spruce Street and apparently also at 162 Nassau Street.* *The Globe* is on Spruce, and *Globe and Evening Press* on Nassau, around the corner.

McGowan describes the steam-powered elevated railroad that went from City Hall to Harlem. Steam cars started in 1867 and ran until 1906, according to the New York Historical Society, and there were two lines fitting his description, "Harlem, From Park Row to ... E. 86th Street" and "Third Avenue, from Ann Street through Park Row to ... Harlem Bridge.*

McGowan was right in describing Harlem as a nice neighborhood in his day. Harlem did not become a poor section until the mid-twentieth century.

McGowan also acknowledged at once that he had been to the Waldorf-Astoria, and correctly identified its position at Fifth

Avenue and 33rd Street. The Waldorf-Astoria came into being on March 14th, 1893. Consequently, McGowan *was alive then,* and evidently sane, if he could visit such places as the Waldorf, Brevoort, and others.

McGowan refers to a (later) landlord as Costi. In 1895, a real-estate firm by the name of George and John Coster was situated at 173 Fifth Avenue, a few houses down the street from McGowan's place.**

As for the carriage smith named Herman, a little later referred to as Herman Gray, there was a carriage maker named William H. Gray from 1872 or earlier, and existing beyond the turn of the century, whose shop was at first at 20 Wooster Street,* and who lived at 258 West Fourth Street, until at least 1882. In 1895 he is listed as living at 275 West 94th Street. Not all *Trow* volumes in between are available, so that residence in McGowan's neighborhood can neither be confirmed nor denied. At one time, Gray's shops were on West Broadway. As for Corrigan Brown, the lawyer neighbor, McGowan's mispronouncing of names almost tripped me up. There was no such lawyer. There was, however, one Edmond Congar Brown, lawyer, listed for the first time as such in 1886, and before that only as a clerk. No home is, unfortunately, listed for his later years.** McGowan stated that the editor of the *Globe* was named White-and-something, and that he lived near his (McGowan's) house on Fifth Avenue.

Well, one Horace P. Whitney, editor, business, 128 Fulton Street, home, 287 Fifth Avenue, is listed in *Trow.** And 128 Fulton Street is the place of the *Globe*'s competitor, the *New York Mercury,* published by Cauldwell and Whitney.*

That McGowan did not die in 1873 seems certain to me, as the above information proves. But if he did not die in 1873, something very traumatic must have been done to him at that time. Or perhaps the murder, if such it was, took place in 1897?

It could well be that General McGowan will take this ultimate secret with him into the Great Land where he now dwells safely forever.

* Trow's New York City Directory for 1872/73
** Trow's New York City Directory for 1895/96

Good Mediums
Are Rare

B Y NOW MY READERS MUST REALIZE that a ghost hunt is nothing without a good medium. True, occasionally apparitions materialize to outsiders without, apparently, a medium present. I say apparently, because I am convinced that *somebody* is mediumistic, when people see or hear ghosts. The catalyst in a group may be the very person believing the least in the supernatural, but being endowed with certain characteristics that make him, or her, the natural intermediary between the Two Worlds!

When I investigate a "haunted house," I do not sit around for days on end and hope for a fortunate moment when the discarnate entity has gathered up enough energy from the people in the house, or maybe passersby, or maybe me, to reveal himself. I am not usually asked to stay for a week. With me, it is tonight or never.

Therefore I like to make sure some sort of communication occurs at our first "sitting." To help matters along, I bring along a medium, preferably someone who does not earn his living in the capacity, although that is not absolutely necessary, provided he or she knows nothing about the location to be looked into.

Good mediums are rare. The talent, the innate inclination toward the psychic, is present in many of us, perhaps all. But the development to a stage where it can be of practical value is another matter. Good mediumship depends on rigorous training of the powers, discipline, and regular attempts at using it. Sporadic psychic application remains spotty. People who feel they have that sixth sense often ask me how to make it work for them. I usually advise them to put aside a few minutes every day, or every week, or even every two weeks, to "withdraw," and allow the power to come to the surface, in a moment of undisturbed silence. The important thing is to "sit" at precisely the same time, and to establish a certain rhythm in these sessions.

If the rhythm is interrupted, all the gains of previous weeks are lost; thus one must carefully choose a time and day when one is sure to be able to "sit" quietly. Sooner or later, mediumship will develop in one of its many forms.

Very few individuals attain the high development of a truly remarkable clairvoyant or trance medium, and there is of course a crying need in psychic research for such people. Thus a part of my attempts to look into ghosts and haunted houses has always been to replenish the supply of good mediums available to me for this work.

Whenever an individual, spurred on by one of my lectures or an article about me, contacted me because he or she has psychic talents, I followed up promptly in the hope of discovering, and perhaps encouraging, a new medium. So this is what I am to talk about now, and please forget your visions of mediums along Giancarlo Menotti lines. My mediums are all normal, everyday people who, by the very fact that they are mediumistic, need to be a bit more "normal" than you or me.

Mrs. Meyers, who appears in a large portion of the cases related in this book, was my first choice for a medium. Even Mrs. Meyers had her limitations, however, since she pursues a tiring career as a vocal coach and teacher. She devoted a great deal of time to psychic work, not only with me but with other researchers. Still, there were moments when the spirit—hers, that is—was only too willing, but the flesh isn't. By and large, however, she scored very highly, and her mediumship was enhanced by a good working knowledge of the scientific aspects of her rare gifts.

Among the half dozen or more mediums I investigated or "sat" with in the course of the Grant Year and the following year, when assembling one of my books, I found personalities as different as day and night. There was a kindly black woman, Nancy Hendricks, who told me on first meeting that a woman with the initial M., very close to me, wanted me to know that "life begins at forty." My mother's name was Martha, and I had turned forty the week before.

A lovely young woman by the name of Marina Brian Agostini wrote to me as a consequence of a newspaper article about my work. I went to see her at her artistically appointed apartment on the Lower Eastside of New York, and was told that her first psychic experience had been at age seventeen, when she heard "a voice" telling her a cousin would soon die—and the cousin did. The night poet Maxwell Bodenheim was murdered, she dreamed of it, only to find the morning headlines confirming her dream!

While living at 307 Sixth Avenue, she noticed a "bearded beggar" leaning over her child's crib. Her husband, an artist, failed to see the stranger, but Marina insisted he had something to do with the house "being on fire." Shortly after, a fire was discovered next door. The apparition was a warning, evidently. Intrigued with the Unknown, Marina and three friends held a seance, during which she felt the presence of Eugene O'Neill, Junior, who had committed suicide in the apartment. She felt herself drawn to the bookcase and heard him say, "Look in my father's play for a message!" The message, the only line on the page indicated by the vision, was found to read, "There is no death"!

It was common for Mrs. Agostini to know the name of a caller before she picked up the telephone (in the days before caller ID), or to see people she had dreamed of the night before, in the street the following day dressed exactly as they were in her dreams.

In the 1960s, Mrs. Agostini visited an allegedly haunted house in Center Moriches, Long Island, which belonged then to an advertising executive, but was later turned into an inn. The owner had been plagued by psychic phenomena, including the doors opening seemingly by their own volition, while securely locked. His wife once saw a person walk down the stairs, while she knew the maid was safely asleep in her quarters, and no one else about.

Unperturbed, Marina went up to the attic to look at the old house. To her amazement she found herself not alone. There, in front of a mirror, stood a young blond woman, dressed in blue, combing her hair. All Marina could see was the woman's back; when she turned, however, Marina was frightened out of her wits by a face so full of unbridled hatred that it made her run down the stairs in stark terror!

Reporting her uncanny experience to her hosts, she was then told of the reputation of the house. A woman exactly like the one Marina had described was killed in this house the very night before her scheduled wedding!

One of her eerie experiences occurred when she was asked to read for the part of "Joan of Arc" in a play—but became uncontrollably agitated, and felt somehow that she was *present* when Joan died at the stake! Taken back to "an earlier life" hypnotically, she once spoke fluent ancient French—which she did not know in her ordinary state!

I arranged for a seance a few days later, to test her psychic abilities. The seance proved her to be a trance medium and highly susceptible. A personality calling himself "John" took her over, and told us that "I was killed . . . God help me." Later, Mrs. Agostini, who did not remember her trance utterances too well, thought the man was her uncle, whose death had been shrouded in mystery for some time.

I asked Marina whether she ever had a clairvoyant experience that prevented misfortune.

"Yes," she answered, "not long ago—in fact, last week. I planned to ride out to Easthampton in my uncle's car. The night before, as I was about to go to sleep, I had a sudden vision of a head-on collision involving his car, which I thought would happen the next day. I dismissed it from my mind, and didn't think of it again until the next day at about 5:30 when we were out in Easthampton, and about to start back to New York.

"We had just eaten in a restaurant out there, and were about to get back into the car, when my thirteen-year-old daughter Diane stated that she would rather sit *in the back* of the car with me than with my aunt and uncle in the front seat. I thought this *strange*, as she always prefers to sit in the front! Then I remembered my vision, and was disturbed by it again. As she got in, I wondered if some intuition made her choose the back seat, if we were to have an accident. I was happy she was back with me, but I was very concerned for my aunt and uncle in the front seat. I had of course not mentioned my vision to anyone.

"As we started to drive, I mentally put a protection (or a magic circle, as I refer to it) around the car, and felt a little better, but still uneasy. We had gone about twenty or thirty miles when a car coming quite fast from the opposite direction suddenly seemed to sway.

"I thought *this is the accident,* and had what seemed to be a blackout. The last thing I saw was the hub cap from the other car coming across the road and our hitting it. Then our car stopped, and my uncle got out to see the man in the other car, which also stopped, to reclaim his hub cap, but we had smashed it. I was trembling, and no one in the car could understand my overreaction, for it seemed a slight thing, hitting a hub cap. I felt very relieved, for I knew the accident had somehow been averted, with nothing more serious than a dented hub cap. I wondered if my 'magic circle' had saved us from the head-on collision that I had seen the night before in my vision!"

The day before our seance, Marina wrote me a note in which she described a series of dreamlike experiences she had had that night. Of particular interest to me was an apparition or spirit she described as "a young, slim, very beautiful, redheaded Scottish woman. I awoke with a terrible blow on the head, and I felt a 'presence' hovering over me. I told her to go away. She said she could take me to beautiful places; why did I want to get rid of her? This woman, I felt, was a seductress. She reminds me strongly of these lines from Keats' 'La Belle Dame Sans Merci':

'I met a lady in the meads,

Full beautiful—a fairy's child

Her hair was long, her foot was light,

and her eyes were wild.' "

It is true that we had sat down after the seance and talked about Scotland, for some reason. I had told Marina that I had always been drawn to things Scottish, and that I had constant and vague "impressions" of a woman somehow connected with me—perhaps in a previous life, if such can be proven. I did not go into any great details, however.

Now the woman Marina described so vividly to me hit me exactly as the "impression" I had had for several years. Moreover, years earlier I wrote a song which went like this:

"One day, in the meadow, I met a fair Maid

I saw not her shadow, I saw not her shade

I bowed to the Maiden, and asked for her name,

And when she denied it, I asked whence she came.

She laughed and said, "Nowheres," and not one more word,

But when she had spoken, no echo was heard.

I swore that I loved her, she said I was sweet,

Then off she ran nimbly, though silent her feet.

Now if she be human, or if she be fay,
I'll love her, and truly, until my last day.
I'll be all her echo, her shadow, and sound—
To the Maid of the Meadow I've never since found!"
I had never heard of the Keats poem quoted to me by Marina. Coincidence? Psychic connections?

Clara Howard, sister of the justly famed West Coast medium, Sophia Williams, and undoubtedly possessed by similar gifts, once gave me a most complicated message that only I could properly place. It was her habit to tell a visitor on first contact all about his or her family.

Before I had time to collect my thoughts, she had rattled off things like, "A man in your mother's family died of a heart condition, and then there is also a Karl, and I get a name like Strauss, only it isn't quite that. You have two grandmothers, one you remember, one you don't, and your father was born just outside Vienna."

I was startled, for all this was correct. The name she had tried to "get," was Stransky, my mother's maiden name. I asked that my mother, whom she claimed to see, identify herself in some unmistakable way.

To my surprise, Clara Howard, who did not know the German language beyond a few broken words, came out with a sentence in perfect German: *"Kennst Du das Land wo die Zitronen Bluehn?"* (Do you know the land where the lemons bloom?) I instantly recognized this as the title of a very lovely aria from the opera *Mignon,* and my mother's great favorite over the years.

At the time that I knew her, Dorothy Jackson was a woman in her late forties working as a secretary. She was of good intelligence and in good health. Her records of paranormal experiences started in 1942; her father had passed on in 1941. She woke up one night, and, *while fully awake,* saw her father standing by her bedside. Thinking he had come for her, she said, "I'm not ready yet." However, it was not for her that her father had apparently come, but for her brother, who died soon after. Her father's apparition seemed exactly as he was in life, wearing a gray suit, but not quite as solid; she had the feeling that if she touched him, her hand would go through him, even though he looked solid enough. There was a luminous outline around his body.

Another favorite brother died in 1946. When in the hospital, he sent for her. On her return from the hospital, she saw her father's materialized head on her shoulder. The brother died the same night.

Several other times in past years she "saw" neighbors or friends, usually only their heads; they died shortly thereafter. She had these visions only when she was very relaxed, in the evenings.

Very often she dreamed of visiting strange places and seeing people both known and unknown to her; when she awoke in the morning, she found her feet *physically tired as if from long walking about!*

One time, she had a dream in which she saw four rooms. In each of the first three rooms was one of the three men in her life up to that time; in the fourth room she saw a man she had been corresponding with, and with whom she was then on excellent terms. Nevertheless she knew in that dream that their relationship was to end. Six months later it did.

One of the more gifted mediums I have ever met was Betty Ritter, whose particular phase was a combination of clairvoyance and trance. I sat with her many times, and never went home empty-handed. I remember our first meeting, at an experimental session conducted at the quarters of the Association for Research and Enlightenment. At that time, she came toward me at the close of the session and asked, rather abruptly—"Are you Hans Holzer?"

When I nodded, she said, in a puzzled voice, "There is a man here who claims to be an uncle of yours."

I have many uncles. I asked for some details so I could recognize the caller.

Betty closed her eyes for a moment. "His initials are O. S.," she then said quietly, "and he's got a blond wife. Her name is Alice!"

I was taken aback. My late uncle Otto Stransky, the composer, had died under tragic circumstances in a streetcar accident. His wife's name was indeed Alice, but—so many years having gone by— she was no longer a blonde. Her hair was by now a mature gray. Still, to the memory of my uncle, she would always be a blonde!

Years went by until I had occasion to meet Betty Ritter again. She described to me a young woman with the name of Lisa. Now the curious thing was that this friend, who died under tragic circumstances, too, had not been named Lisa but Joan. But with her close friends, she preferred to be called Lisa instead!

Florence, the psychometrist, on occasion showed how good a clairvoyant she could be. I remember one night when a large number of people were present at the home of Dr. S. Kahn, the psychiatrist, of Harmon, New York. Florence looked around, not recognizing any of the faces. "There's been a controversy about a grave," she said with determination. Florence always seems sure of her facts.

"About seven or eight years ago, a five-year-old child was paralyzed in the legs and passed on. Someone said 'I can't go on much longer.' I think the mother is in this room."

With this, Florence looked into the semidarkened room, waiting. She didn't have to wait long. A Mrs. Harry Davies rose and acknowledged that her six-year-old boy had been run over by a car, and that the sentence Florence had quoted was spoken exactly seven years earlier!

Then the medium turned to her host and said, "There's a man named Felder, or something like it, here; he says he was a patient in your hospital."

Dr. Kahn nodded gravely. "His name was Feldman," he replied, "and he died recently."

Carolyn Chapman was often considered the dean of mediums. This wonderfully spunky Southern lady received me one day, after a lapse of more than six years. We talked about the family contacts that might be received by her clairvoyantly, and immediately she spoke of my grandmother, Anna; my mother, Martha; my cousins, Albert and Fred; my Uncle, Julius; and Karl. That's five names out of five. Naturally, I had not mentioned any names to her!

Interesting, too, was Marion Klein, a diminutive psychic who likes to help people find the spiritual way. Once, during a seance held at the Burr Galleries in mid-Manhattan, she turned to a man she was seeing for the first time in her life, and inquired—"Are you a stone mason?"

Luigi Bartolomo is a sculptor.

"I seem to be talking to a Mr. and Mrs. Martino," Marion Klein continued. "Do you know them?"

"Yes," the sculptor nodded, "I do. They've been dead for some time."

Not all seance experiences are of a grim nature. Some, in fact, do not lack a sense of humor. Such was the case when Ethel Johnson Meyers and I descended upon the West 56th Street premises of a fancy restaurant called the Da Vinci. It appeared that a certain advertising executive, who had been a frequent guest at the place, and who was given to much drinking, had recently killed himself in his Eastside apartment. A close friend, Juleen Compton, actually "saw" his ghost there, but that is not unusual, from my point of view. Lots of apartments are haunted.

However, the ghost of the ad man was not content to roam his former home; he decided to descend as well upon his home-away-from-home, where he had spent many a long night in the company of a good drink, or a series of them.

Before long, the proprietors found empty Martini glasses on the bar, when they *knew* none had been there at closing time. Advertising slogans were found scribbled on the walls, but no one had seen the scribbler.

When Mrs. Meyers had seated herself behind the long table that runs the entire length of the place, the ghost took hold of her speech mechanism and immediately demanded a drink! In fact, he behaved in such an alcoholic manner that Mrs. Meyer, a very proper lady, would have been horrified to see her face and actions, under the influence of the discarnate gentleman! Pressed by me about his last day on earth, he finally mumbled that he had spent it with Allan. On later investigation, Allan was found to be his closest friend—a fact Mrs. Meyers could not possibly have known!

A ghost hunter without mediums is like an angler without fish—but the important thing is to be always on the alert against deception, both willful and innocent. Nothing is as dangerous as self-delusion, and I have always allowed more than a generous margin for error in psychic evidence. Still, with all these allowances, the fact remains—there are a number of medically healthy individuals who can make contact with what Dr. J. Rhine calls "The World of the Mind."

No chapter on mediums would be complete without an account of psychic photography. There are those researchers who firmly believe it is all fraud. Then there are those who think every psychic photography medium is genuine. Neither is the case, in my opinion. But twice I have had firsthand proof, from medium John Myers, who produced exact likenesses of my late aunt and mother—without of course having access to my family album or any other source of supply.

On one occasion during the 60s, John Myers demonstrated his gift for psychic photography on a television program hosted by Mike Wallace called "PM—EAST." Millions of viewers saw Myers, heard him discuss his past achievements, and then saw him show some of the outstanding psychic photography and skotographs taken by Myers over the years.

Among the remarkable pictures shown was the one taken by Myers at the funeral of Lady Caillard, where he did not even get near the plates used, which were placed on the coffin by a news photographer at the funeral. This picture had the "extras" of Lord Caillard and Lady Caillard. On this same television program, John Myers and I also showed the psychic photograph of Myers' mother, the first such picture received through his mediumship, and several others taken in his presence by experimenters in England, to demonstrate the differences between normal and psychic photographs.

After that, Mike Wallace produced an uncut package of photographic paper from his pocket, and held it up to the camera, asserting for all to hear that he himself had purchased this ordinary photographic paper that afternoon, and had kept the sealed and signed package in his possession continuously. And now, on camera, he would open it on the instructions of John Myers. Before us we had three trays, filled with developing fluid, hypo, and water. Overhead, only a single 60-watt yellow bulb illuminated the somewhat eerie scene as Mike Wallace, flanked on either side by John Myers and myself, proceeded to open the package of sensitive papers. Then he plunged them one by one into the liquid.

At first, nothing happened, and the silence hung heavy as millions of people all over the United States watched in awe. Wallace started to joke about unwillingness of spirits to show themselves on his show. But then, suddenly, forms began to appear on the papers.

Excitement mounted. At first, only amorphous shapes came up; but one or two rapidly took on the appearance of heads, and there was a figure and an arm beginning to take form. But, alas—air time being precious, we could no longer stay on camera; the program had to continue. It was live TV. Although Wallace admitted publicly that these "shapes" shouldn't be there to begin with, and that they did indeed look somewhat like faces, we could not wait for them to clearly develop, as clearly as previous Myers psychic photographs have done.

Nevertheless, it was a coup of the first order—psychic photography on live television for the first time, anywhere.

When we went off the air, we scooped up the psychic photographs, and Myers put them into the envelope they had come in. Not thinking anything further about the matter—for psychic photographs are "old hat" to Myers by now—he took them home with him: there he decided to wash them, since there had been insufficient time on the air to clean them of the hypo. When he withdrew the pictures from the water, he discovered that several heads had come up much clearer, and others had been added, somehow, during the journey from the studio to his home.

Casually, John Myers showed me the results. To my amazement, I found that one of the psychic pictures was that of my own mother, who had passed years before. I located a very similar photograph of her in my family album, taken when she was still in good health, about fifteen years before!

The Ghostly Lover

O NE OF THE MOST FANTASTIC CASES was a case involving Betty Ritter and the well-known psychoanalyst Dr. Nandor Fodor. Dr. Fodor had been treating a certain Edith Berger, in Long Island, for what seemed at first disturbing symptoms of split personality. But Dr. Fodor was a trained parapsychologist as well, and he did not fail to recognize the case for what it was, possession!

He suggested that the Bergers call in a good medium, and recommended Betty Ritter.

Half in tears, Edith Berger's mother told Betty on the telephone how a possessive spirit personality had been annoying her and her daughter for the past four months. It seemed that Edith, the daughter, had a gentleman friend, a medical doctor, who had died in the tropics not long before.

The very day after his death, the young woman found that her erstwhile suitor had attached himself to her, and was forcing himself on her—physically! The attacks were so violent, the mother said, that she had to sleep in the same bed with her daughter for protection, but to no avail. The mother also *felt* the physical contact experienced by her daughter!

Betty concentrated her psychic powers immediately on what can only be called a form of exorcism. Although there was some relief, the ghostly boy friend was still around.

To Betty's horror, she woke up that same night to find the restless one standing before her bed, stark naked, in a menacing mood. Betty's contacts on "the other side," however, protected her and took the erring one away.

Telling Edith Berger of her experience the next day, she accurately described the visitor. Her efforts seemed to weaken the attacks somewhat, and several days later she saw him again, this time, however, fully clothed! He wore riding boots and carried a whip. The Bergers confirmed that the man had been a lover of horses. On April 20th, Betty Ritter telephoned the Bergers to find out how things were going. The moment Edith answered the telephone, the ghost started to pull her hair in a most painful fashion, as if to prove he was still very much in evidence!

But the violent mind of the young doctor would not accept the separation from his physical body and its pleasures. The haunting continued; thus Betty Ritter asked me to accompany her to the Berger home for another go at the case.

The Bergers turned out to be very level-headed middle-class people, and completely ignorant of anything psychic. Edith seemed to be a highly nervous, but quite "normal" human being. Almost immediately, the entity got hold of the medium and yelled through her—"I shall not be pulled away from you. I won't go."

I learned that the father had at first been highly skeptical of all this, but his daughter's behavior changed so much, and became so different from her previous character, that he had to admit to himself that something uncanny was happening in his house. Edith, who was far from tidy, suddenly became the very model of tidyness, started to clean up things, and behaved like a nurse—the profession her late boy friend had wanted her to follow. At times, she assumed his ailments and "passing symptoms." At times, she would suffer from genuine malaria—just as he had done. Since Edith was mediumistic, it was easy for the dead doctor to have his will. The message he wanted her to deliver most was to tell his mother that he was "still alive." But how could she do that, and not reveal her agony?

One afternoon, while she was praying for him, she felt a clutching sensation on her arm. Later on, in bed, she clearly heard his voice, saying—"It is me, Don!" From that day on, he stayed with her constantly. On one particular amorous occasion, *her mother clearly discerned a man's outline in the empty bed.* She quickly grabbed a fly swatter and chased the earthbound spirit out of her daughter's bed!

Once, when she was about to put on her coat to go out, the coat, apparently of its own volition, came toward her—as if someone were holding it for her to slip on!

Whenever she was with other men, he kissed her, and she would hear his angry voice.

But this time the seance cracked his selfish shell. "I haven't been able to finish what I started," he sobbed, referring to his important medical experiments. He then asked forgiveness, and that he be allowed to come back to be with Edith now and then.

After we left—Dr. Fodor had come along, too—we all expressed hope that the Bergers would live in peace. But a few weeks later, Edith telephoned me in great excitement. The doctor had returned once more.

I then explained to her that she had to sacrifice—rid herself of her own *desire* to have this man around, unconscious though it may be—and in closing the door on this chapter of her life, make it impossible for the earthbound one to take control of her psychic energies. I heard nothing further.

The Case of the Murdered Financier

I REMEMBER THE NIGHT WE WENT to visit the house where financier Serge Rubinstein was killed. It was a year after his death but
only I, among the group, had knowledge of the exact date of the
anniversary. John Latouche, my much-too-soon departed friend, and
I picked up Mrs. Meyers at her Westside home and rode in a taxi to
Fifth Avenue and 60th Street. As a precaution, so as not to give away
the address where we were headed, we left the taxi two blocks south
of the Rubinstein residence.

Our minds were careful blanks, and the conversation was
about music. But we didn't fool our medium. "What's the pianist
doing here?" she demanded to know. What pianist, I countered.
"Rubinstein," said she. For to our medium, a professional singing
teacher, that name could only stand for the great pianist, Arthur
Rubinstein. It showed that our medium was, so to speak, on-the-
beam, and already entering into the "vibration," or electrically
charged atmosphere of the haunting.

Latouche and I looked at each other in amazement. Mrs. Meyers
was puzzled by our sudden excitement. Without further delay, we
rang the bell at the stone mansion, hoping the door would open
quickly so that we would not be exposed to curiosity-seekers who

were then still hanging around the house where one of the most pub-licized murders had taken place just a year before, to the hour.

It was now near midnight, and my intention had been to try and make contact with the spirit of the departed. I assumed, from the manner in which he died, that Serge Rubinstein might still be around his house, and I had gotten his mother's permission to attempt the contact.

The seconds on the doorstep seemed like hours, as Mrs. Meyers questioned me about the nature of tonight's "case." I asked her to be patient, but when the butler came and finally opened the heavy gate, Mrs. Meyers suddenly realized where we were. "It isn't the pianist, then!" she mumbled, somewhat dazed. "It's the *other* Rubinstein!" With these words we entered the forbidding-looking building for an evening of horror and ominous tension.

A year after the murder, it was still officially unsolved, and as much an enigma to the world as it was on that cold winter night when the newspaper headlines screamed of "bad boy" financier Serge Rubinstein's untimely demise. That night, after business conferences and a night on the town with a brunette, Rubinstein had some unex-pected visitors. Even the District Attorney couldn't name them for sure, but there were suspects galore, and the investigation never ran out of possibilities.

Evidently Serge had a falling-out with the brunette, Estelle Gardner, and decided the evening was still young, so he felt like continuing it with a change of cast. Another woman, Pat Wray, later testified that Rubinstein telephoned her to join him, after he had got-ten rid of Estelle, *and that she refused.*

The following morning, the butler, William Morter, found Rubinstein dead in his third-floor bedroom. He was wearing pajamas, and evidently the victim of some form of torture—for his arms and feet were tied, and his mouth and throat thickly covered by adhesive tape. The medical examiner dryly ruled death caused by strangulation.

The police found themselves with a first-rate puzzle on their hands. Lots of people wanted to kill Rubinstein, lots of people had said so publicly without meaning it—but who actually did? The financier's reputation was not the best, although it must be said that he did no more nor less than many others; but his manipulations were neither elegant nor quiet, and consequently, the glaring light of publicity and exposure created a public image of a monster that did not exactly fit the Napoleonic-looking young man from Paris.

Rubinstein was a possessive and extremely jealous man. A tiny microphone was placed by him in the apartment of Pat Wray, sending sound into a tape recorder hidden in a car parked outside the building. Thus, Rubinstein was able to monitor her every word!

Obviously, his dealings were worldwide, and there were some 2,000 names in his private files. The usual sensational news accounts had been seen in the press the week prior to our seance, but none of them contained anything new or definite. Mrs. Meyers' knowledge of the case was as specific as that of any ordinary newspaper reader.

We were received by Serge's seventy-nine-year-old mother, Stella Rubinstein; her sister, Eugenia Forrester; the Rubinstein attorney, Ennis; a secretary; a guard named Walter; and a newspaper reporter from a White Russian paper, Jack Zwieback. After a few moments of polite talk downstairs—that is, on the second floor where the library of the sumptuous mansion was located—I suggested we go to the location of the crime itself.

We all rose, when Mrs. Meyers suddenly stopped in her tracks. "I feel someone's grip on my arm," she commented.

We went upstairs without further incidents. The bedroom of the slain financier was a medium-size room in the rear of the house, connected with the front sitting room through a large bathroom. We formed a circle around the bed, occupying the center of the room. The light was subdued, but the room was far from dark. It was just twenty minutes after nine. Mrs. Meyers insisted on sitting in a chair close to the bed, and remarked that she "was directed there."

Gradually her body relaxed, her eyes closed, and the heavy, rhythmic breathing of onsetting trance was heard in the silence of the room, heavily tensed with fear and apprehension of what was to come.

Several times, the medium placed her arm before her face, as if warding off attacks; symptoms of choking distorted her face and a struggle seemed to take place before our eyes!

Within a few minutes, this was over, and a new strange voice came from the lips of the medium. "I can speak . . . over there, they're coming!" The arm pointed toward the bathroom.

I asked who "they" were.

"They're no friends . . . Joe, Stan . . . cheap girl . . . in the door, they—" The hand went to the throat, indicating choking.

Then, suddenly, the person in command of the medium added: "The woman should be left out. There was a calendar with serial numbers . . . box numbers, but they can't get it! Freddie was here, too!"

"What was in the box?"

"Fourteen letters. Nothing for the public."

"Give me more information."

"Baby-Face . . . I don't want to talk too much . . . they'll pin it on Joe."

"How many were there?"

"Joe, Stan, and Freddie . . . stooges. Her bosses' stooges! London . . . let me go, let me go . . . I'm too frantic here . . . not up here. . . I'll come again."

With a jolt, the medium awoke from her trance. Perspiration stood on her forehead, although the room was cold. Not a word was said by the people in the room. Mrs. Meyers leaned back and thought for a moment.

"I feel a small, stocky man here, perverted minds, and there is fighting all over the room. He is being surprised by the bathroom door. They were hiding in the next room, came through this window and fire escape."

We descended again to the library, where we had originally assembled. The conversation continued quietly, when suddenly Mrs. Meyers found herself rapidly slipping into trance again.

"Three men, one wiry and tall, one short and very stocky, and one tall and stout—the shorter one is in charge. Then there is Baby-Face . . . she has a Mona Lisa-like face. Stan is protected. I had the goods on them. . . . Mama's right, it's getting hot. . . ."

"Give us the name!" I almost shouted. Tension gripped us all.

The medium struggled with an unfamiliar sound. "Kapoich . . . ?" Then she added, "The girl here . . . poker face."

"But what is her name?"

"Ha ha . . . tyrant."

When Mrs. Meyers came out of her trance, I questioned Rubinstein's mother about the seance. She readily agreed that the voice had indeed sounded much like her late son's. Moreover, there was that girl—named in the investigation—who had a "baby face." She never showed emotion, and was, in fact, poker-faced all the time. Her name?

"My son often called her his tyrant," the mother said, visibly shaken. "What about the other names?"

"My son used a hired limousine frequently. The chauffeur was a stocky man, and his name was Joe or Joey. Stan? I have heard that name many times in business conversations." One of the men involved in the investigation was named Kubitschek. Had the deceased tried to pronounce that name?

A wallet once belonging to Serge had been handed to Mrs. Meyers a few minutes before, to help her maintain contact with the deceased. Suddenly, without warning, the wallet literally *flew out of her hands* and hit the high ceiling of the library with tremendous impact.

Mrs. Meyers' voice again sounded strange, as the late financier spoke through her in anger. "Do you know how much it costs to sell a man down the river?"

Nobody cared to answer. We had all had quite enough for one evening!

We all left in different directions, and I sent a duplicate of the seance transcript to the police, something I have done with every subsequent seance as well. Mrs. Meyers and I were never the only ones to know what transpired in trance. The police knew, too, and if they did not choose to arrest anyone, that was their business.

We were sure our seance had not attracted attention, and Mrs. Rubinstein herself, and her people, certainly would not spread the word of the unusual goings-on in the Fifth Avenue mansion on the anniversary of the murder.

But on February 1, society columnist Cholly Knickerbocker headlined—"Serge's Mother Holds A Seance"!

Not entirely accurate in his details—his source turned out to be one of the guards—Mr. Cassini, nevertheless, came to the point in stating: "To the awe of all present, no less than four people were named by the medium. If this doesn't give the killers the chills, it certainly does us."

We thought we had done our bit toward the solution of this baffling murder, and were quite prepared to forget the excitement of that evening. Unfortunately, the wraith of Rubinstein did not let it rest at that.

During a routine seance then held at my house on West 70th Street, he took over the medium's personality, and elaborated on his statements. He talked of his offices in London and Paris, his staff, and his enemies. One of his lawyers, Rubinstein averred, knew more than he *dared* disclose!

I called Mrs. Rubinstein and arranged for another, less public sitting at the Fifth Avenue house. This time only the four of us—the two elderly ladies, Mrs. Meyers, and I, were present. Rubinstein's voice was again recognized by his mother.

"It was at 2:45 on the nose. 2:45!" he said, speaking of the time of his death. "Pa took my hand, it wasn't so bad. I want to tell the little angel woman here, I don't always listen like a son should—she told me always, 'You go too far, don't take chances!' "

Then his voice grew shrill with anger. "Justice will be done. I have paid for that."

I asked, what did this fellow Joey, whom he mentioned the first time, do for a living?

"Limousines. He knew how to come. He brought them here, they were not invited."

He then added something about Houston, Texas, and insisted that a man from that city was involved. He was sure "the girl" would eventually talk and break the case.

There were a number of other sittings, at my house, where the late Serge put his appearance into evidence. Gradually, his hatred and thirst for revenge gave way to a calmer acceptance of his untimely death. He kept us informed of "poker face's moves"—whenever the girl moved, Serge was there to tell us. Sometimes his language was rough, sometimes he held back.

"They'll get Mona Lisa," he assured me on March 30th. I faithfully turned the records of our seances over to the police. They always acknowledged them, but were not eager to talk about this help from so odd a source as a psychical researcher!

Rubinstein kept talking about a Crown Street Headquarters in London, but we never were able to locate this address. At one time, he practically insisted on taking his medium with him into the street, to look for his murderers! It took strength and persuasion for me to calm the restless one, for I did not want Mrs. Meyers to leave the safety of the big armchair by the fireplace, which she usually occupied at our seances.

"Stan is on this side now," he commented on April 13th.

I could never fathom whether Stan was his friend or his enemy, or perhaps both at various times. Financier Stanley died a short time after our initial seance at the Fifth Avenue mansion.

Safe deposit boxes were mentioned, and numbers given, but somehow Mrs. Rubinstein never managed to find them.

On April 26th, we held another sitting at my house. This time the spirit of the slain financier was particularly restless.

"Vorovsky," he mumbled, "yellow cab, he was paid good for helping her get away from the house. Doug paid him, he's a friend of Charley's. Tell mother to hire a private detective."

I tried to calm him. He flared up at me. "Who're you talking to? The Pope?"

The next day, I checked these names with his mother. Mrs. Rubinstein also assured me that the expression "who do you think I am—the Pope?" was one of his favorite phrases in life!

"Take your nose down to Texas and you'll find a long line to London and Paris," he advised us on May 10th.

Meanwhile, Mrs. Rubinstein increased the reward for the capture of the murderer to $50,000. Still, no one was arrested, and the people the police had originally questioned had all been let go. Strangely enough, the estate was much smaller than at first anticipated. Was much money still in hiding, perhaps in some unnamed safe deposit box? We'll never know. Rubinstein's mother has gone on to join him on the Other Side of the Veil, too.

My last contact with the case was when columnist Hy Gardner asked me to appear on his television program. We talked about the Rubinstein seances, and he showed once more the eerie bit of film he called "a collector's item"—the only existing television interview with Rubinstein, made shortly before his death.

The inquisitive reporter's questions are finally parried by the wily Rubinstein with an impatient—"Why, that's like asking a man about his own death!"

Could it be that Serge Rubinstein, in addition to all his other "talents," also had the gift of prophecy?

The Rockland County Ghost

I T WAS OVER A DINNER TABLE in a Manhattan restaurant that this writer heard for the first time of the haunted house belonging to Danton Walker, the well-known Broadway newspaper man.

It was then that the strange goings-on in the Rockland County house were discussed with me for the first time, although they had been observed over the ten years preceding our dinner meeting. The manifestations had come to a point where they had forced Mr. Walker to leave his house to the ghost and build himself a studio on the other end of his estate, where he was able to live unmolested.

A meeting with Mrs. Garrett was soon arranged, but due to her indisposition, it had to be postponed. Despite her illness, Mrs. Garrett, in a kind of "traveling clairvoyance," did obtain a clairvoyant impression of the entity. His name was "Andreas," and she felt him to be rather attached to the present owner of the house. These findings Mrs. Garrett communicated to Mr. Walker, but nothing further was done on the case. A "rescue circle" operation was finally organized, and successfully concluded the case, putting the disturbed soul to rest, and allowing Mr. Walker to return to the main house without further fear of manifestations.

Before noting the strange phenomena that had been observed in the house, it will be necessary to describe this house a bit, as the nature of the building itself has a great deal to do with the subsequent occurrences.

Mr. Walker's house is a fine example of colonial architecture, of the kind that was built in the country during the second half of the eighteenth century. Although Walker was sure only of the first deed to the property, dated 1813 and naming the Abrams family, of pre-Revolutionary origin in the country, the house itself is unquestionably much older.

When Mr. Walker bought the house in upstate New York, it was in the dismal state of disrepair typical of some dwellings in the surrounding Ramapo Mountains. It took the new owner several years and a great deal of money to rebuild the house to its former state and to refurbish it with the furniture, pewter, and other implements of the period. I am mentioning this point because the house was a completely livable and authentic colonial building of the kind that would be an entirely familiar and a welcome sight to a man living toward the end of the eighteenth century, were he to set foot into it today.

The house stands on a hill which was once part of a farm. During the War for Independence, this location was the headquarters of a colonial army. In fact, "Mad" Anthony Wayne's own headquarters stood near this site, and the Battle of Stony Point (1779) was fought a few miles away. Most likely, the building restored by Mr. Walker was then in use as a fortified roadhouse, used both for storage of arms, ammunitions, and food supplies, and for the temporary lodging of prisoners.

After the house passed from the hands of the Abrams family in the earlier part of the nineteenth century, a banker named Dixon restored the farm and the landscaping, but paid scant attention to the house itself. By and by, the house gave in to the ravages of time and weather. A succession of mountain people made it their living quarters around the turn of the twentieth century, but did nothing to improve its sad state of disrepair. When Mr. Walker took over in the mid-twentieth century, only the kitchen and a small adjoining room were in use; the rest of the house was filled with discarded furniture and other objects. The upstairs was divided into three tiny rooms and a small attic, which disgorged bonnets, hoop skirts, and crudely carved wooden shoe molds and toys, dating from about the Civil War period.

While the house was being reconstructed, Mr. Walker was obliged to spend nights at a nearby inn, but would frequently take naps during the day on an army cot upstairs. On these occasions he received distinct impressions of "a Revolutionary soldier" being in the room.

Mr. Walker's moving in touched off the usual country gossip, some of which later reached his ears. *It seemed that the house was haunted.* One woman who had lived in the place told of an "old man" who frightened the children, mysterious knocks at the front door, and other mysterious happenings. But none of these reports could be followed up. For all practical purposes, we may say that the phenomena started with the arrival of Mr. Walker.

Though Mr. Walker was acutely sensitive to the atmosphere of the place from the time he took over, it was not until the manifestations resulted in both visible and audible phenomena. Later that year, during an afternoon when he was resting in the front room downstairs, he was roused by a violent summons to the front door, which has a heavy iron knocker. Irritated by the intrusion when no guest was expected, he called "Come in!" then went to the front door and found no one there.

About this time, Mr. Walker's butler, Johnny, remarked to his employer that the house was a nice place to stay in "if they would let you alone." Questioning revealed that Johnny, spending the night in the house alone, had gone downstairs three times during the night to answer knocks at the front door. An Italian workman named Pietro, who did some repairs on the house, reported sounds of someone walking up the stairs in midafternoon "with heavy boots on," at a time when there definitely was no one else in the place. Two occasional guests of the owner also were disturbed, while reading in the living room, by the sound of heavy footsteps overhead.

A few years later Mr. Walker and his secretary were eating dinner in the kitchen, which is quite close to the front door. There was a sharp rap at the door. The secretary opened it and found nobody there. On another occasion, when there were guests downstairs but no one upstairs, sounds of heavy thumping were heard from upstairs, *as if someone had taken a bad fall.* Of course, when the thumping was investigated, no one was found.

Though Mr. Walker, his butler, and his guests never saw or fancied they saw any ghostly figures, the manifestations did not restrict themselves to audible phenomena. Unexplainable dents in pewter pieces occurred from time to time. A piece of glass in a door pane, the same front door of the house, was cracked but remained solidly in place for some years. One day it was missing and could not be located in the hall indoors, nor outside on the porch. A week later this four-by-four piece of glass was accidentally found resting on a plate rail eight feet above the kitchen floor. How it got there is as much of a mystery now as it was then.

On one occasion, when Johnny was cleaning the stairs to the bedroom, a picture that had hung at the top of the stairs for at least two years tumbled down, almost striking him. A woman guest who had spent the night on a daybed in the living room, while making up the bed next morning, was almost struck by a heavy pewter pitcher which fell ("almost as if thrown at her") from a bookshelf hanging behind the bed. There were no unusual vibrations of the house to account for these things.

On the white kitchen wall there were heavy semicircular black marks where a pewter salt box, used for holding keys, had been violently swung back and forth. A large pewter pitcher, which came into the house in perfect condition, now bears five heavy imprints, four on one side, one on the other. A West Pointer with unusually large hands fitted his own four fingers and thumb into the dents!

Other phenomena include the gripping chills felt from time to time by Mr. Walker and his more sensitive guests. These chills, not to be confused with drafts, were felt in all parts of the house by Mr. Walker when alone. They took the form of a sudden paralyzing cold, as distinct as a cramp. Such a chill once seized him when he had been ill and gone to bed early. Exasperated by the phenomenon, he unthinkingly called out aloud, "Oh, for God's sake, let me alone!" The chill abruptly stopped.

But perhaps the most astounding incident took place only a few days before the rescue circle met at the house.

Two of Mr. Walker's friends, down-to-earth men with no belief in the so-called supernatural, were weekend guests. Though Walker suggested that they both spend the night in the commodious studio about three hundred feet from the main house, one of them insisted on staying upstairs in the "haunted" room. Walker persuaded him to leave the lights on.

An hour later, the pajama-clad man came rushing down to the studio, demanding that Mr. Walker put an end "to his pranks." The light beside his bed was blinking on and off. All *other lights* in the house were burning steadily!

Assured that this might be caused by erratic power supply and that no one was playing practical jokes, the guest returned to the main house. But an hour or so later, he came back to the studio and spent the rest of the night there. In the morning he somewhat sheepishly told that he had been awakened from a sound sleep by the sensation of someone slapping him violently in the face. Sitting bolt upright in bed, he noticed that the shirt he had hung on the back of a rocking chair was being agitated by the "breeze." Though admitting that this much might have been pure imagination, he also seemed to notice the chair gently rocking. Since all upstairs windows were closed, there definitely was no "breeze."

"The sensation described by my guest," Mr. Walker remarked, "reminded me of a quotation from one of Edith Wharton's ghost stories. Here is the exact quote:

" 'Medford sat up in bed with a jerk which resembles no other. Someone was in his room. The fact reached him not by sight or sound . . . but by a peculiar faint disturbance of the invisible currents that enclose us.'

"Many people in real life have experienced this sensation. I myself had not spent a night alone in the main house in four years. It got so that I just couldn't take it. In fact, I built the studio specifically to get away from staying there. When people have kidded me about my 'haunted house,' my reply is, would I have spent so much time and money restoring the house, and then built another house to spend the night in, if there had not been some valid reason?"

On many previous occasions, Mr. Walker had remarked that he had a feeling that someone was trying "desperately" to get into the house, as if for refuge. The children of an earlier tenant had mentioned some agitation "by the lilac bush" at the corner of the house. The original crude walk from the road to the house, made of flat native stones, passed this lilac bush and went to the well, which, according to local legend, was used by soldiers in Revolutionary times.

"When I first took over the place," Mr. Walker observed, "I used to look out of the kitchen window twenty times a day to see who was at the well. Since the old walk has been replaced by a stone walk and driveway, no one could now come into the place without being visible for at least sixty-five feet. Following the reconstruction, the stone wall blocking the road was torn down several times at the exact spot where the original walk reached the road."

In all the disturbances which led to the efforts of the rescue circle, I detected one common denominator. Someone was attempting to get into the house, and to call attention to something. Playing pranks, puzzling people, or even frightening them, were not part of the "ghost's" purpose; they were merely his desperate devices for getting attention, attention for something he very much wanted to say.

On a bleak and foreboding day in November, the little group comprising the rescue circle drove out into the country for the sitting. They were accompanied by Dr. L., a prominent Park Avenue psychiatrist and psychoanalyst, and of course by Mr. Walker, the owner of the property.

The investigation was sponsored by the Parapsychology Foundation, Inc., of New York City. Participants included Mrs. Eileen J. Garrett; Dr. L., whose work in psychiatry and analysis is well known; Miss Lenore Davidson, assistant to Mrs. Garrett, who was responsible for most of the notes taken; Dr. Michel Pobers, then Secretary General of the Parapsychology Foundation; and myself.

The trip to the Rockland County home of Mr. Walker took a little over an hour. The house stood atop a wide hill, not within easy earshot of the next inhabited house, but not too far from his own "cabin" and two other small houses belonging to Mr. Walker's estate. The main house, small and compact, represents a perfect restoration of Colonial American architecture.

A plaque in the ground at the entrance gate calls attention to the historical fact that General Wayne's headquarters at the time of the Battle of Stony Point, 1779, occupied the very same site. Mr. Walker's house was possibly part of the fortification system protecting the hill, and no doubt served as a stronghold in the war of 1779 and in earlier wars and campaigns fought around this part of the country. One feels the history of many generations clinging to the place.

We took our places in the upstairs bedroom, grouping ourselves so as to form an imperfect circle around Mrs. Garrett, who sat in a heavy, solid wooden chair with her back to the wall and her face toward us.

The time was 2:45 P.M. and the room was fully lit by ample daylight coming in through the windows.

After a moment, Mrs. Garrett placed herself in full trance by means of autohypnosis. Quite suddenly her own personality vanished, and the medium sank back into her chair completely lifeless, very much like an unused garment discarded for the time being by its owner. But not for long. A few seconds later, another personality "got into" the medium's body, precisely the way one dons a shirt or coat. It was Uvani, one of Mrs. Garrett's two spirit guides who act as her control personalities in all of her experiments. Uvani, in his own lifetime, was an East Indian of considerable knowledge and dignity, and as such he now appeared before us.

As "he" sat up—I shall refer to the distinct personalities now using the "instrument" (the medium's body) as "he" or "him"—it was obvious that we had before us a gentleman from India. Facial expression, eyes, movements, the folded arms, and the finger movements that accompanied many of his words were all those of a native of India. As Uvani addressed us, he spoke in perfect English, except for a faltering word now and then or an occasional failure of idiom, but his accent was typical.

At this point, the tape recorder faithfully took down every word spoken. The transcript given here is believed to be complete, and is certainly so where we deal with Uvani, who spoke clearly and slowly. In the case of the ghost, much of the speech was garbled because of the ghost's unfortunate condition; some of the phrases were repeated several times, and a few words were SO badly uttered that they could not be made out by any of us. In order to present only verifiable evidence, I have eliminated all such words and report here nothing which was not completely understandable and clear. But at least seventy percent of the words uttered by the ghost, and of course all of the words of Uvani, are on record. The tape recording is supplemented by Miss Davidson's exacting transcript, and in the final moments her notes replace it entirely.

Uvani: It is I, Uvani. I give you greetings, friends. Peace be with you, and in your lives, and in this house!

Dr. L.: And our greetings to you, Uvani. We welcome you.

Uvani: I am very happy to speak with you, my good friend. (Bows to Dr. L.) You are out of your native element.

Dr. L.: Very much so. We have not spoken in this environment at all before. . . .

Uvani: What is it that you would have of me today, please?

Dr. L.: We are met here as friends of Mr. Walker, whose house this is, to investigate strange occurrences which have taken place in this house from time to time, which lead us to feel that they partake of the nature of this field of interest of ours. We would be guided by you, Uvani, as to the method of approach which we should use this afternoon. Our good friend and instrument (Mrs. Garrett) has the feeling that there was a personality connected with this house whose influence is still to be felt here.

Uvani: Yes, I would think so. I am confronted myself with a rather restless personality. In fact, a very strange personality, and one that might appear to be in his own life perhaps not quite of the right mind—I think you would call it.

I have a great sense of agitation. I would like to tell you about this personality, and at the same time draw your attention to the remarkable—what you might call—atmospherics that he is able to bring into our environment. You, who are my friend and have worked with me very much, know that when I am in control, we are very calm—yes? Yet it is as much as I can do to maintain the control, as you see—for such is the atmosphere produced by this personality, that you will note my own difficulty to restrain and constrain the instrument. (The medium's hand shakes in rapid palsy. Uvani's voice trembles.) This one, in spite of me, by virtue of his being with us brings into the process of our field of work a classical palsy. Do you see this?

Dr. L.: I do.

Uvani: This was his condition, and that is why it may be for me perhaps necessary (terrific shaking of medium at this point) to ask you to—deal—with this—personality yourself—while I withdraw—to create a little more quietude around the instrument. Our atmosphere, as you notice, is charged. . . . You will not be worried by anything that may happen, please. You will speak, if you can, with this one—and you will eventually return the instrument to my control.

Dr. L.: I will.

Uvani: Will you please to remember that you are dealing with a personality very young, tired, who has been very much hurt in life, and who was, for many years prior to his passing, unable—how you say—to think for himself. Now will you please take charge, so that I permit the complete control to take place. . . .

Uvani left the body of the medium at this point. For a moment, all life seemed gone from it as it lay still in the chair. Then, suddenly, another personality seemed to possess it. Slowly, the new personality sat up, hands violently vibrating in palsy, face distorted in extreme pain, eyes blinking, staring, unable to see anything at first, looking straight through us all without any sign of recognition. All this was accompanied by increasing inarticulate outcries, leading later into halting, deeply emotional weeping.

For about ten seconds, the new personality maintained its position in the chair, but as the movements of the hands accelerated, it suddenly leaned over and crashed to the floor, narrowly missing a wooden chest nearby. Stretched out on the floor before us, "he" kept uttering inarticulate sounds for perhaps one or two minutes, while vainly trying to raise himself from the floor.

One of Dr. L.'s crutches, which he uses when walking about, was on the floor next to his chair. The entity seized the crutch and tried to raise himself with its help, but without success. Throughout the next seconds, he tried again to use the crutch, only to fall back onto the floor. One of his legs, the left one, continued to execute rapid convulsive movements typical of palsy. It was quite visible that the leg had been badly damaged. Now and again he threw his left hand to his head, touching it as if to indicate that his head hurt also.

Dr. L.:   We are friends, and you may speak with us. Let us help you in any way we can. We are friends.

Entity: Mhh—mhh—mhh—(inarticulate sounds of sobbing and pain).

Dr. L.:   Speak with us. Speak with us. Can we help you? (More crying from the entity.) You will be able to speak with us. Now you are quieter. You will be able to talk to us. (The entity crawls along the floor to Mr. Walker, seems to have eyes only for him, and remains at Walker's knee throughout the interrogation. The crying becomes softer.) Do you understand English?

Entity: Friend . . . friend . . . friend. Mercy . . . mercy . . . mercy. . . . (The English has a marked Polish accent, the voice is rough, uncouth, bragging, emotional.) I know ... I know ... I know. ... (pointing at Mr. Walker)

Dr. L.: When did you know him before?

Entity: Stones ... stones. ... Don't let them take me!

Dr. L.: No, we won't let them take you.

Entity: (More crying) Talk. ...

Mr. Walker: You want to talk to me? Yes, I'll talk to you.

Entity: Can't talk. ...

Mr. Walker: Can't talk? It is hard for you to talk?

Entity: (Nods) Yes.

Dr. L.: You want water? Food? Water?

Entity: (Shakes head) Talk! Talk! (To Mr. Walker) Friend? You?

Mr. Walker: Yes, friend. We're all friends.

Entity: (Points to his head, then to his tongue.) Stones ... no?

Dr. L.: No stones. You will not be stoned.

Entity: No beatin'?

Dr. L.: No, you won't be stoned, you won't be beaten.

Entity: Don't go!

Mr. Walker: No, we are staying right here.

Entity: Can't talk. ...

Mr. Walker: You can talk. We are all friends.

Dr. L.: It is difficult with this illness that you have, but you can talk. Your friend there is Mr. Walker. And what is your name?

Entity: He calls me. I have to get out. I cannot go any further. In God's name I cannot go any further. (Touches Mr. Walker)

Mr. Walker: I will protect you. (At the word "protect" the entity sits up, profoundly struck by it.) What do you fear?

Entity: Stones. ...

Mr. Walker: Stones thrown at you?

Dr. L.:	That will not happen again.
Entity:	Friends! Wild men . . . you know. . . .
Mr. Walker:	Indians?
Entity:	No.
Dr. L.:	White man?
Entity:	Mh . . . teeth gone—(shows graphically how his teeth were kicked in)
Mr. Walker:	Teeth gone.
Dr. L.:	They knocked your teeth out?
Entity:	See? I can't. . . . Protect me!
Mr. Walker:	Yes, yes. We will protect you. No more beatings, no more stones.
Dr. L.:	You live here? This is your house?
Entity:	(Violent gesture, loud voice) No, oh no! I hide here.
Mr. Walker:	In the woods?
Entity:	Cannot leave here.
Dr. L.:	Whom do you hide from?
Entity:	Big, big, strong . . . big, big, strong. . . .
Dr. L.:	Is he the one that beat you?
Entity:	(Shouts) All . . . I know . . . I know . . . I know. . . .
Dr. L.:	You know the names?
Entity:	(Hands on Mr. Walker's shoulders) Know the plans . . .
Dr. L.:	They tried to find the plans, to make you tell, but you did not tell? And your head hurts?
Entity:	(Just nods to this) Ah . . . ah. . . .
Dr. L.:	And you've been kicked, and beaten and stoned. (The entity nods violently.)
Mr. Walker:	Where are the plans?
Entity:	I hid them . . . far, far. . . .
Mr. Walker:	Where did you hide the plans? We are friends, you can tell us.
Entity:	Give me map.

(The entity is handed note pad and pen, which he uses in the
        stiff manner of a quill. The drawing, showing the
        unsteady and vacillating lines of a palsy sufferer, is
        on hand.)

Entity: In your measure . . . Andreas Hid. . . . (drawing)

Mr. Walker: Where the wagon house lies?

Entity: A house . . . not in the house . . . timber house . . . log . . .

Mr. Walker: Log house?

Entity: (Nods) Plans . . . log house . . . under . . . under . . .
        stones . . . fifteen . . . log . . . fifteen stones . . . door . . .
        plans—for whole shifting of. . . .

Mr Walker: Of ammunitions?

Entity: No . . . men and ammunitions . . . plans—I have for
        French. . . . I have plans for French . . . plans I have
        to deliver to log house . . . right where sun strikes win-
        dow. . . .

Dr. L.:   Fifteen stones from the door?

Entity: Where sun strikes the window. . . . Fifteen stones . . .
        under . . . in log house. . . . There I have put away. . . .
        plans. . . . (agitated) Not take again!

Mr. Walker: No, no, we will not let them take you again. We will
        protect you from the English.

Entity: (Obviously touched) No one ever say—no one ever
        say—I will protect you. . . .

Mr. Walker: Yes, we will protect you. You are protected now for
        always.

Entity: Don't send me away, no?

Dr. L.:   No, we won't send you away.

Entity: Protect . . . protect . . . protect. . . .

Dr. L.:   You were not born in this country?

Entity: No.

Dr. L.:   You are a foreigner?

Entity:	(Hurt and angry, shouts) Yeah . . . dog! They call me dog. Beasts!
Dr. L.:	Are you German? (The entity makes a disdainful negative gesture.) Polish?
Entity:	Yes.
Dr. L.:	You came here when you were young?
Entity:	(His voice is loud and robust with the joy of meeting a countryman.) Das . . . das . . . das! Yes . . . brother? Friends? Pole? Polski, yeah?
Mr. Walker:	Yes, yes.
Entity:	(Throws arms around Walker) I hear . . . I see . . . like . . . like brother . . . like brother Jilitze . . . Jilitze. . . .
Mr. Walker:	What is your name?
Entity:	Gospodin! Gospodin! (Polish for "master")
Mr. Walker:	What's the name? (in Polish) *Zo dje lat?*
Entity:	(Touching Mr. Walker's face and hands as he speaks) Hans? Brother . . . like Hans . . . like Hans . . . me Andre—you Hans.
Mr. Walker:	I'm Hans?
Entity:	My brother . . . he killed too . . . I die . . . I die . . . die . . . die. . . .
Mr. Walker:	Where? At Tappan? Stony Point?
Entity:	Big field, battle. Noise, noise. Big field. Hans like you.
Mr. Walker:	How long ago was this battle?
Entity:	Like yesterday . . . like yesterday . . . I lie here in dark night . . . bleed . . . call Hans. . . call Hans . . . Polski?
Mr. Walker:	Did you die here?
Entity:	Out there. . . . (pointing down) Say again protect, friend. . . . (points at himself) Me, me . . . you . . . Andreas? You like Hans . . . friend, brother . . . you . . . Andreas?
Dr. L.:	Do you know anything about dates?

Entity: Like yesterday. English all over. Cannot . . . they are terrible. . . . (hits his head)

Dr. L.:   You were with the Americans?

Entity: No, no.

Dr. L.:   Yankees?

Entity: No, no. . . Re . . . Re . . . Republic. . . . (drops back to the floor with an outcry of pain)

Dr. L.:   You are still with friends. You are resting. You are safe.

Entity: Protection . . . protection . . . the stars in the flag . . . the stars in the flag . . . Republic . . . they sing. . . .

Dr. L.:   How long have you been hiding in this house?

Entity: I go to talk with brother later. . . . Big man say, you go away, he talk now. . . . I go away a little, he stays . . . he talk . . . he here part of the time. . . .

By "big man" the entity was referring to his guide, Uvani. The entity rested quietly, becoming more and more lifeless on the floor. Soon all life appeared to be gone from the medium's body. Then Uvani returned, took control, sat up, got back up into the chair without trouble, and addressed us in his learned and quiet manner as before.

Uvani: (Greeting us with bended arms, bowing) You will permit me. You do not very often find me in such surroundings. I beg your pardon. Now let me tell to you a little of what I have been able to ascertain. You have here obviously a poor soul who is unhappily caught in the memory of perhaps days or weeks or years of confusion. I permit him to take control in order to let him play out the fantasy . . . in order to play out the fears, the difficulties. . . . I am able thus to relax this one. It is then that I will give you what I see of this story.

165

He was obviously kept a prisoner of . . . a hired army. There had been different kinds of soldiers from Europe brought to this country. He tells me that he had been in other parts of this country with French troops, but they were friendly. He was a friend for a time with one who was friendly not only with your own people, but with Revolutionary troops. He seems, therefore, a man who serves a man . . . a mercenary.

He became a jackboot for all types of men who have fought, a good servant. He is now here, now there.

He does not understand for whom he works. He refers to an Andre, with whom he is for some time in contact, and he likes this Andre very much because of the similar name . . . because he is Andre(w)ski. There is this similarity to Andre. It is therefore he has been used, as far as I can see, as a cover-up for this man. Here then is the confusion.

He is caught two or three times by different people because of his appearance—he is a "dead ringer" . . . a double. His friend Andre disappears, and he is lost and does what he can with this one and that one, and eventually he finds himself in the hands of the British troops. He is known to have letters and plans, and these he wants me to tell you were hidden by him due east of where you now find yourselves, in what he says was a temporary building of sorts in which were housed different caissons. In this there is also a rest house for guards. In this type kitchen he . . . he will not reveal the plans and is beaten mercilessly. His limbs are broken and he passes out, no longer in the right mind, but with a curious break on one side of the body, and his leg is damaged.

It would appear that he is from time to time like one in a coma—he wakes, dreams, and loses himself again, and I gather from the story that he is not always aware of people. Sometimes he says it is a long dream. Could it therefore be that these fantasies are irregular? Does he come and go? You get the kind of disturbance—"Am I dreaming? What is this? A feeling that there is a tempest inside of me. . . ." So I think he goes into these states, suspecting them himself. This is his own foolishness . . . lost between two states of being.

(To Mr. Walker who is tall and blue-eyed)

He has a very strong feeling that you are like his brother. This may account for his desire to be near you. He tells me, "I had a brother and left him very young, tall, blue-eyed," and he misses him in a battlefield in this country.

Now I propose with your prayers and help to try to find his brother for him. And I say to him, "I have asked for your protection, where you will not be outcast, degraded, nor debased, where you will come and go in freedom. Do as your friends here ask. In the name of that God and that faith in which you were brought up, seek salvation and mercy for your restlessness. Go in peace. Go to a kindlier dream. Go out where there is a greater life Come with us you are not with your kind. In mercy let us go hand in hand."

Now he looks at me and asks, "If I should return, would he like unto my brother welcome me?" I do not think he will return, but if you sense him or his wildness of the past, I would say unto you, address him as we have here. Say to him, "You who have found the God of your childhood need not return." Give him your love and please with a prayer send him away.

May there be no illness, nor discord, nor unhappiness in this house because he once felt it was his only resting place. Let there indeed be peace in your hearts and let there be understanding between here and there. It is such a little way, although it looks so far. Let us then in our daily life not wait for this grim experience, but let us help in every moment of our life.

Mr. Walker was softly repeating the closing prayer. Uvani relinquished control, saying, "Peace be unto you . . . until we meet again." The medium fell back in the chair, unconscious for a few moments. Then her own personality returned.

Mrs. Garrett rose from the chair, blinked her eyes, and seemed none the worse for the highly dramatic and exciting incidents which had taken place around her—none of which she was aware of. Every detail of what had happened had to be told to Mrs. Garrett later, as the trance state is complete and no memory whatsoever is retained.

It was 2:45 P.M. when Mrs. Garrett went into trance, and 4 P.M. when the operation came to an end. After some discussion of the events of the preceding hour and a quarter, mainly to iron out differing impressions received by the participants, we left Mr. Walker's house and drove back to New York.

About a month later, Mr. Walker informed me that "the atmosphere about the place does seem much calmer." It seems reasonable to assume that the restless ghost had at last found that "sweeter dream" of which Uvani spoke.

In cases of this nature, where historical names and facts are part of the proceedings, it is always highly desirable to have them corroborated by research in the available reference works. In the case of "The Ghost of Ash Manor," for example, this was comparatively easy, as we were dealing with a personality of some rank and importance in his own lifetime. In this case, however, we were dealing with an obscure immigrant servant, whose name is not likely to appear in any of the regimental records available for the year and place in question. In fact, extensive perusal of such records shows no one who might be our man. There were many enlisted men with the name Andreas serving in the right year and in the right regiment for our investigation, but none of them seems to fit.

And why should it? After all, our Andrewski was a very young man of no particular eminence who served as ordinary jackboot to a succession of colonial soldiers, as Uvani and he himself pointed out. The search for Andreas' brother Hans was almost as negative. Pursuing a hunch that the Slavic exclamation *"Jilitze . . . Jilitze . . ."* which the ghost made during the interrogation, might have been "Ulica . . . Ulica. . . ." I found that a Johannes Ulick (Hans Ulick could be spelled that way) did indeed serve in 1779 in the Second Tryon County Regiment.

The "fifteen stones to the east" to which the ghost referred as the place where he hid the plans may very well have been the walk leading from the house to the log house across the road. Some of these stone steps are still preserved. What happened to the plans, we shall never know. They were probably destroyed by time and weather, or were found and deposited later in obscure hands. No matter which— it is no longer of concern to anyone.

The Haunted
Night Club

PTLY NAMED THE CAFE BIZARRE, this Greenwich Village artists' hangout was the scene of a seance held on the instigation
of the owner, Rick Allmen, whose wife, Renee, was apparently psychic.

One summer night, in 1961, at two o'clock in the morning,
she and her husband had been alone in the cafe, locking up. While
already outside, she recalled having forgotten a package inside the
place, and ran back alone. There was nobody in the dark cafe as
she unlocked the doors again, yet she was overcome by an uncanny
feeling of a "presence."

She put on the lights, took her package, and walked back
toward the front door. Halfway down the long room, she glanced
back toward the rear.

There stood an apparition, a man with piercing black eyes,
wearing a white ruffled shirt of an earlier age, just staring at her.
When she called out to him, he did not answer, he did not move.
This was too much for the woman. Hurriedly she ran out of
the cafe, locked up again, and told her husband what she had
been through.

Together they returned once more, but there was no one in the place. They later learned that a waiter working there had also met the stranger.

On the evening of the seance, about twenty people were present, including representatives of the *New York Journal-American,* the Associated Press, and two small local papers. Mrs. Ethel Johnson Meyers was the medium, and I had carefully kept her in the dark about our purpose and destination.

Clairvoyantly at first, later in full trance, Mrs. Meyers described what she called a previous owner of the place, his son, and a girl that had been murdered.

Curiously enough, she described a man with penetrating dark eyes as the owner, and gave the period of 1804, and before. Yet she knew nothing of the apparition the owner's wife had seen. Also, she insisted that the house was different in those days, shorter; and that also was proven correct.

The initials of a man connected with the place were given as A. B.

In full trance the fact that the building was used as stables was brought out, also not known to the medium. Later, Richard Mardus, historian of the Village, confirmed that the place had been the location of the stables of Aaron Burr, who killed Alexander Hamilton in a duel.

The Riverside Ghost

"**P**LEASE HELP ME FIND OUT what this is all about," pleaded the stranger on the telephone. "I'm being attacked by a ghost!" The caller turned out to be a young jeweler, Edward Karalanian of Paris, then living in an old apartment building on Riverside Drive.

For the past two years, he had lived there with his mother; occasionally he had heard footsteps where no one could have walked. Five or six times he would wake up in the middle of the night to find several strangers in his room. They seemed to him people in conversation, and disappeared as he challenged them on fully awakening.

In one case, he saw a man coming toward him, and threw a pillow at the invader. To his horror, the pillow did not go through the ghostly form, but slid off it and fell to the floor, as the spook vanished!

The man obviously wanted to attack him; there was murder in his eyes—and Mr. Karalanian was frightened by it all. Although his mother could see nothing, he was able to describe the intruder as a man wearing a white "uniform" like a chef, with a hat like a chef, and that his face was mean and cruel.

On March 9, I organized a seance at the apartment, at which a teacher at Adelphi College, Mr. Dersarkissian, and three young ladies were also present; Mrs. Ethel Meyers was the medium.

Although she knew nothing of the case, Mrs. Meyers immediately described a man and woman arguing in the apartment and said there were structural changes, which Mr. Karalanian confirmed.

"Someone is being strangled . . . the man goes away . . . now a woman falls and her head is crushed they want to hide something from the family." Mrs. Meyers then stated that someone had gone out through the twelfth floor window, after being strangled, and that the year was about 1910.

In trance, the discarnate victim, Lizzy, took over her voice and cried pitifully for help. Albert, Mrs. Meyers' control, added that this was a maid who had been killed by a hired man on the wife's orders. Apparently, the girl had had an affair with the husband, named Henry. The murderer was a laborer working in a butcher's shop, by the name of Maggio. The family's name was Brady, or O'Brady; the wife was Anne.

After the seance, I investigated these data, and found to my amazement that the 1812 *City Directory* listed an "A. Maggio, poultry," and both an Anne Brady and Anne O'Grady. The first name was listed as living only one block away from the house! Oh, yes—Mr. Karalanian found out that a young girl, accused of stealing, had killed herself by jumping from that very room!

The Haunted
Chair

B ERNARD SIMON WAS A YOUNG WRITER with great interest in
the occult, and very definitely a budding trance medium. He
has done highly evidential trance work in a strange language
that turned out, on later investigation, to be authentic medieval Inca
speech of Peru, and he had a number of astral projections as well as
clairvoyant dreams.

His wife, Joan, who was known professionally on the stage
under the name of Joan Lowe, and was the niece of screen lumi-
nary Joan Crawford, whom she greatly resembled, also had psychic
talents in addition to her artistic ones. Over the years, we shared a
number of seance experiences.

Shortly after the Simons moved into a brand-new building on
West 12th Street, Bernard found himself drawn to a certain neighbor-
hood antique shop, where he saw a peculiarly shaped wooden chair.
He immediately felt he must buy this chair, which was said to be of
Mexican Indian workmanship.

He brought the chair, a thronelike seat with a round back, arm
pieces and a strange base of crossed staves, to his newly furnished
apartment, and thought no more of the peculiar force that made him
acquire the unusual chair.

A few days later, Bernard awoke rather suddenly in the middle of the night from a deep sleep. There was enough light in the small apartment to distinguish solid objects from each other.

His eyes were drawn to the chair. In it sat an extremely tall man. His back was turned to the observer, but it was clear to Bernard that the man was unusually tall. Before he could get up and challenge the intruder, he had vanished into thin air.

Both Bernard and Joan Simon continually felt a "presence" and told me about their strange guest. I promised to arrange for a seance, and invited Ethel Johnson Meyers to come down with me, without, however, telling her any of the details of the case.

But, before the seance had taken place, I got an urgent telephone call from Joan. Something startling had just happened before her very eyes.

Her husband, laughingly and tongue in cheek, had remarked that he didn't believe in ghosts, and there was nothing to their "visitor." With that he got up and went to the kitchen, leaving Joan in the room.

There was a small but fairly heavy metal figurine, a pagoda, placed in the middle of a small table near one of the walls. As Joan looked on, that figurine *flew off* the table, and on to the floor, *with such violence that it broke in two!*

Three days later, the seance took place.

Mrs. Meyers took the chair, and within moments was in deep trance. Suddenly she sat bolt upright and Native American words came out of her mouth—words that Bernard immediately recognized as Kichua language, the dialect spoken in ancient Peru. Having learned a few words and prayer formulas himself, he managed to quiet the ghost.

It appeared that the man was Huaska, and that he recognized Bernard as his "son," apparently through reincarnation. He had been instrumental in getting Bernard to buy the chair, and then was anxious to make himself known. This having now been accomplished, there followed a joyful embrace, and then the Native American was gone.

The following day, all knocks and other strange noises that had accompanied the feeling of a "presence" prior to the seance were gone. The chair no longer moved and squeaked. All was then quiet since at the Simons'.

The Ghost at the Window

OUT ON LONG ISLAND, an expedition including Mrs. Meyers, Brian Flood (he edited the *New Voice*), My wife Catherine and myself descended upon a dilapidated manor house in the town of West Islip.

A man committed suicide there in 1948; many times since he had been seen at the window facing a busy highway; and several times, at night, motorists had seen him and, diverted momentarily from the road, crashed as a result.

On the second floor of the large wooden structure, Mrs. Meyers felt the presence of the ghost and stated that he had been shot in the left temple—this proved to be correct. At the same time, I had the distinct impression that the stock market had a great deal to do with his death.

Within minutes of searching through the house, we found a yellowed page from a newspaper, the investor's column, dated March 17, 1948. In the basement, the portrait of a well-known stockbroker was located.

A Rendezvous with Houdini

F OR MANY YEARS, EVERY YEAR on the anniversary of Houdini's death, a determined effort was made by the late escape artist's friend, Joseph Dunninger, to contact the departed, while at the same time giving a psychic the opportunity to obtain from the Other Side the code message contained in a sealed package in the possession of Mr. Dunninger, who was holding it in trust for a committee of scientists interested in obtaining positive evidence of Houdini's continued existence. On one particular occasion, I attended the ceremony.

The group, which consisted of people from several countries, and laymen as well as scientists, met at the Park Sheraton Hotel in New York City at midnight on October 31. The Sensitive, who was to try to make contact with Houdini, was the well-known psychometrist Florence, of Edgewater, New Jersey.

Mr. Dunninger had brought along, in addition to a sealed code message, two pairs of handcuffs used by the late Harry Houdini in his work. Florence immediately seized upon one of these and said, "I am impelled to say, 'How much longer will I go on with this work?'"

Mr. Dunninger confirmed that this was indeed one of Houdini's favorite expressions. Florence, who knew Houdini slightly herself, then expressed a feeling of difficulty around the neck, and Mr. Dunninger confirmed that Houdini suffered in that region as a consequence of his work.

I then asked Florence, "Do you feel Houdini present among us?" and she answered in the affirmative. Touching the handcuffs again, she then said, "I get a man's name around him . . . Burke. . . ."

After a moment of reflection, in an effort to associate the name, Mr. Dunninger confirmed that Burke was one of Houdini's teachers of tricks.

Mr. Dunninger then asked Florence to describe some incident that might have puzzled the late Harry Houdini, who did not believe in Survival or Spiritualism.

Florence proceeded to describe "two balls breaking in half." Mr. Dunninger then confirmed that some years ago and unknown to the general public, Houdini had sat in a seance, at which time a departed medium friend of Houdini's was asked to give some evidence of her presence. The medium then materialized two spheres against a black background, which Houdini never was able to account for by so-called "natural" explanations. It was indeed a puzzlement to the great escape artist.

I then repeated a direct challenge to the spirit of Houdini to come forward and make contact, but nothing further happened.

Regretfully, Mr. Dunninger took the sealed envelope containing the code message, which incidentally carried a reward of 10,000 dollars, and hoped for better luck the next time.

The Bayberry Perfume
Ghost

I F THERE IS ANYTHING MORE STAID than a Philadelphia banker
I wouldn't know it. But even bankers are human and sometimes
psychic. In William Davy's case there had been little or no occasion to consider such a matter except for one long forgotten incident
when he was eight years of age. At that time he lived with his parents
in Manchester, England. On one particular morning, little William
insisted that he saw a white shadow in the shape of a man passing
in front of the clock. The clock, it so happened, was just striking the
hour of 8:30 A.M. His mother, reminded by the sound of the clock,
hurriedly sent the boy off to school, telling him to stop his foolishness
about white shadows.

By the time the boy returned home, word had reached the
house that his favorite grandfather, who lived halfway across England
in Devon, had passed away. The time of his death was 8:30 A.M.
Eventually, Mr. Davy moved to Philadelphia where he became an
officer in a local bank, much respected in the community and not the
least bit interested in psychic matters. His aged father, William Sr.,
came to live with him and his family in the home they bought in 1955.
The house is a splendid example of Victorian architecture, built on
three levels on a plot surrounded by tall trees in what is now part of

North Philadelphia, but what was at the time the house was built a separate community, and originally just farmland.

The ground floor has a large kitchen to one side, a large living room, with fireplace, separated from a dining room by a sliding double door. Upstairs are bedrooms on two floors, with the third floor the one-time servant quarters, as was customary in Victorian houses. The Davy family did some remodeling downstairs, but essentially the house was as it was when it was first built, sometime in the late 1880's, according to a local lawyer named Huston, an expert on such things. At any rate, in 1890 it already stood on the spot.

William Sr. was a true English gentleman given to historical research, and a lover of ghost stories, with which he liked to regale his family on many occasions. But what started as a purely literary exercise soon turned into grim reality. Shortly after his arrival, William Sr. complained of hearing unusual noises in the house. He had a room on the third floor and was constantly hearing strange noises and floor boards creaking as if someone were walking on them.

His son laughed at this and ascribed it to his father's vivid imagination, especially after his many fictional ghost stories had set the mood for that sort of thing. But the older Davy insisted to his last day that he was being troubled by an unseen entity. After he passed away in February of 1963, Mr. and Mrs. Davy thought no more of the matter. The house was a peaceful home to them and they enjoyed life.

Several months later, Mr. Davy was sitting by himself in the living room, reading. He was tired, and the time was 10 P.M. He decided to call it a day, and got up to go to bed. As he walked toward the hallway between the living room and the staircase, he literally stepped into a cloud of very pungent perfume which he instantly identified as a very strong bayberry smell. For a moment he stood in utter amazement, then slowly continued into the hall and up the stairs. The perfume still surrounded him, as if someone invisible, wearing this heavy perfume, were walking alongside him!

Upon reaching the first landing he went into the bedroom. At that point, the perfume suddenly left him, just as suddenly as it had come.

"Mary," he asked his wife, "did you by any chance spill some perfume?" She shook her head emphatically. She did not even own any such scent, and there had been no one else in the house that day or evening.

Puzzled but not particularly upset, Mr. Davy let the matter drop and he would have forgotten it entirely had not another event taken him by surprise.

Several months later he was again sitting in the living room, the time being around 10 P.M. He put down his book, and went toward the hallway. Again, he walked into a heavy cloud of the same perfume! Again it followed him up the stairs. As he climbed he felt something— or someone—brush against his right leg. It made a swishing sound but he could not see anything that could have caused it. When he got to the landing, he stopped and asked Mary to come out to him.

His wife had suffered a fractured skull when she was young and as a consequence had lost about seventy percent of her sense of smell.

When Mary joined him at the landing, he asked her if she smelled anything peculiar. "Oh my word," she said, immediately, "what a heavy perfume!" They were standing there looking at each other in a puzzled state. "What on earth is it?" Mary finally asked. He could only shrug his shoulders.

At that precise moment, they clearly heard footsteps going up the stairs from where they were standing, to the third floor!

Since neither of them saw any person causing the footsteps, they were completely unnerved, and refused to investigate. They did not follow the footsteps up to the third floor. They knew only too well that there wasn't any living soul up there at the moment.

One evening Mary was reading in bed, on the second floor, when she found herself surrounded by the same bayberry perfume. It stayed for several seconds, then died away. Since she was quite alone in the house and had been all evening, this was not very reassuring. But the Davys were not the kind of people that panic easily, if at all, so she shrugged it off as something she simply could not explain. On another occasion, Mr. Davy saw a patch of dull, white light move through the living room. From the size of the small cloud it resembled in height either a large child or a small adult, more likely a woman than a man. This was at 3 A.M. when he had come downstairs because he could not sleep that night.

In April of 1966 the Davys had gone to Williamsburg, Virginia, for a visit. On their return, Mr. Davy decided to take the luggage directly upstairs to their bedroom. That instant he ran smack into the cloud of bayberry perfume. It was if some unseen presence wanted to welcome them back!

One of Mary's favorite rings, which she had left in her room, disappeared only to be discovered later in the garden. How it got there was as much of a mystery then as it is now, but no one of flesh and blood moved that ring. Naturally, the Davys did not discuss their unseen visitor with anyone. When you're a Philadelphia banker you don't talk about ghosts.

In September of the same year, they had a visit from their niece and her husband, Mr. and Mrs. Clarence Nowak. Mr. Nowak was a U.S. government employee, by profession a chemical engineer. Their own house was being readied and while they were waiting to move in, they spent two weeks with their uncle and aunt. The niece was staying on the second floor, while Mr. Nowak had been assigned the room on the third floor that had been the center of the ghostly activities in the past. After they had retired, Mr. Nowak started to read a book. When he got tired of this, he put the book down, put the lights out and got ready to doze off.

At that precise moment, he clearly heard footsteps coming up and he was so sure it was his aunt Mary coming up to say goodnight that he sat up and waited. But nobody came into his room and the footsteps continued!

Since he was a man of practical outlook, this puzzled him and he got out of bed and looked around. The corridor was quite empty, yet the footsteps continued right in front of him. Moreover, they seemed to enter the room itself and the sound of steps filled the atmosphere of the room as if someone were indeed walking in it. Unable to resolve the problem, he went to sleep.

The next night, the same thing happened. For two weeks, Mr. Nowak went to sleep with the footsteps resounding promptly at 10 P.M. But he had decided to ignore the whole thing and went to sleep, steps or no steps.

"It seemed, when I was in bed," he explained to his aunt, somewhat sheepishly, "the footsteps were coming up the stairs, and when I was lying there it seemed as if they were actually in the room, but I could not distinguish the actual location. When I first heard them I thought they were Mary's, so I guess they must have been the footsteps of a woman."

Mr. Nowak was not given to any interest in psychic phenomena, but on several occasions his wife, also named Mary, as is her aunt, did have a rapport bordering on telepathic communication with him. These were minor things, true, but they were far beyond the possibilities of mere chance. Thus it was very likely that the chemist's natural tendency towards extrasensory perception played a role in his ability to hear the steps, as it certainly did in the case of the banker, Mr. Davy, whose own childhood had shown at least one marked incident of this sort.

But if the ghostly presence favored anyone with her manifestations, it would seem that she preferred men. Mary Nowak slept soundly through the two weeks, with nary a disturbance or incident.

Clifford Richardson, another nephew of the Davys, came from Oklahoma to visit the Nowaks one time, and in the course of the visit he decided to stay a night at the Davys. Mr. Richardson was the owner of an insurance agency and not the least bit interested in the occult. On his return to the Nowaks the following day, he seemed unusually pensive and withdrawn. Finally, over coffee, he opened up.

"Look, Mary," he said, "your husband Bucky has stayed over at Uncle Ned's house for a while. Did he sleep well?"

"What do you mean?" Mary asked, pretending not to know.

"Did he ever hear any sounds?"

Mary knew what he meant and admitted that her husband had indeed "heard sounds."

"Thank God," the insurance man sighed. "I thought I was going out of my mind when I heard those footsteps."

He, too, had slept in the third floor bedroom.

What was the terrible secret the little bedroom held for all these years?

The room itself was plainly but adequately furnished as a guest room. It was small and narrow and undoubtedly was originally a maid's room. There was a small window leading to the tree-studded street below. It must have been a somewhat remote room originally where a person might not be heard, should he or she cry for help for any reason.

The Davys began to look into the background of their house. The surrounding area had been known as Wright's Farm, and a certain Mrs. Wright had built houses on the property towards the late 1880's. The house was owned by four sets of occupants prior to their buying it and despite attempts to contact some of those who were still alive, they failed to do so. They did not discuss their "problem" with anyone, not even Mary's aged mother who was now staying with them. No sense frightening the frail old lady. Then again the Davys weren't really frightened, just curious. Mary, in addition to being a housewife, was also a student of group dynamics and education at nearby Temple University, and the phenomena interested her mildly from a researcher's point of view. As for William Davy, it was all more of a lark than something to be taken seriously, and certainly not the sort of thing one worries about.

When their inquiries about the history of the house failed to turn up startling or sensational details, they accepted the presence as something left over from the Victorian age and the mystique of it all added an extra dimension, as it were, to their fine old home.

Then one day, in carefully looking over the little room on the third floor, Mr. Davy made an interesting discovery. At waist height, the door to the room showed heavy dents, as if someone had tried to batter it down! No doubt about it, the damage showed clear evidence of attempted forcing of the door.

Had someone violated a servant up there against her wishes? Was the door to the bedroom battered down by one of the people in the house, the son, perhaps, who in that age was sacrosanct from ordinary prosecution for such a "minor" misdeed as having an affair with the maid?

The strong smell of bayberry seemed to indicate a member of the servant class, for even then, as now, an overabundance of strong perfume is not a sign of good breeding.

Many years have passed with no further incidents, but this does not mean the ghost is gone. For a Victorian servant girl to be able to roam the *downstairs* at will is indeed a pleasure not easily abandoned—not even for the promised freedom of The Other Side!

The Ghost-Servant
Problem at
Ringwood Manor

RINGWOOD, IN THE SOUTH OF ENGLAND, has an American counterpart in New Jersey. I had never heard of Ringwood Manor in New Jersey until Mrs. Edward Tholl, a resident of nearby Saddle River, brought it to my attention. An avid history buff and a talented geographer and map maker, Mrs. Tholl had been to the Manor House and on several occasions felt "a presence." The mountain people who still inhabited the Ramapo Mountains of the region wouldn't go near the Manor House at night.

"Robert Erskine, geographer to Washington's army, is buried on the grounds," Mrs. Tholl told me.

The Manor House land was purchased by the Ogden family of Newark in 1740, and an iron-smelting furnace was built on it two years later. The area abounds in mine deposits and was at one time a center of iron mining and smelting. In 1762, when a second furnace was built, a small house was also built. This house still stands and now forms part of the haphazard arrangement that constitutes the Manor House today. One Peter Hasenclever bought the house and iron works in 1764. He ran the enterprise with such ostentation that he was known as "The Baron." But Hasenclever did not produce enough iron to suit his backers, and was soon replaced by Robert Erskine. When the War of Independence broke out, the iron works were forced to close. Erskine himself died "of exposure" in 1780.

By 1807, the iron business was going full blast again, this time under the aegis of Martin Ryerson, who tore down the ramshackle old house and rebuilt it completely. After the iron business failed in the 1830s, the property passed into the hands of famed Peter Cooper in 1853. His son-in-law Abram S. Hewitt, one-time Mayor of New York, lived in the Manor House.

Mrs. Hewitt, Cooper's daughter, turned the drab house into an impressive mansion of 51 rooms, very much as it appears today. Various older buildings already on the grounds were uprooted and added to the house, giving it a checkered character without a real center. The Hewitt family continued to live at Ringwood until Erskine Hewitt deeded the estate to the State of New Jersey in 1936, and the mansion became a museum through which visitors were shown daily for a small fee.

During troubled times, tragedies may well have occurred in and around the house. There was a holdup in 1778, and in the graveyard nearby, many French soldiers were buried who died there during an epidemic. There is also on record an incident, in later years, when the cook was threatened by a butler with a knife, and there were disasters that took many lives in the nearby iron mines.

One of the Hewitt girls, Sally, had been particularly given to mischief. If anyone were to haunt the place, she'd be a prime candidate for the job. I thanked Claire Tholl for her help, and called on Ethel Johnson Meyers to accompany me to New Jersey. Of course, I didn't give her any details. We arranged to get to the house around dusk, after all the tourists had gone.

My wife Catherine and I, with Ethel Meyers as passenger, drove out to the house on a humid afternoon in May, 1965. Jim Byrne joined us at the house with *Saturday Review* writer Haskell Frankel in tow.

We were about an hour late, but it was still light, and the peaceful setting of the park with the Manor House in its center reminded one indeed of similar houses gracing the English countryside.

We stood around battling New Jersey mosquitoes for a while, then I asked Catherine to take Ethel away from the house for a moment, so I could talk to Mrs. Tholl and others who had witnessed ghostly goings-on in the house.

"I've had a feeling in certain parts of the house that I was not alone," Mrs. Tholl said, "but other than that I cannot honestly say I have had uncanny experiences here."

Alexander Waldron had been the superintendent of Ringwood Manor for many years, until a year before, in fact. He consented to join us for the occasion. A jovial, gray-haired man, he seemed rather deliberate in his report, giving me only what to him were actual facts.

"I was superintendent here for eighteen years," Mr. Waldron began. "I was sitting at my desk one day, in the late afternoon, like today, and the door to the next room was closed. My office is on the ground floor. I heard two people come walking toward me at a fast pace. That did not seem unusual, for we do have workmen here frequently. When the steps reached my door, nothing happened. Without thinking too much, I opened the door for them. But there was no one there. I called out, but there was no answer. Shortly after, two workmen did come in from outside, and together we searched the whole building, but found no one who could have made the sound."

"Could anyone have walked away without being seen by you?"

"Impossible. There was good light."

"Did anything else happen after that?"

"Over the years we've had a few things we could not explain. For instance, doors we had shut at night, we found open the next morning. Some years ago, when I had my boys living here with me, they decided to build a so-called monster down in the basement. One boy was of high-school age, the other in grammar school—sixteen and thirteen. One of them came in by himself one night, when he heard footsteps overhead, on the ground floor. He thought it was his brother who had come over from the house.

"He thought his brother was just trying to scare him, so he continued to work downstairs. But the footsteps continued and finally he got fed up with it and came upstairs. All was dark, and nobody was around. He ran back to the house, where he found his brother, who had never been to the Manor at all."

Bradley Waldron probably never worked on his "monster" again after that.

There are stories among the local hill folk of Robert Erskine's ghost walking with a lantern, or sitting on his grave half a mile down the road from the Manor House, or racing up the staircase in the house itself.

Wayne Daniels, who had accompanied Mrs. Tholl to the House, spoke up now. Mr. Daniels had lived in the region all his life, and was a professional restorer of early American structures.

"I have felt strange in one corner of the old dining room, and in two rooms upstairs," he volunteered. "I feel hostility in those areas, somehow."

It was time to begin our search in the house itself.

I asked Ethel Meyers to join us, and we entered the Manor House, making our way slowly along the now-deserted corridors and passages of the ground floor, following Ethel as she began to get her psychic bearings.

Suddenly, Ethel remarked that she felt a man outside the windows, but could not pin down her impression.

"Someone died under a curse around here," she mumbled, then added as if it were an afterthought, "Jackson White . . . what does that mean?"

I had never heard the name before, but Claire Tholl explained that "Jackson White" was a peculiar local name for people of mixed blood, who live in the Ramapo hills. Ethel added that someone had been in slavery at one time.

Ethel was taken aback by the explanation of "Jackson White." She had taken it for granted that it was an individual name. Jackson Whites, I gathered, are partly Native American and partly black, but not white.

We now entered a large bedroom elegantly furnished in the manner of the early nineteenth century, with a large bed against one wall and a table against the other. Ethel looked around the room uncertainly, as if looking for something she did not yet see.

"Someone with a bad conscience died in this room," she said. "A man and a woman lived here, who were miles apart somehow."

It was Mrs. Erskine's bedroom we were in. We went through a small door into another room that lay directly behind the rather large bedroom; it must have been a servant's room at one time. Nevertheless, it was elegant, with a marble fireplace and a heavy oak table, around which a number of chairs had been placed. We sat down but before I had time to adjust my tape recorder and camera, Ethel Meyers fell into deep trance. From her lips came the well-modulated voice of Albert, her control. He explained that several layers of consciousness covered the room, that there were blacks brought here by one Jackson, who came in the eighteenth century. One of them seemed present in the room, he felt.

"One met death at the entrance . . . a woman named Lucy Bell, she says. She was a servant here."

Suddenly, Albert was gone. In his stead, there was a shrill, desperate female voice, crying out to all who would listen.

"No . . . I didn't . . . before my God I didn't . . . I show you where . . . I didn't touch it . . . never . . ."

She seemed to be speaking to an unseen tormentor now, for Ethel, possessed by the ghost, pulled back from the table and cried:

"No . . . don't . . . don't!" Was she being beaten or tortured?

"He didn't either!" the ghost added.

I tried to calm her.

"I didn't touch . . . I didn't touch . . ." she kept repeating.

I asked for her name.

"Lucy," she said in a tormented, high-pitched voice completely different from Ethel Meyers' normal tones.

"I believe you," I said, and told the ghost who we were and why we had come. The uncontrollable crying subsided for the moment.

"He's innocent too," she finally said. "I can't walk," she added. Ethel pointed to her side. Had she been hurt?

"I didn't take it," she reiterated. "It's right there."

What didn't she take? I coaxed her gently to tell me all about it. "I've come as a *friend*," I said, and the word finally hit home. She got very excited and wanted to know where I was since she could not see me.

"A friend, Jeremiah, do you hear?" she intoned.

"Who is Jeremiah?"

"He didn't do it either," she replied. Jeremiah, I gathered, lived here, too, but she did not know any family name—just Jeremiah. Then Ethel Meyers grabbed my hand, mumbling "friend," and almost crushed my fingers. I managed to pull it away. Ethel ordinarily has a very feminine, soft grip—a great contrast to the desperately fierce gasp of the ghost possessing the medium!

"Don't go!"

I promised to stay if she would talk.

"I have never stolen," she said. "It's dark . . . I can't see now . . . where do I go to see always?"

"I will show you the way," I promised.

"Marie . . . Marie . . . where are you?" she intoned pleadingly.

"What is Jeremiah doing?"

"He is begging for his honor."

"Where is he now?"

"Here with me."

"Who is the person you worked for?" I asked.

"Old lady . . . I don't want her . . ."

"If she did you wrong, should we punish her? What is her name?"

"I never wished evil on anyone . . . I would forgive her . . . if she forgives me. She is here . . . I saw her, and she hates me . . ."

The voice became shrill and emotional again. I started to send her away, and in a few moments, she slipped out. Suddenly, there was an entirely different person occupying Ethel's body. Proudly sitting up, she seemed to eye us, with closed eyes, of course, as if we were riffraff invading her precincts.

"What is your name?" I demanded.

"I am in no court of justice," was the stiff reply in a proper upper-class accent. "I cannot speak to you. I have no desire. It is futile for you to give me any advice."

"What about this servant girl?" I asked.

"You may take yourself away," the lady replied, haughtily. "Depart!"

"What did the girl take?" I asked, ignoring her outburst of cold fury.

"I am not divulging anything to you."

"Is she innocent then?"

This gave her some thought, and the next words were a little more communicative.

"Why are you in my house?" she demanded.

"Is it your house?"

"I will call the servants and have you taken out by the scruff of your neck," she threatened.

"Will the servants know who you are?" I countered.

"I am lady in my own."

"What is your name?"

"I refuse to reveal myself or talk to you!"

I explained about the passage of time. It made no impression.

"I will call her . . . Old Jeremiah is under his own disgrace. You are friend to him?"

I explained about Ethel Meyers and how she, the ghost, was able to communicate with us.

She hit the table hard with Ethel's fist.

"The man is mad," the ghost said. "Take him away!"

I didn't intend to be taken away by ghostly men-in-white. I continued to plead with "the lady" to come to her senses and listen. She kept calling for her servants, but evidently nobody answered her calls.

"Jeremiah, if you want to preserve yourself in my estimation and not stand by this girl, take this . . ."

Somehow the medium's eyes opened for a moment, and the ghost could "see." Then they closed again. It came as a shock, for "the lady" sullenly stopped her angry denunciation and instead "looked" at me in panic.

"What is this? Doctor . . . where is he . . . Laura! Laura! I am ill. Very ill. I can't see. I can't see. I hear something talking to me, but I can't see it. Laura, call a doctor. I'm going to die!"

"As a matter of fact," I said calmly, "you have died already. "

"It was my mother's." The ghost sobbed hysterically. "Don't let her keep it. Don't let it go to the scum! I must have it. Don't let me die like this. Oh, oh . . ."

I called on Albert, the control, to take the unhappy ghost away and lead her to the other side of the veil, if possible. The sobbing slowly subsided as the ghost's essence drifted away out of our reach in that chilly Georgian room at Ringwood.

It wasn't Albert's crisp, precise voice that answered me. Another stranger, obviously male, now made his coughing entry and spoke in a lower-class accent.

"What's the matter?"

"Who is this?" I asked.

The voice sounded strangely muffled, as if coming from far away.

"Jeremiah . . . What's the matter with everybody?" The voice sounded like it was an African-American speaking.

"I'm so sleepy," the voice said.

"Who owns this house?" I asked.

"Ho, ho, I do," the ghost said. "I have a funny dream, what's the matter with everybody?" Then the voice cleared up a little, as he became more aware of the strange surroundings into which he had entered.

"Are you one of these white trashes?" he demanded.

"What is the old lady's name?" I asked.

"She's a Bob," he replied, enigmatically, and added, "real bumby, with many knots in it, many knots in the brain."

"Who else is here?"

"I don't like you. I don't know you and I don't like who I don't know," the servant's ghost said.

"You're white trash," he continued. "I see you!" The stress was on *white*.

"How long have you been living here?"

"My father. . . Luke."

Again, I explained about death and consequences, but the reception was even less friendly than I had received from "the lady."

Jeremiah wanted no truck with death.

"What will the old squaw say? What will she say?" he wondered. "She needs me."

"Not really," I replied. "After all, she's dead, too." He could hardly believe the news. Evidently, the formidable "squaw" was immune to such events as death in his mind.

"What do you have against my mother?" he demanded now. Things were getting confusing. Was the "old lady" his mother?

"Lucy white trash too," he commented.

"Was she your wife?"

"Call it that."

"Can you see her?"

"She's here."

"Then you know you have died and must go from this house?" I asked.

"'dominable treek, man, 'dominable treek," he said, furiously.

"This house is no longer yours."

"It never was," he shot back. "The squaw is here. We're not dead, great white spirit—laugh at you."

"What do you want in this house?"

"Squaw very good," he said. "I tell you, my mother, squaw very good. Lucy Bell, white trash, but good. Like Great White Spirit. Work my fingers down to the bone. I am told! I am thief, too. Just yesterday. Look at my back! Look at my squaw! Red Fox, look at her. Look at my back, look at it!"

He seemed to have spent his anger. The voice became softer now.

"I am so sleepy," he said. "So sleepy. . . my Lucy will never walk again . . . angel spirit . . . my people suffer . . . her skin should be like mine . . . help me, help my Lucy . . . "

I promised to help and to send him to his father, Luke, who was awaiting him.

"I should have listened to my father," the ghost mumbled.

Then he recognized his father, evidently come to guide him out of the house, and wondered what he was doing here.

I explained what I thought was the reason for his father's presence. There was some crying, and then they all went away.

"Albert," I said. "Please take over the instrument."

In a moment, the control's cool voice was heard, and Ethel was brought out of trance rather quickly.

"My hip," she complained. "I don't think I can move."

"Passing conditions" or symptoms the ghost brings are sometimes present for a few moments after a medium comes out of trance. It is nothing to be alarmed about.

I closed Ethel's eyes again, and sent her back into trance, then brought her out again, and this time all was "clear." However, she still recalled a scream in a passage between the two rooms.

I wondered about the Indian nature of the ghost. Were there any Native Americans in this area?

"Certainly," Mr. Waldron replied. "They are of mixed blood, often mixed with African Americans, and are called Jackson Whites. Many of them worked here as servants."

The footsteps the superintendent had heard on the floor below were of two persons, and they could very well have come from this area, since the room we were in was almost directly above his offices.

There was, of course, no record of any servants named Jeremiah or Lucy. Servants' names were rarely recorded unless they did something that was most unusual.

I asked Mrs. Tholl about ladies who might have fit the description of the haughty lady who had spoken to us through Ethel Meyers in trance.

"I associate this with the Hewitt occupancy of the house," she explained, "because of the reference to a passage connecting two parts of the house, something that could not apply to an early structure on the spot. Amelia Hewitt, whose bedroom we had come through, was described in literature of the period as 'all placidity and kindliness.' Sarah Hewitt, however, was quite a cut-up in her day, and fitted the character of 'the lady' more accurately."

But we cannot be sure of the identity of the ghost-lady. She elected to keep her name a secret and we can only bow to her decision and let it remain so.

What lends the accounts an air of reality and evidence is, of course, the amazing fact that Ethel Meyers spoke of "Jackson Whites" in this house, an appellation completely new to her and me.

I am also sure that the medium had no knowledge of mixed-blood Native Americans living in the area. Then, too, her selecting a room above the spot where the ghostly steps had been heard was also interesting, for the house was sprawling and had many, many rooms and passages.

"Ocean-Born" Mary

AMONG THE GHOSTLY LEGENDS OF the United States, that of "Ocean-Born" Mary and her fascinating house at Henniker, New Hampshire, is probably one of the best known. To the average literate person who has heard about the colorful tale of Mary Wallace, or the New Englander who knows of it because he lives "Down East," it is, of course, a legend not to be taken too seriously.

I had a vague idea of its substance when I received a note from a lady named Corinne Russell, who together with her husband, David, had bought the Henniker house and wanted me to know that it was still haunted.

That was in October of 1963. It so happens that Halloween is the traditional date on which the ghost of six-foot Mary Wallace is supposed to "return" to her house in a coach drawn by six horses. On many a Halloween, youngsters from all around Henniker have come and sat around the grounds waiting for Mary to ride in. The local press had done its share of Halloween ghost hunting, so much so that the Russells had come to fear that date as one of the major nuisance days of their year.

After all, Halloween visitors do not pay the usual fee to be shown about the house, but they do leave behind them destruction and litter at times. Needless to say, nobody has ever seen Mary ride in her coach on Halloween. Why should she when she lives there *all year round*?

To explain this last statement, I shall have to take you back to the year 1720, when a group of Scottish and Irish immigrants was approaching the New World aboard a ship called the *Wolf*, from Londonderry, Ireland. The ship's captain, Wilson, had just become the father of a daughter, who was actually born at sea. Within sight of land, the ship was boarded by pirates under the command of a buccaneer named Don Pedro. As the pirates removed all valuables from their prize, Don Pedro went below to the captain's cabin. Instead of gold, he found Mrs. Wilson and her newborn baby girl.

"What's her name?" he demanded.

Unafraid, the mother replied that the child had not yet been baptized, having been recently born.

"If you will name her after my mother, Mary," the pirate said, overcome with an emotion few pirates ever allow into their lives, "I will spare everybody aboard this ship."

Joyously, the mother made the bargain, and "Ocean-Born" Mary received her name. Don Pedro ordered his men to hand back what they had already taken from their prisoners, to set them free, and to leave the captured ship. The vicious-looking crew grumbled and withdrew to their own ship.

Minutes later, however, Don Pedro returned alone. He handed Mrs. Wilson a bundle of silk.

"For Mary's wedding gown," he said simply, and left again.

As soon as the pirate ship was out of sight, the *Wolf* continued her voyage for Boston. Thence Captain and Mrs. Wilson went on to their new home in Londonderry, New Hampshire, where they settled down, and where Mary grew up.

When she was 18, she married a man named Wallace, and over the years they had four sons. However, shortly after the birth of the fourth son, her husband died and Mary found herself a widow.

Meanwhile, Don Pedro—allegedly an Englishman using the Spanish *nom de pirate* to disguise his noble ancestry—had kept in touch with the Wilsons. Despite the hazards of pirate life, he survived to an old age when thoughts of retirement filled his mind. Somehow he managed to acquire a land grant of 6,000 acres in what is now Henniker, New Hampshire, far away from the sea. On this land, Pedro built himself a stately house. He employed his ship's carpenters, as can be seen in the way the beams are joined. Ship's carpenters have a special way of building, and "Ocean-Born" Mary's house, as it later became known, is an example of this.

The house was barely finished when the aging pirate heard of Mary Wallace's loss of her husband, and he asked Mary and her children to come live with him. She accepted his invitation, and soon became his housekeeper.

The house was then in a rather isolated part of New England, and few callers, if any, came to interrupt the long stillness of the many cold winter nights. Mary took up painting and with her own hands created the eagle that can still be seen gracing the house.

The years went by peacefully, until one night someone attacked Don Pedro and killed him. Whether one of his men had come to challenge the pirate captain for part of the booty, or whether the reputation of a retired pirate had put ideas of treasure in the mind of some local thief, we may never know. All we know is that by the time Mary Wallace got out into the grove at the rear of the house, Don Pedro was dying with a pirate cutlass in his chest. He asked her to bury him under the hearthstone in the kitchen, which is in the rear of the house.

Mary herself inherited the house and what went with it, treasure, buried pirate, and all. She herself passed on in 1814, and ever since then the house had been changing hands.

Unfortunately, we cannot interview the earlier owners of the house, but during the 1930s, it belonged to one Louis Roy, retired and disabled and a permanent guest in what used to be his home. He sold the house to the Russells in the early sixties.

During the great hurricane of 1935, Roy claims that Mary Wallace's ghost saved his life 19 times. Trapped outside the house by falling trees, he somehow was able to get back into the house. His very psychic mother, Mrs. Roy, informed him that she had actually seen the tall, stately figure of "Ocean-Born" Mary moving behind him, as if to help him get through. In the 1950s, *Life* told this story in an illustrated article on famous ghost-haunted houses in America. Mrs. Roy claimed she had seen the ghost of Mary time and again, but since she herself passed on in 1948, I could not get any details from *her*.

Then there were two state troopers who saw the ghost, but again I could not interview them, as they, too, were also on the other side of the veil.

A number of visitors claimed to have felt "special vibrations" when touching the hearthstone, where Don Pedro allegedly was buried. There was, for instance, Mrs. James Nisula of Londonderry, who visited the house several times. She said that she and her "group" of ghost buffs had "felt the vibrations" around the kitchen. Mrs. David Russell, the owner who contacted me, felt nothing.

I promised to look into the "Ocean-Born" Mary haunting the first chance I got. Halloween or about that time would be all right with me, and I wouldn't wait around for any coach!

"There is a lady medium I think you should know," Mrs. Russell said when I spoke of bringing a psychic with me. "She saw Mary the very first time she came here."

My curiosity aroused, I communicated with the lady. She asked that I not use her married name, although she was not so shy several months after our visit to the house, when she gave a two-part interview to a Boston newspaper columnist. (Needless to say, the interview was not authorized by me, since I never allow mediums I work with to talk about their cases for publication. Thus Lorrie shall remain without a family name and anyone wishing to reach this medium will have to do so without my help.)

Lorrie wrote me she would be happy to serve the cause of truth, and I could count on her. There was nothing she wanted in return.

We did not get up to New Hampshire that Halloween. Mr. Russell had to have an operation, the house was unheated in the winter except for Mr. Roy's room, and New England winters are cold enough to freeze any ghost.

Although there was a caretaker at the time to look after the house and Mr. Roy upstairs, the Russells did not stay at the house in the winter, but made their home in nearby Chelmsford, Massachusetts.

I wrote Mrs. Russell postponing the investigation until spring. Mrs. Russell accepted my decision with some disappointment, but she was willing to wait. After all, the ghost at "Ocean-Born" Mary's house is not a malicious type. Mary Wallace just lived there, ever since she died in 1814, and you can't call a lady who likes to hold on to what is hers an intruder.

"We don't want to drive her out," Mrs. Russell repeatedly said to me. "After all, it is her house!"

Not many haunted-house owners make statements like that.

But something had happened at the house since our last conversation.

"Our caretaker dropped a space heater all the way down the stairs at the 'Ocean-Born' Mary house, and when it reached the bottom, the kerosene and the flames started to burn the stairs and climb the wall. There was no water in the house, so my husband went out after snow. While I stood there looking at the fire and powerless to do anything about it, the fire went right out all by itself right in front of my eyes; when my husband got back with the snow it was out. It was just as if someone *had smothered it with a blanket.*"

This was in December of 1963. I tried to set a new date, as soon as possible, and February 22 seemed possible. This time I would bring Bob Kennedy of WBZ, Boston, and the "Contact" producer Squire Rushnell with me to record my investigation.

Lorrie was willing, asking only that her name not be mentioned.

"I don't want anyone to know about my being different from them," she explained. "When I was young my family used to accuse me of spying because I knew things from the pictures I saw when I touched objects."

Psychometry, I explained, is very common among psychics, and nothing to be ashamed of.

I thought it was time to find out more about Lorrie's experiences at the haunted house.

"I first saw the house in September of 1961," she began. "It was on a misty, humid day, and there was a haze over the fields."

Strange, I thought, I always get my best psychic results when the atmosphere is moist.

Lorrie, who was in her early forties, was Vermont born and raised; she was married and had one daughter, Pauline. She was a tall redhead with sparkling eyes, and, come to think of it, not unlike the accepted picture of the ghostly Mary Wallace. Coincidence?

A friend of Lorrie's had seen the eerie house and suggested she go and see it also. That was all Lorrie knew about it, and she did not really expect anything uncanny to occur. Mr. Roy showed Lorrie and her daughter through the house and nothing startling happened. They left and started to walk down the entrance steps, crossing the garden in front of the house, and had reached the gate when Pauline clutched at her mother's arm and said:

"Mamma, what is that?"

Lorrie turned to look back at the house. In the upstairs window, a woman stood and looked out at them. Lorrie's husband was busy with the family car. Eventually, she called out to him, but as he turned to look, the apparition was gone.

She did not think of it again, and the weeks went by. But the house kept intruding itself into her thoughts more and more. Finally she could not restrain herself any longer, and returned to the house—even though it was 120 miles from her home in Weymouth, Massachusetts.

She confessed her extraordinary experience to the owner, and together they examined the house from top to bottom. She finally returned home.

She promised Roy she would return on All Hallow's Eve to see if the legend of Mary Wallace had any basis of fact. Unfortunately, word of her intentions got out, and when she finally arrived at the house, she had to sneak in the back to avoid the sensation-hungry press outside. During the days between her second visit and Halloween, the urge to go to Henniker kept getting stronger, as if someone were possessing her.

By that time the Russells were negotiating to buy the house, and Lorrie came up with them. Nothing happened to her that Halloween night. Perhaps she was torn between fear and a desire to fight the influence that had brought her out to Henniker to begin with.

Mediums, to be successful, must learn to relax and not allow their own notions to rule them. All through the following winter and summer, Lorrie fought the desire to return to "Ocean-Born" Mary's house. To no avail. She returned time and again, sometimes alone and sometimes with a friend.

Things got out of hand one summer night when she was home alone.

Exhausted from her last visit—the visits always left her an emotional wreck—she went to bed around 9:30 P.M.

"What happened that night?" I interjected. She seemed shaken even now.

"At 11 P.M., Mr. Holzer," Lorrie replied, "I found myself driving on the expressway, wearing my pajamas and robe, with no shoes or slippers, or money, or even a handkerchief. I was ten miles from my home and heading for Henniker. Terrified, I turned around and returned home, only to find my house ablaze with light, the doors open as I had left them, and the garage lights on. I must have left in an awful hurry."

"Have you found out why you are being pulled back to that house?"

She shook her head.

"No idea. But I've been back twice, even after that. I just can't seem to stay away from that house."

I persuaded her that perhaps there was a job to be done in that house, and the ghost wanted her to do it.

We did not go to Henniker in February, because of bad weather. We tried to set a date in May, 1964. Meanwhile, the people from WBZ decided Henniker was too far away from Boston and dropped out of the planning.

Summer came around, and I went to Europe instead of Henniker. However, the prospect of a visit in the fall was very much in my mind.

It seemed as if someone were keeping me away from the house very much in the same way someone was pulling Lorrie toward it!

Come October, and we were really on our way, at last. Owen Lake, a public relations man who dabbles in psychic matters, introduced himself as "a friend" of mine and told Lorrie he'd come along, too. I had never met the gentleman, but in the end he could not make it anyway. So just four of us—my wife Catherine and I, Lorrie, and her nice, even-tempered husband, who had volunteered to drive us up to New Hampshire—started out from Boston. It was close to Halloween, all right, only two days before. If Mary Wallace were out haunting the countryside in her coach, we might very well run into her. The coach is out of old Irish folktales; it appears in numerous ghost stories of the Ould Sod. I'm sure that in the telling and retelling of the tale of Mary and her pirate, the coach got added. The countryside is beautiful in a New England fall. As we rolled toward the New Hampshire state line, I asked Lorrie some more questions.

"When you first saw the ghost of 'Ocean-Born' Mary at the window of the house, Lorrie," I said, "what did she look like?"

"A lovely lady in her thirties, with auburn-colored hair, smiling rather intensely and thoughtfully. She stayed there for maybe three minutes, and then suddenly, *she just wasn't there.*"

"What about her dress?"

"It was a white dress."

Lorrie never saw an apparition of Mary again, but whenever she touched anything in the Henniker house, she received an impression of what the house was like when Mary had it, and she had felt her near the big fireplace several times.

Did she ever get an impression of what it was Mary wanted?

"She was a quick-tempered woman; I sensed that very strongly," Lorrie replied. "I have been to the house maybe twenty times altogether, and still don't know why. She just keeps pulling me there."

Lorrie had always felt the ghost's presence on these visits.

"One day I was walking among the bushes in the back of the house. I was wearing shorts, but I never got a scratch on my legs, because I kept feeling heavy skirts covering my legs. I could feel the brambles pulling at this invisible skirt I had on. I felt enveloped by something, or someone."

Mrs. Roy, the former owner's mother, had told of seeing the apparition many times, Lorrie stated.

"As a matter of fact, I have sensed her ghost in the house, too, but it is not a friendly wraith like Mary is."

Had she ever encountered this other ghost?

"Yes, my arm was grabbed one time by a malevolent entity," Lorrie said emphatically. "It was two years ago, and I was standing in what is now the living room, and my arm was taken by the elbow and pulled.

"I snatched my arm back, because I felt she was not friendly."

"What were you doing at the time that she might have objected to?"

"I really don't know."

Did she know of anyone else who had had an uncanny experience at the house?

"A strange thing happened to Mrs. Roy," Lorrie said. "A woman came to the house and said to her, 'What do you mean, the *rest* of the house?' The woman replied, 'Well, I was here yesterday, and a tall woman let me in and only showed me half of the house.' But, of course, there was nobody at the house that day."

What about the two state troopers? Could she elaborate on their experience?

"They met her walking down the road that leads to the house. She was wearing a Colonial-type costume, and they found that odd. Later they realized they had seen a ghost, especially as no one of her description lived in the house at the time."

Rudi D., Lorrie's husband, was a hospital technician. He was with her on two or three occasions when she visited the house. Did he ever feel anything special?

"The only thing unusual I ever felt at the house was that I wanted to get out of there fast," he said.

"The very first time we went up," Lorrie added, "something kept pulling me toward it, but my husband insisted we go back. There was an argument about our continuing the trip, when suddenly the door of the car flew open of its own volition. Somehow we decided to continue on to the house."

An hour later, we drove up a thickly overgrown hill and along a winding road at the end of which the "Ocean-Born" Mary house stood in solitary stateliness, a rectangular building of gray stone and brown trim, very well preserved.

We parked the car and walked across the garden that sets the house well back from the road. There was peace and autumn in the air. We were made welcome by Corinne Russell, her husband David, and two relatives who happened to be with them that day. Entering the main door beneath a magnificent early American eagle, we admired the fine wooden staircase leading to the upstairs—the staircase on which the mysterious fire had taken place—and then entered the room to the left of it, where the family had assembled around an old New England stove.

During the three years the Russells had lived at the house, nothing uncanny had happened to Mrs. Russell, except for the incident with the fire. David Russell, a man almost typical of the shrewd New England Yankee who weighs his every word, was willing to tell me about *his* experiences, however.

"The first night I ever slept in what we call the Lafayette room, upstairs, there was quite a thundershower on, and my dog and I were upstairs. I always keep my dog with me, on account of the boys coming around to do damage to the property.

"Just as I lay down in bed, I heard very heavy footsteps. They sounded to me to be in the two rooms which we had just restored, on the same floor. I was quite annoyed, almost frightened, and I went into the rooms, but there was nobody there or anywhere else in the house."

"Interesting," I said. "Was there more?"

"Now this happened only last summer. A few weeks later, when I was in that same room, I was getting undressed when I suddenly heard somebody pound on my door. I said to myself, 'Oh, it's only the house settling,' and I got into bed. A few minutes later, the door knob turned back and forth. I jumped out of bed, opened the door, and there was absolutely nobody there. The only other people in the house at the time were the invalid Mr. Roy, locked in his room, and my wife downstairs."

What about visual experiences?

"No, but I went to the cellar not long ago with my dog, about four in the afternoon, or rather tried to—this dog never leaves me, but on this particular occasion, something kept her from going with me into the cellar. Her hair stood up and she would not budge."

The Lafayette room, by the way, was the very room in which the pirate, Don Pedro, is supposed to have lived. The Russells did nothing to change the house structurally, only restored it as it had been and generally cleaned it up.

I now turned to Florence Harmon, an elderly neighbor of the Russells, who had some recollections about the house. Mrs. Harmon recalls the house when she herself was very young, long before the Russells came to live in it.

"Years later, I returned to the house and Mrs. Roy asked me whether I could help her locate 'the treasure' since I was reputed to be psychic."

Was there really a treasure?

"If there was, I think it was found," Mrs. Harmon said. "At the time Mrs. Roy talked to me, she also pointed out that there were two elm trees on the grounds—the only two elm trees around. They looked like some sort of markers to her. But before the Roys had the house, a Mrs. Morrow lived here. I know this from my uncle, who was a stone mason, and who built a vault for her."

I didn't think Mrs. Harmon had added anything material to knowledge of the treasure, so I thanked her and turned my attention to the other large room, on the right hand side of the staircase. Nicely furnished with period pieces, it boasted a fireplace flanked by sofas, and had a rectangular piano in the corner. The high windows were curtained on the sides, and one could see the New England landscape through them.

We seated ourselves around the fireplace and hoped that Mary would honor us with a visit. Earlier I had inspected the entire house, the hearthstone under which Don Pedro allegedly lay buried, and the small bedrooms upstairs where David Russell had heard the footsteps. Each of us had stood at the window in the corridor upstairs and stared out of it, very much the way the ghost must have done when she was observed by Lorrie and her daughter.

And now it was Mary's turn.

"This was her room," Lorrie explained, "and I do feel her presence." But she refused to go into trance, afraid to "let go." Communication would have to be via clairvoyance, with Lorrie as the interpreter. This was not what I had hoped for. Nevertheless we would try to evaluate whatever material we could obtain.

"Sheet and quill," Lorrie said now, and a piece of paper was handed her along with a pencil. Holding it on her lap, Lorrie was poised to write, if Mary wanted to use her hand, so to speak. The pencil suddenly jumped from Lorrie's hand with considerable force.

"Proper quill," the ghost demanded.

I explained about the shape of quills these days, and handed Lorrie my own pencil.

"Look, lady," Lorrie explained to the ghost. "I'll show you it writes. I'll write my name."

And she wrote in her own, smallish, rounded hand, "Lorrie."

There was a moment of silence. Evidently, the ghost was thinking it over. Then Lorrie's hand, seemingly not under her own control, wrote with a great deal of flourish "Mary Wallace." The "M" and "W" had curves and ornamentation typical of eighteenth-century calligraphy. It was not at all like Lorrie's own handwriting.

"Tell her to write some more. The quill is working," I commanded.

Lorrie seemed to be upset by something the ghost told her.

"No," she said. "I can't do that. No."

"What does she want?" I asked.

"She wants me to sleep, but I won't do it."

Trance, I thought—even the ghost demands it. It would have been so interesting to have Mary speak directly to us through Lorrie's entranced lips. You can lead a medium to the ghost, but you can't make her go under if she's scared.

Lorrie instead told the ghost to tell *her*, or to write through her. But no trance, thank you. Evidently, the ghost did not like to be told how to communicate. We waited. Then I suggested that Lorrie be very relaxed and it would be "like sleep" so the ghost could talk to us directly.

"She's very much like me, but not so well trimmed," the ghost said of Lorrie. Had she picked her to carry her message because of physical resemblance, I wondered.

"She's waiting for Young John," Lorrie now said. Not young John. The stress was on young. Perhaps it was one name—Young john.

"It happened in the north pasture," Mary said through Lorrie now. "He killed Warren Langerford. The Frazier boys found the last bone."

I asked why it concerned her. Was she involved? But there was no reply.

Then the ghost of Mary introduced someone else standing next to her.

"Mrs. Roy is with her, because she killed her daughter," Lorrie said, hesitatingly, and added, on her own, "but I don't believe she did." Later we found out that the ghost was perhaps not lying, but of course nobody had any proof of such a crime if it were indeed a crime.

"Why do you stay on in this house?" I asked.

"This house is my house, h-o-u-s-e!" "Ocean-Born" Mary reminded me.

"Do you realize you are what is commonly called dead?" I demanded. As so often with ghosts, the question brought on resistance to face reality. Mary seemed insulted and withdrew.

I addressed the ghost openly, offering to help her, and at the same time explaining her present position to her. This was her chance to speak up.

"She's very capricious," Lorrie said. "When you said you'd bring her peace, she started to laugh."

But Mary was gone, for the present anyway.

We waited, and tried again a little later. This time Lorrie said she heard a voice telling her to come back tonight.

"We can't," I decided. "If she wants to be helped, it will have to be now."

Philip Babb, the pirate's real name (as I discovered later), allegedly had built a secret passage under the house. The Russells were still looking for it. There were indeed discrepancies in the thickness of some of the walls, and there were a number of secret holes that didn't lead anywhere. But no passage. Had the pirate taken his secrets to his grave?

I found our experience at Henniker singularly unsatisfactory since no real evidence had been forthcoming from the ghost herself. No doubt another visit would have to be made, but I didn't mind that at all. "Ocean-Born" Mary's place was a place one can easily visit time and again. The rural charm of the place and the timeless atmosphere of the old house made it a first-rate tourist attraction. Thousands of people came to the house every year.

We returned to New York and I thought no more about it until received a letter from James Caron, who had heard me discuss the house on the "Contact" program in Boston. He had been to the house in quest of pirate lore and found it very much haunted.

James Caron was in the garage business at Bridgewater, Massachusetts. He had a high school and trade school education, and was married, with two children. Searching for stories of buried treasure and pirates was a hobby of his, and he sometimes lectured on it. He had met Gus Roy about six years before. Roy complained that his deceased mother was trying to contact him for some reason. Her picture kept falling off the wall where it was hung, and he constantly felt "a presence." Would Mr. Caron know of a good medium?

In August of 1959, James Caron brought a spiritualist named Paul Amsdent to the "Ocean-Born" Mary house. Present at the ensuing séance were Harold Peters, a furniture salesman; Hugh Blanchard, a lawyer; Ernest Walbourne, a fireman, and brother-in-law of Caron; Gus Roy; and Mr. Caron himself. Tape recording the séance, Caron had trouble with his equipment. Strange sounds kept intruding. Unfortunately, there was among those present someone with hostility toward psychic work, and Gus Roy's mother did not manifest. However, something else did happen.

"There appear to be people buried somewhere around or in the house," the medium Amsdent said, "enclosed by a stone wall of some sort."

I thought of the hearthstone and of Mrs. Harmon's vault. Coincidence?

Mr. Caron used metal detectors all over the place to satisfy Gus Roy that there was no "pirate treasure" buried in or near the house.

A little later, James Caron visited the house again. This time he was accompanied by Mrs. Caron and Mr. and Mrs. Walbourne. Both ladies were frightened by the sound of a heavy door opening and closing with no one around and no air current in the house.

Mrs. Caron had a strong urge to go to the attic, but Mr. Caron stopped her. Ernest Walbourne, a skeptic, was alone in the so-called "death" room upstairs, looking at some pictures stacked in a corner. Suddenly, he clearly heard a female voice telling him to get out of the house. He looked around, but there was nobody upstairs. Frightened, he left the house at once and later required medication for a nervous condition!

Again, things quieted down as far as "Ocean-Born" Mary was concerned, until I saw a lengthy story—two parts, in fact—in the *Boston Record-American,* in which my erstwhile medium Lorrie had let her hair down to columnist Harold Banks.

It seemed that Lorrie could not forget Henniker, after all. With publicist Owen Lake, she returned to the house in November, 1964, bringing with her some oil of wintergreen, which she claimed Mary Wallace asked her to bring along.

Two weeks later, the report went on, Lorrie felt Mary Wallace in her home in Weymouth near Boston. Lorrie was afraid that Mary Wallace might "get into my body and use it for whatever purpose she wants to. I might wake up some day and *be* Mary Wallace."

That's the danger of being a medium without proper safeguards. They tend to identify with a personality that has come through them. Especially when they read all there is in print about them.

I decided to take someone to the house who knew nothing about it, someone who was not likely to succumb to the wiles of amateur "ESP experts," inquisitive columnists and such, someone who would do exactly what I required of her: Sybil Leek, famed British psychic.

It was a glorious day late in spring when we arrived at "Ocean Born" Mary's house in a Volkswagen station wagon driven by two alert young students from Goddard College in Vermont: Jerry Weener and Jay Lawrence. They had come to Boston to fetch us and take us all the way up to their campus, where I was to address the students and faculty. I proposed that they drive us by way of Henniker, and the two young students of parapsychology agreed enthusiastically. It was their first experience with an actual séance and they brought with them a lively dose of curiosity.

Sybil Leek brought with her something else: "Mr. Sasha," a healthy four-foot boa constrictor someone had given her for a pet. At first I thought she was kidding when she spoke with tender care of her snake, coiled peacefully in his little basket. But practical Sybil, author of some nine books, saw still another possibility in "Life with Sasha" and for that reason kept the snake on with her. On the way to Henniker, the car had a flat tire and we took this opportunity to get acquainted with Sasha, as Sybil gave him a run around the New Hampshire countryside.

Although I have always had a deep-seated dislike for anything reptilian, snakes, serpents, and other slitherers, terrestrial or maritime, I must confess that I found this critter less repulsive than I had thought he would be. At any rate, "Mr. Sasha" was collected once more and carefully replaced in his basket and the journey continued to Henniker, where the Russells were expecting us with great anticipation.

After a delightful buffet luncheon—"Mr. Sasha" had his the week before, as snakes are slow digesters—we proceeded to the large room upstairs to the right of the entrance door, commonly called the Lafayette room, and Sybil took the chair near the fireplace. The rest of us—the Russells, a minister friend of theirs, two neighbors, my wife Catherine and I, and our two student friends—gathered around her in a circle.

It was early afternoon. The sun was bright and clear. It didn't seem like it would be a good day for ghosts. Still, we had come to have a talk with the elusive Mary Wallace in her own domain, and if I knew Sybil, she would not disappoint us. Sybil is a very powerful medium, and something *always* happens.

Sybil knew nothing about the house since I had told our hosts not to discuss it with her before the trance session. I asked her if she had any clairvoyant impressions about the house.

"My main impressions were outside," Sybil replied, "near where the irises are. I was drawn to that spot and felt very strange. There is something outside this house which means more than things inside!"

"What about inside the house? What do you feel here?"

"The most impressive room I think is the loom room," Sybil said, and I thought, that's where Ernest Walbourne heard the voice telling him to get out, in the area that's also called the "death" room.

"They don't want us here . . . there is a conflict between two people . . . somebody wants something he can't have . . ."

Presently, Sybil was in trance. There was a moment of silence as I waited anxiously for the ghost of Mary Wallace to manifest itself through Sybil. The first words coming from the lips of the entranced medium were almost unintelligible.

Gradually, the voice became clearer and I had her repeat the words until I could be sure of them.

"Say-mon go to the lion's head," she said now. "To the lion's head. Be careful."

"Why should I be careful?"

"In case he catches you."

"Who are you?"

"Mary Degan."

"What are you doing here?"

"Waiting. Someone fetch me."

She said *"Witing"* with a strong cockney accent, and suddenly I realized that the *"say-mon"* was probably a seaman.

"Whose house is this?" I inquired.

"Daniel Burn's." (Perhaps it was "Birch.")

"What year is this?"

"1798."

"Who built this house?"

"Burn . . ."

"How did you get here?"

"All the time, come and go . . . to hide . . . I have to wait. He wants the money, Burn. Daniel Burn."

I began to wonder what had happened to Mary Wallace. Who was this new member of the ghostly cast? Sybil knew nothing whatever of a pirate or a pirate treasure connected by legend to this house. Yet her very first trance words concerned a *seaman and money*. Did Mary Degan have someone else with her, I hinted. Maybe this was only the first act and the lady of the house was being coy in time for a second act appearance.

But the ghost insisted that she was Mary Degan and that she lived here, "with the old idiot."

"Who was the old idiot?" I demanded.

"Mary," the Degan girl replied.

"What is Mary's family name?"

"Birch," she replied without hesitation.

I looked at Mrs. Russell, who shook her head. Nobody knew of Mary Wallace by any other name. Had she had another husband we did not know about?

Was there anyone else with her, I asked.

"Mary Birch, Daniel, and Jonathan," she replied.

"Who is Jonathan?"

"Jonathan Harrison Flood," the ghostly girl said.

A week or so later, I checked with my good friend Robert Nesmith, expert in pirate lore. Was there a pirate by that name? There had been, but his date is given as 1610, far too early for our man. But then Flood was a very common name. Also, this Flood might have used another name as his *nom de pirate* and Flood might have been his real, civilian name.

"What are they doing in this house?" I demanded.

"They come to look for their money," Sybil in trance replied. "The old idiot took it."

"What sort of money was it?"

"Dutch money," came the reply. "Very long ago."

"Who brought the money to this house?"

"Mary. Not me."

"Whose money was it?"

"Johnny's."

"How did he get it?"

"Very funny. . . he helped himself . . . so we did."

"What profession did he have?"

"Went down to the sea. Had a lot of funny business. Then he got caught, you know. So they did him in."

"Who did him in?"

"The runners. In the bay."

"What year was that?"

"Ninety-nine."

"What happened to the money after that?"

"She hid it. Outside. Near the lion's head."

"Where is the lion's head?"

"You go down past the little rocks, in the middle of the rocks, a little bit like a lion's head."

"If I left this house by the front entrance, which way would I turn?"

"The right, down past the little rock on the right. Through the trees, down the little . . ."

"How far from the house?"

"Three minutes."

"Is it under the rock?"

"Lion's head."

"How far below?"

"As big as a boy."

"What will I find there?"

"The gold. Dutch gold."

"Anything else?"

"No, unless she put it there."

"Why did she put it there?"

"Because he came back for it."

"What did she do?"

"She said it was hers. Then he went away. Then they caught him, a good thing, too. He never came back and she went off, too."

"When did she leave here?"

"Eighteen three."

"What was she like? Describe her."

"Round, not as big as me, dumpy thing, she thought she owned everything."

"How was Jonathan related to Daniel?"

"Daniel stayed here when Johnny went away and then they would divide the money, but they didn't because of Mary. She took it."

"Did you see the money?"

"I got some money. Gold. It says 1747."

"Is anyone buried in this ground?"

"Sometimes they brought them back here when they got killed down by the river."

"Who is buried in the house?"

"I think Johnny."

I now told Mary Degan to fetch me the other Mary, the lady of the house. But the girl demurred. The other Mary did not like to talk to strangers.

"What do you look like?" I asked. I still was not sure if Mary Wallace was not masquerading as her own servant girl to fool us.

"Skinny and tall."

"What do you wear?"

"A gray dress."

"What is your favorite spot in this house?"

"The little loom room. Peaceful."

"Do you always stay there?"

"No." The voice was proud now. "I go where I want."

"Whose house is this?" Perhaps I could trap her if she was indeed Mary Wallace.

"Mary Birch."

"Has she got a husband?"

"They come and go. There's always company here that's why I go to the loom room."

I tried to send her away, but she wouldn't go.

"Nobody speaks to me," she complained. "Johnny . . . she won't let him speak to me. Nobody is going to send me away."

"Is there a sea captain in this house?" I asked.

She almost shouted the reply.

"Johnny!"

"Where is he from?"

"Johnny is from the island."

She then explained that the trouble with Johnny and Mary was about the sea. Especially about the money the captain had.

"Will the money be found?" I asked.

"Not until I let it."

I asked Mary Degan to find me Mary Wallace. No dice. The lady wanted to be coaxed. Did she want some presents, I asked. That hit a happier note.

"Brandy . . . some clothes," she said. "She needs some hair . . . hasn't got much hair."

"Ask her if she could do with some oil of wintergreen," I said, sending up a trial balloon.

"She's got a bad back," the ghost said, and I could tell from the surprised expression on Mrs. Russell's face that Mary Wallace had indeed had a bad back.

"She makes it . . . people bring her things . . . rub her back . . . back's bad . . . she won't let you get the money . . . not yet , . . may want to build another house, in the garden . . . in case she needs it . . . sell it . . . she knows she is not what she used to be because her back's bad . . . she'll never go. Not now."

I assured her that the Russells wanted her to stay as long as she liked. After all, it was her house, too.

"Where is Johnny's body buried?" I now asked.

"Johnny's body," she murmured, "is under the fireplace."

Nobody had told Sybil about the persistent rumors that the old pirate lay under the hearthstone.

"Don't tell anyone," she whispered.

"How deep?"

"Had to be deep."

"Who put him there?"

"I shan't tell you."

"Did you bury anything with him?"

"I shan't tell. He is no trouble now. Poor Johnny."

"How did Johnny meet Mary?"

"I think they met on a ship."

"Ocean-Born" Mary, I thought. Sybil did not even know the name of the house, much less the story of how it got that name.

"All right," I said. "Did Mary have any children?"

"Four . . . in the garden. You can never tell with her."

"Did anyone kill anyone in this house at any time?"

"Johnny was killed, you know. Near the money. The runners chased him and he was very sick, we thought he was dead, and then he came here. I think she pushed him when he hurt his leg. We both brought him back here and put him under the fireplace. I didn't think he was dead."

"But you buried him anyway?" I said.

"She did," the ghost servant replied. "Better gone, she said. He's only come back for the money."

"Then Mary and Johnny weren't exactly friendly?"

"They were once."

"What changed things?"

"The money. She took his money. The money he fought for. Fighting money."

Suddenly, the tone of voice of the servant girl changed.

"I want to go outside," she begged. "She watches me. I can go out because her back is bad today. Can't get up, you see. So I can go out."

I promised to help her.

Suspiciously, she asked, "What do you want?"

"Go outside. You are free to go," I intoned.

"Sit on the rocks," the voice said. "If she calls out? She can get very angry."

"I will protect you," I promised.

"She says there are other places under the floor . . ." the girl ghost added, suddenly.

"Any secret passages?" I asked.

"Yes. Near the old nursery. First floor. Up the stairs, the loom room, the right hand wall. You can get out in the smoke room!"

Mr. Russell had told me of his suspicions that on structural evidence alone there was a hidden passage behind the smoke room. How would Sybil know this? Nobody had discussed it with her or showed her the spot.

I waited for more. But she did not know of any other passages, except one leading to the rear of the house.

"What about the well?"

"She did not like that either, because she thought he put his money there."

"Did he?"

"Perhaps he did. She used to put money in one place, he into another, and I think he put some money into the smoke room. He was always around there. Always watching each other. Watch me, too. Back of the house used to be where he could hide. People always looking for Johnny. Runners."

"Who was Mr. Birch?"

"Johnny had a lot to do with his house, but he was away a lot and so there was always some man here while he was away."

"Who paid for the house originally?"

"I think Johnny."

"Why did he want this house?"

"When he got enough money, he would come here and stay forever. He could not stay long ever, went back to the sea, and she came."

I tried another tack.

"Who was Don Pedro?" That was the name given the pirate in the popular tale.

She had heard the name, but could not place it.

"What about Mary Wallace?"

"Mary Wallace was Mary Birch," the ghost said, as if correcting me. "She had several names."

"Why?"

"Because she had several husbands."

Logical enough, if true.

"Wallace lived here a little while, I think," she added.

"Who was first, Wallace or Birch?"

"Birch. Mary Wallace, Mary Birch, is good enough."

Did the name Philip Babb mean anything to her? That allegedly was the pirate's real name.

"She had a little boy named Philip," the ghost said, and I thought, why not? After all, they had named Mary for the pirate's mother, why not reciprocate and name *her* son for the old man? Especially with all that loot around.

"If I don't go now, she'll wake up," the girl said. "Philip Babb, Philip Babb, he was somewhere in the back room. That was his room. I remember him."

How did Philip get on with Johnny? I wanted to know if they were one and the same person or not.

"Not so good," the ghost said. "Johnny did not like men here, you know."

I promised to watch out for Mary, and sent the girl on her way.

I then brought Sybil out of trance.

A few moments later, we decided to start our treasure hunt in the garden, following the instructions given us by Mary Degan, girl ghost.

Sybil was told nothing more than to go outside and let her intuition lead her toward any spot she thought important. The rest of us followed her like spectators at the National Open Golf Tournament.

We did not have to walk far. About twenty yards from the house, near some beautiful iris in bloom, we located the three stones.

The one in the middle looked indeed somewhat like a lion's head, when viewed at a distance. I asked the others in the group to look at it. There was no doubt about it. If there was a lion's head on the grounds, this was it. What lay underneath? What indeed was underneath the hearthstone in the house itself?

The Russells promised to get a mine detector to examine the areas involved. If there was metal in the ground, the instrument would show it. Meanwhile, the lore about "Ocean-Born" Mary had been enriched by the presence in the nether world of Mary Degan, servant girl, and the intriguing picture of two pirates—Johnny and Philip Babb. Much of this is very difficult to trace. But the fact is that Sybil Leek, who came to Henniker a total stranger, was able, in trance, to tell about a man at sea, a Mary, a pirate treasure, hidden passages, a child named Philip, four children of Mary, and the presence of a ghost in the loom room upstairs. All of this had been checked.

Why should not the rest be true also? Including, perhaps, the elusive treasure?

Only time will tell.

The Ghost Clock

NEW ENGLAND IS FULL OF GHOSTS. A young woman with the improbable first name of Dixie-Lee, and the acquired-by-marriage second name of Danforth, lived in the small town of Milford, just over the border in New Hampshire. She chanced to hear me on a Boston radio program, and presto, there was a note in the mail about something pretty eerie that had happened to her.

In 1954, when Dixie-Lee was 17, she took on a two-week job as companion to an elderly lady by the name of Mrs. William Collar. Mrs. Collar, then 82 years old, had been a fine artist, and had lived a happy life all over the world. Dixie-Lee found being a companion an easy way to make some extra money. Mrs. Collar's housekeeper went home nights, and the elderly lady wanted someone with her in the large, rambling house, at least until she could find a full-time housekeeper who would sleep in.

The Collars had met in France, both studying there, and though they married against the wishes of their parents, they had a wonderful and happy life together. When Mr. William Collar died, things were never the same. They had occupied a large double room on the second floor, with a bed on either side, and a wash basin for each. They truly lived close together.

After her husband's death, Mrs. Collar moved out of the room, and never slept in it again. She left everything as it was, including a big grandfather clock, which was never wound again after Mr. Collar's passing. Finally, in 1958, she joined her Bill. She may have been able to prepare herself for it, for she was often heard talking to "her Bill" when no one else could be seen in the room.

There was a fight over the will. The Collars had had no children, and a niece inherited the house.

But let me get back to Dixie-Lee and 1954. The young girl had moved into Mrs. Collar's imposing white house at New Ipswich, as the section was called, and given a room on the second floor next to the large bedroom once occupied by Mr. and Mrs. Collar. She had barely enough time to admire the expensive antique furniture around the house, when it was time to retire for the night.

Mrs. Dixie-Lee Danforth had come to Boston to meet me, and I questioned her about what happened then.

"I went to bed," she said, "and in the wee hours of the morning I awoke to the faint sound of footsteps and ticking of a clock. The sound of both kept getting louder—louder—till it seemed to beat against my brain."

At first she thought she was dreaming, but, biting her own hand, she realized she was fully awake. Cold sweat stood on her forehead when she realized that Mrs. Collar was an invalid *who could not walk.* What was more, the big clock had not worked for years. Suddenly, just as suddenly as it had come, it ceased. Dixie-Lee lay still for a while in sheer terror, then she turned on the light. Her bedroom door was firmly closed, just as she had left it before going to bed. She checked the door leading to what was once the Collars' big bedroom. It was shut tight, too. She ventured out onto the narrow landing of the staircase leading to the lower floor. It was shut off from the downstairs part of the house by a hall door. That, too, was shut.

She retraced her steps and suddenly noticed a rope and pulley. She pulled it and another door appeared.

"I opened it, heart in my mouth," Dixie-Lee said, "and was relieved to find a pretty, light bedroom behind it. It was furnished with modern furniture, and seemed to me much gayer and more peaceful than the rest of the house. The room was empty."

"What did you do then?" I wondered.

"First, I checked the big clock in my room. It was not going. Just as dead as it had been all those years. I looked around the house for other clocks. The only one in going condition was downstairs in the room occupied by Mrs. Collar, and I'd have to have had superhearing to hear that one tick all the way up to the second floor through three sets of closed doors and a heavy wooden floor!"

I readily agreed that was not very likely, and wondered if she had told anyone of her frightening experience that night.

"I told the daytime housekeeper, with whom I was friendly, and she laughed. But I refused to stay another moment unless someone else stayed with me. She and her young daughter moved in with me upstairs, and stayed the full two weeks. I never heard the footsteps or the ticking of the clock again while they were with me. But after I left, housekeepers came and went." Nobody seemed to stay very long at the big white house in New Ipswich. Possibly they, too, heard the uncanny noises.

I nodded and asked about Mrs. Collar. Could she have gotten out of bed somehow?

"Not a chance," Dixie-Lee replied. "She was a total invalid. I checked on her in the morning. She had never left her bed. She couldn't have. Besides, the footsteps I heard weren't those of a frail old woman. *They were a man's heavy footfalls.* I never told Mrs. Collar about my experience though. Why frighten her to death?"

"Quite so," I agreed, and we talked about Dixie-Lee now. Was she psychic to any degree?

Dixie-Lee came from a most unusual family. Her great-grandmother knew how "to work the table." Her grandfather saw the ghost of his sister, and Dixie-Lee herself had felt her late grand-father in his house whenever she visited, and she had numerous premonitions of impending danger.

On at least one such occasion she had a feeling she should not go on a certain trip, and insisted on stopping the car. On investigation, she found the wheels damaged. She might have been killed had she not heeded the warning!

We parted. Mrs. Danforth returned to her somewhat-more-than skeptical husband in Milford, and I took the next plane back to New York.

But the haunted house in New Ipswich never left my mind. I was due back in New England around Halloween, 1963, and decided to join Mrs. Danforth in a little trip up to the New Hampshire border country. A friend of hers, their children, a Boston-teacher friend of ours named Carol Bowman, and my wife and I completed the party that drove up to New Ipswich on that warm fall day. We weren't exactly expected, since I did not know the name of the present owner of the house. But Mrs. Danforth had sent word of our coming ahead. It turned out the word was never received, and we actually were lucky to find anyone in, luckier yet to be as cordially welcomed as we were by the lady of the house, whom we shall call Mrs. F.

Mrs. Jeanette F. was a sophisticated, well-educated lady whose husband was a psychiatrist, who was once also interested in parapsy-chology. She asked that I not use her full name here. A strange "feeling" of expecting us made her bid us a cordial welcome. I wasn't surprised to hear this—in this business, nothing surprises me anymore.

The F.'s had only had the house for a year when we visited them. They had not intended to buy the house, although they were on the lookout for a home in New England. But they passed it in their car, and fell in love with it . . . or rather were somehow made to buy the place. They discovered it was built in 1789. That wasn't all they discovered after they moved in.

"I always had the feeling," Mrs. F. said, "that we were only *allowed* to live here . . . but never really alone. Mrs. Collar's bedroom, for instance. I had the distinct feeling something was buried there under the floorboards. My sister-in-law slept upstairs. The next morning she told me she had 'heard things.' Right after we moved in, I heard footsteps upstairs."

"You too?" marveled Dixie-Lee, shooting a triumphant side glance at me, as if I had doubted her story.

"Last winter at dusk one day, I heard a woman scream. Both of us heard it, but we thought—or rather, *liked* to think—that it was a bobcat. Soon thereafter, we heard it again, only now it sounded more like a *child crying*. We heard it on several occasions and it gave us the willies."

On another occasion, there had been five people in the house when they heard the scream, followed by a growl. They went out to look for a bobcat . . . but there were absolutely no traces in the fresh snow, of either animal or human. There had also been all sorts of noises in the basement.

"Something strange about this child crying," Mrs. F. continued. "When we moved in, a neighbor came to see us and said when they saw we had a child, 'You've brought life back to the Collar house.'"

Dixie-Lee broke in.

"I seem to recall there was something about a child. I mean that they had a child."

"And it died?" I asked.

"I don't know," Mrs. F. said. "But there were diaries—they were almost lost, but one of Bill Collar's best friends, Archie Eaton, saved them. Here they are."

Mrs. F. showed us the remarkable books, all written in longhand. On cursory examination I did not uncover the secret of the child.

There is a hollow area in the basement. We went down to get "impressions," and Dixie-Lee felt very uneasy all of a sudden, and didn't feel like joining us downstairs, even though moments before she had been the spirit of adventure personified.

We returned to the ground floor and had some coffee.

I decided to return with a medium, and hold a séance next to the chimney down in the basement, underneath the room where Mrs. F. felt the floorboards held a secret.

But somehow we were thwarted in this effort.

In December of 1963, we were told that our visit would have to be postponed, and Mrs. F. asked us to come later in the winter. Too many living relatives in the house were making it difficult to listen for the dead.

"Something happened yesterday," she added, "that will interest you. My housekeeper is a very bright and trusted woman. She has never mentioned anything strange about the house. Yesterday I was telling her about our plans to sell the house. As I spoke, she was looking in the room next to me—I was standing in the kitchen. She was looking into the dining room, when she turned pale and interrupted me. She had seen a short, old woman in a long gray dress walk through the dining room. Now I questioned her about anything she might have seen in the past. She admitted she had seen figures on several occasions, but was afraid to be ridiculed. Strangely enough, she wants to buy the house despite these experiences. She calls it 'the house that watches,' because she always feels she is being observed while she cares for the children, even when she has them in the garden."

Later, we tried to fix a new date to visit the house. My letters remained unanswered. Had the house changed hands again?

But no matter who actually *lived* there. It seemed the *real* owner was still Mrs. Collar.

The Haunted Organ
at Yale

YALE UNIVERSITY IN NEW HAVEN, Connecticut, is an austere and respectable institution, which does not take such matters as ghostly manifestations very lightly. I must, therefore, keep the identity of my informant a secret, but anyone who wishes to visit Yale and admire its magnificent, historical organ is, of course, at liberty to do so, provided he or she gets clearance from the proper authorities. I would suggest, however, that the matter of ghostly goings-on not be mentioned at such a time. If you happen to experience something out of the ordinary while visiting the organ, well and good, but let it not be given as the reason to the university authorities for your intended visit.

I first heard about this unusual organ in 1969 when a gentleman who was then employed as an assistant organist at Yale had been asked to look after the condition and possible repairs of the huge organ, a very large instrument located in Woolsey Hall. This is the fifth largest organ in the world and has a most interesting history.

Woolsey Hall was built as part of a complex of three buildings for Yale's two-hundredth anniversary in 1901 by the celebrated architects, Carere and Hastings. Shortly after its completion the then university organist, Mr. Harry B. Jepson, succeeded in getting the Newberry family, of the famous department store clan, to contribute a large sum of money for a truly noble organ to be built for the hall.

Even in 1903 it was considered to be an outstanding instrument because of its size and range. By 1915, certain advances in the technology of pipe organs made the 1903 instruments somewhat old-fashioned. Again Jepson contacted the Newberry family about the possibility of updating their gift so that the organ could be rebuilt and the hall enlarged. This new instrument was then dedicated in 1916 or thereabouts.

By 1926 musical tastes had again shifted toward romantic music, and it became necessary to make certain additions to the stops as well as the basic building blocks of the classical ensemble. Once again the Newberry family contributed toward the updating of the instrument. The alterations were undertaken by the Skinner Organ Company of Boston, in conjunction with an English expert by the name of G. Donald Harrison. Skinner and Harrison did not get on well together and much tension was present when they restored and brought the venerable old organ up-to-date.

Professor Harry Jepson was forced to retire in the 1940s, against his wishes, and though he lived down the street only two blocks from Woolsey Hall, he never again set foot in it to play the famous organ that he had caused to be built. He died a bitter and disappointed man sometime in 1952.

The last university organist, Frank Bozyan, retired in the 1970s, with great misgivings. He confided to someone employed by the hall that he felt he was making a mistake; within six months after his retirement he was dead. As time went on, Woolsey Hall, once a temple of beauty for the fine arts, was being used for rock and roll groups and mechanically amplified music. Undoubtedly, those connected with the building of the hall and the organ would have been horrified at the goings-on had they been able to witness them.

The gentleman who brought all of this to my attention, and who shall remain nameless, had occasion to be in the hall and involved with the organ itself frequently. He became aware of a menacing and melancholic sensation in the entire building, particularly in the basement and the organ chambers. While working there at odd hours late at night, he became acutely aware of some sort of unpleasant sensation just lurking around the next corner or even standing behind him! On many occasions he found it necessary to look behind him in order to make sure he was alone. The feeling of a presence became so strong he refused to be there by himself, especially in the evenings. Allegedly, the wife of one of the curators advised him to bring a crucifix whenever he had occasion to go down to the organ chambers. She also claimed to have felt someone standing at the entrance door to the basement, as if to keep strangers out.

I visited Yale and the organ one fine summer evening in the company of my informant, who has since found employment elsewhere. I, too, felt the oppressive air in the organ chambers, the sense of a presence whenever I moved about. Whether we were dealing here with the ghost of the unhappy man who was forced to retire and who never set foot again into his beloved organ chamber, or whether we were dealing with an earlier influence, is hard to say. Not for a minute do I suggest that Yale University was haunted or that there were any evil influences concerning the university itself. But it is just possible that sensitive individuals visiting the magnificent organ at Woolsey Hall might pick up some remnant of an unresolved past.

The Ship Chandler's
Ghost

IT IS A WELL-KNOWN FACT AMONG ghost hunting experts that structural changes in a house can have dire effects. Take out a wall, and you've got a poltergeist mad as a wet hen. If the ghost is inside the house before the changes are realized, he may bump into walls and doors that weren't there before—not the way he remembered things at all.

But move a whole house several yards away from the shore where it belongs, and you're asking for trouble. Big trouble. And big trouble is what the historical society in Cohasset, Massachusetts, got when they moved the old Ship's Chandlery in Cohasset. With my good friend Bob Kennedy of station WBZ, Boston, I set out for the quaint old town south of Boston on a chilly evening in the fall of 1964.

When we arrived at the wooden structure on a corner of the Post Road—it had a nautical look, its two stories squarely set down as if to withstand any gale—we found several people already assembled. Among them were Mrs. E. Stoddard Marsh, the lively curator of the museum, which was what the Ship's Chandlery became, and her associate, lean, quiet Robert Fraser. The others were friends and neighbors who had heard of the coming of a parapsychologist, and didn't want to miss anything. We entered the building and walked around the downstairs portion of it, admiring its displays of nautical supplies, ranging from fishing tackle and scrimshaw made from walrus teeth to heavy anchors, hoists, and rudders—all the instruments and wares of a ship chandler's business.

Built in the late eighteenth century by Samuel Bates, the building was owned by the Bates family; notably by one John Bates, second of the family to have the place, who had died 78 years before our visit. Something of a local character, John Bates had cut a swath around the area as a dashing gentleman. He could well afford the role, for he owned a fishing fleet of 24 vessels, and business was good in those far-off days when the New England coast was dotted with major ports for fishing and shipping. A handwritten record of his daily catch can be seen next to a mysterious closet full of ladies' clothes. Mr. Bates led a full life.

After the arrival of Dorothy Damon, a reporter from the *Boston Traveler*, we started to question the curator about uncanny happenings in the building.

"The building used to be right on the waterfront, at Cohasset Cove, and it had its own pier," Mrs. Marsh began, "and in 1957 we moved it to its present site."

"Was there any report of uncanny happenings before that date?"

"Nothing I know of, but the building was in a bad state of disrepair."

"After the building was brought to its present site, then," I said, "what was the first unusual thing you heard?"

"Two years ago we were having a lecture here. There were about forty people listening to Francis Hagerty talk about old sailing boats. I was sitting over here to the left—on this ground floor—with Robert Fraser, when all of a sudden we heard heavy footsteps upstairs and things being moved and dragged—so I said to Mr. Fraser, 'Someone is up there; will you please tell him to be quiet?' I thought it was kids."

"Did you know whether there was in fact anyone upstairs at the time?"

"We did not know. Mr. Fraser went upstairs and after a moment he came down looking most peculiar and said, 'There is no one there.'"

"Now, there is no other way to get down from upstairs, only this one stairway. Nobody had come down it. We were interrupted three times on that evening."

I asked Robert Fraser what he had seen upstairs.

"There was enough light from the little office that is upstairs, and I could see pretty well upstairs, and I looked all over, but there was nobody upstairs."

"And the other times?"

"Same thing. Windows all closed, too. Nobody could have come down or gotten out. But I'm sure those were footsteps."

I returned to Mrs. Marsh and questioned her further about anything that might have occurred after that eventful evening of footsteps.

"We were kept so busy fixing up the museum that we paid scant attention to anything like that, but this summer something happened that brought it all back to us."

"What happened?" I asked, and the lady reporter perked up her ears.

"It was on one of the few rainy Sundays we had last July," Mrs. Marsh began. "You see, this place is not open on Sundays. I was bringing over some things from the other two buildings, and had my arms full. I opened the front door, when I heard those heavy footsteps upstairs."

"What did you do—drop everything?"

"I thought it was one of our committee or one of the other curators, so I called out, 'Hello—who's up there?' But I got no answer, and I thought, well, someone sure is pretty stuffy, not answering me back, so I was a little peeved and I called again."

"Did you get a reply?"

"No, but *the steps hesitated* when I called. But then they continued again, and I yelled, 'For Heaven's sake, why don't you answer?'—and I went up the stairs, but just as I got to the top of the stairs, they stopped."

There was a man who had helped them with the work at the museum who had lately stayed away for reasons unknown. Could he have heard the footsteps too and decided that caution was the better part of valor?

"The other day, just recently, four of us went into the room this gentleman occupies when he is here, and the *door closed on us*, by itself. It has never done that before."

I soon established that Fraser did not hear the steps when he was *alone* in the building, but that Mrs. Marsh did. I asked her about anything psychic in her background.

"My family has been interested in psychic matters since I was ten years old," she said in a matter-of-fact tone. "I could have become a medium, but I didn't care to. I saw an apparition of my mother immediately after she passed away. My brother also appeared to me six months after his death, to let me know he was all right, I guess."

"Since last July has there been any other manifestation?"

"I haven't been here much," Mrs. Marsh replied. "I had a lot of work with our costume collection in the main building. So I really don't know."

We decided to go upstairs now, and see if Mr. Bates—or whoever the ghost might be—felt like walking for us. We quietly waited in the semi-darkness upstairs, near the area where the footsteps had been heard, but nothing happened.

"The steps went back and forth," Mrs. Marsh reiterated. "Heavy, masculine steps, the kind a big man would make."

She showed us how it sounded, allowing of course for the fact she was wearing high heels. It sounded hollow enough for ten ghosts.

I pointed at a small office in the middle of the upstairs floor.

"This was John Bates' office," Mrs. Marsh explained, "and here is an Indian doll that falls down from a secure shelf now and then as if someone were throwing it."

I examined the doll. It was one of those early nineteenth-century dolls that Native Americans in New England used to make and sell.

"The people at the lecture also heard the noises," Mrs. Marsh said, "but they just laughed and nobody bothered thinking about it."

I turned to one of the local ladies, a Mrs. Hudley, who had come up with us. Did she feel anything peculiar up here, since she had the reputation of being psychic?

"I feel disturbed. Sort of a strange sensation," she began, haltingly, "as though there was a 'presence' who was in a disturbed frame of mind. It's a man."

Another lady, by the name of McCarthy, also had a strange feeling as we stood around waiting for the ghost to make himself known. Of course, suggestion and atmosphere made me discount most of what those who were around us that night might say, but I still wanted to hear it.

"I felt I had to get to a window and get some air," Mrs. McCarthy said. "The atmosphere seemed disturbed somehow."

I asked them all to be quiet for a moment and addressed myself to the unseen ghost.

"John Bates," I began, "if this is you, may I, as a stranger come to this house in order to help you find peace, ask that you manifest in some form so I know you can hear me?"

Only the sound of a distant car horn answered me.

I repeated my invitation to the ghost to come forward and be counted. Either I addressed myself to the wrong ghost or perhaps John Bates disliked the intrusion of so many people—only silence greeted us.

"Mr. Bates," I said in my most dulcet tones, "please forgive these people for moving your beautiful house inland. They did not do so out of irreverence for your person or work. They did this so that many more people could come and admire your house and come away with a sense of respect and admiration for the great man that you were."

It was so quiet when I spoke, you could have heard a mouse breathe.

Quietly, we tiptoed down the haunted stairs, and out into the cool evening air. Cowboy star Rex Trailer and his wife, who had come with us from Boston, wondered about the future—would the footsteps ever come back? Or was John Bates reconciled with the fact that the sea breezes no longer caressed his ghostly brow as they did when his house was down by the shore?

Then, too, what was the reason he was still around to begin with? Had someone given him his quietus in that little office upstairs? There were rumors of violence in the famous bachelor's life, and the number of women whose affections he had trifled with was legion. Someone might very well have met him one night and ended the highly successful career of the ship chandlery's owner.

Many years went by, and I heard nothing further from the curator. Evidently, all was quiet at John Bates' old house. Maybe old John finally joined up with one of the crews that sail the ghost ships on the other side of the curtain of life.

The Terror on
the Farm

ORTH WOODSTOCK, CONNECTICUT, was New England at its
best and quietest: rolling farmland seldom interrupted by
the incursions of factories and modern city life.

The village itself seemed to have weathered the passage of time
rather well and with a minimum of change. Except for the inevitable
store signs and other expressions of contemporary bad taste, the
village was as quiet when we visited as it must have been, say, two
hundred years earlier, when America was young.

On Brickyard Road, going toward the outer edges of the village and standing somewhat apart from the inhabited areas, was an
old farmhouse. At the time this incident takes place, it had obviously seen better days; it was totally dilapidated and practically
beyond repair. Still, it was a house of some size and quite obviously
different from the ordinary small farmhouses of the surrounding
countryside.

For the fifty years prior, the sixteen-room house had been the
property of the Duprey family. The house itself was built in pre-
revolutionary times by the Lyons family, who used it as a tavern. The
place was a busy spot on the Boston-Hartford road, and a tavern

here did well indeed in the days when railroads had not yet come into existence.

After the Lyons Tavern changed hands, it belonged successfully to the Potters, Redheads, Ides, and then the Dupreys. But it finally became a private dwelling, the center of the surrounding farm, and no longer a public house.

Very little was known about its early history beyond what I've told here; at least that was what Mrs. Florence Viner discovered when she considered buying the house. She did learn, however, that Mrs. Emery Duprey, a previous owner, had suffered great tragedy in the house. One morning she had taken a group of neighbor children to school. The school was in a one-room house, less than a mile distant. Her fourteen-year-old daughter Laura was left behind at the house because she had not been feeling well that day. When Mrs. Duprey returned home a short time later, she found the girl gone. Despite every effort made, the girl was never seen again nor was any trace found of her disappearance.

Mr. and Mrs. Charles Viner decided to buy the house in 1951 despite its deplorable condition. They wanted a large country house and did not mind putting it in good condition; in fact, they rather looked forward to the challenging task.

It was on Good Friday of that year that they moved in. Although they started the restoration immediately, they stayed at the house and made do, like the pioneers they felt they had now become.

The farm itself was still a working farm, and they retained a number of farm workers from the surrounding area to work it for them. The only people staying at the house at all times were the Viners, their daughter Sandra, and the help.

Two months after their arrival, one evening Mrs. Viner and her daughter, then eleven years old, were alone in the house, sitting in the kitchen downstairs, reading.

"Who is upstairs?" the girl suddenly inquired.

Mrs. Viner had heard furtive footsteps also, but had decided to ignore them. Surely, the old house was settling or the weather was causing all sorts of strange noises.

But the footsteps became clearer. This was no house settling. This was someone walking around upstairs. For several minutes, they sat in the kitchen, listening as the steps walked all over the upper floor. Then Mrs. Viner rose resolutely, went to her bedroom on the same floor and returned with a .22 revolver she had in the drawer of her night table just in case prowlers showed up. The moment she re-entered the kitchen, she clearly heard two heavy thumps upstairs. It sounded as if a couple of heavy objects had fallen suddenly and hit the floor. Abruptly, the walking ceased as if the thumps were the end of a scene being re-enacted upstairs.

Too frightened to go up and look into what she *knew* to be an empty room, Mrs. Viner went to bed. When her husband returned a little later, however, they investigated upstairs together. There was nothing out of place nor indeed any sign that anyone had been up there.

But a few days later, the same phenomenon recurred. First, there were the footsteps of someone walking back and forth upstairs, as if in great agitation. Then two heavy thumps and the sound of a falling object and abrupt silence. The whole thing was so exactly the same each time it almost became part of the house routine, and the Viners heard it so many times they no longer became panicky because of it.

When the house regained its former splendor, they began to have overnight guests. But whenever anyone stayed at the house, inevitably, the next morning they would complain about the constant walking about in the corridor upstairs. Mrs. Ida Benoit, Mrs. Viner's mother, came downstairs the morning after her first night in the house and assured her daughter, "I'll never sleep in *this* house again. Why, it's haunted. Someone kept walking through my bedroom."

Her daughter could only shrug and smile wanly. She knew very well what her mother meant. Naturally, the number of unhappy guests grew, but she never discussed the phenomena with anyone beforehand. After all, it was just possible that *nothing* would happen. But in ten years of occupancy, there wasn't a single instance where a person using a bedroom upstairs was not disturbed.

A year after they had moved in, Mrs. Viner decided to begin to renovate a large upstairs bedroom. It was one of those often used as a guest room. This was on a very warm day in September, and despite the great heat, Mrs. Viner liked her work and felt in good spirits. She was painting the window sash and singing to herself with nothing particular on her mind. She was quite alone upstairs at the time and for the moment the ghostly phenomena of the past were far from her thoughts.

Suddenly, she felt the room grow ice cold. The chill became so intense she began to shudder and pulled her arms around herself as if she were in mid-winter on an icy road. She stopped singing abruptly and at the same time she felt the strong presence of another person in the room with her.

"Someone's resenting very much what I'm doing," she heard herself think.

Such a strong wave of hatred came over her she could not continue. Terrified, she nevertheless knew she had to turn around and see who was in the room with her. It seemed to take her an eternity to muster sufficient strength to move a single muscle.

Suddenly, she felt a cold hand at her shoulder. Someone was standing behind her and evidently trying to get her attention. She literally froze with fear. When she finally moved to see who it was the hand just melted away.

With a final effort, she jerked herself around and stared back into the room. There was no one there. She ran to the door, screaming,

"I don't know who you are or what you are, but you won't drive me out of this house."

Still screaming, she ran down the stairs and onto the porch. There she caught her breath and quieted down. When her daughter came home from school, she felt relieved. The evil in that room had been overpowering, and she avoided going up there as much as possible after that experience.

"I'll never forget that hand, as long as I live," she explained to her husband.

In the years that followed, they came to terms with the unseen forces in the house. Perhaps her determined effort not to be driven out of her home had somehow gotten through to the specter. At any rate, the Viners were staying and making the house as livable as they could. Mrs. Viner gave birth to two more children, both sons, and as Sandra grew up, the phenomena seemed to subside. In 1958, a second daughter was born, and Sandra left for college. But three weeks later the trouble started anew.

One night in September, she was sitting in the downstairs living room watching television with James Latham, their farm worker. The two boys and the baby had been in bed for hours. Suddenly, there was a terrific explosion in the general direction of the baby's room. She ran into the room and found it ice cold—cold as an icebox. From the baby's room another door led out into the hall, which was usually closed for obvious reasons. But now it stood wide open, evidently thrust open with considerable force. The lock was badly bent from the impact and the radiator, which the door had hit in opening, was still reverberating from it. The baby was not harmed in any way, but Mrs. Viner wondered if perhaps the oil burner had blown up.

She went down into the basement to check but found everything normal. As she returned to the baby's room she suddenly had the distinct impression that the phenomenon was somehow connected with the presence of a *young girl.*

She tried to reason this away since no young girl was present in the household, nor was there any indication that this tied in in any way with the tragic disappearance of Mrs. Duprey's girl, of which she, of course, knew about. Try as she might, she could not shake this feeling that a young girl was the focal point of the disturbances at the house.

One night her sister had joined her in the living room downstairs. Suddenly there was a loud crash overhead in what they knew was an empty bedroom. Mrs. Viner left her worried sister downstairs and went up alone. A table in the bedroom had been knocked over. No natural force short of a heavy earthquake could have caused this. The windows were closed, and there was no other way in which the table could topple over by itself. She was so sure that this could not have been caused by anything but human intruders, she called the state police.

The police came and searched the house from top to bottom but found no trace of any intruder.

Mrs. Viner then began to wonder about the goings-on. If these unseen forces had the power to overturn heavy tables, surely they might also harm people. The thought frightened her. She had until then considered living with a ghost or ghosts rather on the chic side; now it took on distinctly threatening overtones. She discussed it with her husband but they had put so much work and money into the house that the thought of leaving again just did not appeal to them.

It was inevitable that she should be alone in the house, except for the children, at various times. Her husband was away on business, and the farm help were out where they belonged. Often Mrs. Viner found herself walking through the rooms hoping against rational reasoning that she would come face to face with the intruder. Then she could address her or him—she was not sure how many there were—and say, "Look, this is my house now, we've bought it and rebuilt it, and we don't intend to leave it. Go away and don't hang around; it's no use." She often rehearsed her little speech for just such a confrontation. But the ghost never appeared when she was ready.

Meanwhile the footsteps followed by the heavy thumps kept recurring regularly, often as many as four times in a single week. It was usually around the same time of the evening, which led her to believe that it represented some sort of tragedy that was being re-enacted upstairs by the ghostly visitors. Or was she merely tuning in on a past tragedy and what she and the others were hearing was in fact only an echo of the distant past? She could not believe this, especially as she still remembered vividly the ice cold hand that grabbed her shoulder in the bedroom upstairs on that hot September day. And a memory would not cause a heavy door to swing open by itself with such violence that it burst the lock.

No, these were not memory impressions they were hearing. These were actual entities with minds of their own, somehow trapped between two states of being and condemned by their own violence to live forever in the place where their tragedy had first occurred. What a horrible fate, Mrs. Viner thought, and for a moment she felt great compassion for the unfortunate ones.

But then her own involvement reminded her that it was, after all, her house and her life that was being disrupted. She had a better right to be here than they had, even if they had been here before.

Defiantly, she continued to polish and refine the appointments in the house until it looked almost as if it had never been a dilapidated, almost hopelessly derelict, house. She decided to repaper one of the bedrooms upstairs, so that her guests would sleep in somewhat more cheerful surroundings. The paper in this particular room was faded and very old and deserved to be replaced. As she removed the dirty wallpaper, the boards underneath became visible again. They were wide and smooth and obviously part of the original boards of the house.

After she had pulled down all the paper from the wall facing away from the window, she glanced up at it. The wall, exposed to light after goodness knows how many years, was spattered with some sort of paint.

"This won't do at all," she decided, and went downstairs to fetch some rags and water. Returning to the room, she started to remove what she took for some very old paint. When she put water on the stains, the spots turned a bright red!

Try as she might, she could not remove the red stains. Finally she applied some bleach, but it only turned the spots a dark brown. It finally dawned on her that this wasn't paint but blood. On closer investigation, her suspicion was confirmed. She had stumbled upon a blood-spattered wall—but what had taken place up here that had caused this horrible reminder?

Somehow she felt that she had gotten a lead in her quest for the solution to the phenomena plaguing the house. Surely, someone had been killed up there, but who and why?

She went into the village and started to talk to the local people. At first, she did not get much help. New Englanders are notoriously shy about family matters. But eventually Mrs. Viner managed to get some information from some of the older, local people who had known about the house on Brickyard Road for a long time.

When the house was still a public tavern, that is somewhere around the turn of the nineteenth century or the very end of the eighteenth, there had been two men at the tavern who stayed overnight as guests. Their names are shrouded in mystery, and perhaps they were very unimportant as history goes.

But there was also a young woman at the tavern, the kind innkeepers used to hire as servant girls in those days. If the woman wanted to be just that, well and good; if she wanted to get involved with some of the men that passed through on their way to the cities, that was her own business. Tavern keepers in those days were not moral keepers and the hotel detective had not yet been conceived by a Puritan age. So the servant girls often went in and out of the guests' rooms, and nobody cared much.

It appears that one such young woman was particularly attractive to two men at the same time. There were arguments and jealousy. Finally the two men retired to a room upstairs and a fight to the finish followed. As it was upstairs, most likely it was in the young woman's own room, with one suitor discovering the other obtaining favors he had sought in vain, perhaps. At any rate, as the horrified girl looked on, the two men killed each other with their rapiers, and their blood, intermingled in death, spattered upon the wall of the room.

As she walked back from the village with this newly gained knowledge, Mrs. Viner understood clearly for the first time, why her house was indeed haunted. The restless footsteps in the room upstairs were the hurried steps of the unhappy suitor. The scuffling noises that followed and the sudden heavy thumps would be the fight and the two falling bodies—perhaps locked in death. The total silence that always ensued after the two heavy falls clearly indicated to her that the stillness of death following the struggle was being re-enacted along with the tragedy itself.

And how right she had been about a girl being the central force in all this!

But why the hostility towards her? Why the icy hand on the shoulder? Did the girl resent her, another woman, in this house? Was she still hoping her suitor would come for her, and did she perhaps take Mrs. Viner for competition? A demented mind, especially when it has been out of the body for a hundred and fifty years, can conjure up some strange ideas.

But her fighting energies were somehow spent, and when an opportunity arose to sell the house, Mrs. Viner agreed readily to do so. The house then passed into the hands of Samuel Beno after the Viners had lived in it from 1951 to 1961. For more than five years, Mr. Beno owned the house but never lived in it. It remained unoccupied, standing quietly on the road.

There was a flurry of excitement about it in 1966; someone made off with $5,000 worth of plumbing and copper piping. The owner entrusted the matter to the state police, hoping the thieves would return for more. The authorities even placed tape recorders in the house in case the thieves did return.

Since then not much has been heard about the house and one can only presume that the tragic story of the servant girl and her two suitors has had its final run. But one can't be entirely sure; after all, blood does not come off easily, either from walls or from men's memories.

Morgan Hall

AT THE TIME THAT I KNEW HER, Alice was a twenty-two-year-old blond, way above average in both looks and intelligence. She lived in Manhattan, had a decent, law-abiding seaman for a father and an Irish heritage going back, way back, but mixed in with some French and various other strains that had blended well in Alice's face, which was one of continual curiosity and alertness. Alice's work was routine, as was that of most of her friends. She took this in her stride, for she had another world waiting for her where nothing was ever ordinary.

Shortly after she was born, her parents moved into an old house in Brooklyn that had a reputation of being strange. Alice was less than a year old when they moved again, but during those months she would not go into her mother's bedroom without a fierce struggle, without breaking into tears immediately—a behavior so markedly different from her otherwise "good" behavior as a baby that it could not help but be noticed by her parents. While her father had no interest in such matters, her mother soon connected the child's strange behavior with the other strange things in the house: the doors that would open by themselves, the footsteps, the strange drafts, especially in the bedroom little Alice hated so much.

When Alice was about twelve years old, and the family had moved from the old neighborhood into still another house, she found

251

herself thinking of her grandmother all of a sudden one day. Her grandparents lived a distance away upstate and there had been no recent contact with them.

"Grandmother is dead," Alice said to her mother, matter-of-factly. Her mother stared at her in disbelief. Hours later the telephone rang. Grandmother, who had been in excellent health, had suddenly passed away.

Her mother gave the girl a queer look but she had known of such gifts and realized her daughter, an only child, was something special. Within six months, the telephone rang twice more. Each time, Alice looked up and said:

"Grandfather's dead."

"Uncle's dead."

And they were.

While her father shook his head over all this "foolishness," her mother did not scoff at her daughter's powers. Especially after Alice had received a dream warning from her dead grandmother, advising her of an impending car accident. She was shown the exact location where it would happen, and told her that if her mother were to sit in front, she would be badly hurt but if Alice were to change places with her, Alice would not be as badly hurt.

After the dream, without telling her mother her reasons, she insisted on changing places with her on the trip. Sure enough, the car was hit by another automobile. Had her mother been where Alice sat, she might not have reacted quickly enough and been badly hurt. But Alice was prepared and ducked—and received only a whiplash.

Afterward, she discussed all this with her mother. Her mother did not scoff, but asked her what grandmother, who had given them the warning, had looked like in the vision.

"She had on a house dress and bedroom slippers," Alice replied. Her mother nodded. Although the grandmother had lost both legs due to diabetes, she had been buried with her favorite bedroom slippers in the coffin. Alice had never seen nor known this.

When she was seventeen years of age, Alice had a strong urge to become a nun. She felt the world outside had little to offer her and began to consider entering a convent. Perhaps this inclination was planted in her mind when she was a camp counselor for a Catholic school on Long Island. She liked the serenity of the place and the apparently quiet, contemplative life of the sisters.

On her very first visit to the convent, however, she felt uneasy. Morgan Hall was a magnificently appointed mansion in Glen Cove, Long Island, that had only been converted to religious purposes a few years before. Prior to that it was the Morgan estate—with all that the name of that wealthy family implies. Nothing about it was either ugly or frightening in the least, and yet Alice felt immediately terrified when entering its high-ceilinged corridors.

As a prospective postulant, it was necessary for her to visit the place several times prior to being accepted, and on each occasion her uneasiness mounted.

But she ascribed these feelings to her lack of familiarity with the new place. One night, her uncle and grandfather appeared to her in a dream and told her not to worry, that everything would be all right with her. She took this as an encouragement to pursue her religious plans and, shortly after, formally entered the convent.

She moved in just a few days before her eighteenth birthday, looking forward to a life totally different from that of her friends and schoolmates. The room she was assigned to adjoined one of the cloisters, but at first she was alone in it as her future roommate was to arrive a week later. Thus she spent her very first days at Morgan Hall alone in the room. The very first night, after she had retired, she heard someone walking up and down outside the door. She thought this strange at that hour of the night, knowing full well that convents like their people to retire early. Finally her curiosity overcame her natural shyness of being in a new place, and she peaked out of her door into the corridor. The footsteps were still audible. But there was no one walking about outside. Quickly, she closed the door and went to bed.

The next morning, she discussed the matter with six other postulants in rooms nearby. They, too, had heard the footsteps that night. In fact, they had heard them on many other nights as well when there was positively no one walking about outside.

As she got used to convent routine, Alice realized how impossible it would be for one of them—or even one of the novices, who had been there a little longer than they— to walk around the place at the hour of the night when she heard the steps. Rigid convent rules included a bell, which rang at 10 P.M. Everybody had to be in their rooms and in bed at that time, except for dire emergencies. One just didn't walk about the corridors at midnight or later for the sheer fun of it at Morgan Hall, if she did not wish to be expelled. All lights go out at ten also and nothing moves.

At first, Alice thought the novices were playing tricks on the new arrivals by walking around downstairs to create the footsteps, perhaps to frighten the postulants in the way college freshmen are often hazed by their elder colleagues. But she soon realized that this was not so, that the novices were no more allowed out after ten than they were.

Her psychic past did not allow Alice to let matters rest there and her curiosity forced her to make further inquiries as best she could under the circumstances. After all, you can't run to the Mother Superior and ask, "Who walks the corridors at night, Ma'am?"

It was then she learned that the house had been J. P. Morgan's mansion originally and later had been used by the Russian Embassy for their staff people. She recalled the battles the Russians had fought with the Glen Cove township over taxes and how they finally vacated the premises in less than perfect condition. As a sort of anticlimax, the Catholic nuns had moved in and turned the Hall into a convent and school.

A conversation with the convent librarian wasn't particularly fruitful, either. Yes, Mr. Morgan built the house in 1910. No, he didn't die here, he died in Spain. Why did she want to know?

Alice wondered about Mr. Morgan's daughter.

Alice Morgan had lived in this house and died here of typhoid fever in the early years of her life.

But try as she might, she never got the librarian to tell her anything helpful. Naturally, Alice did not wish to bring up the real reason for her curiosity. But it seemed as if the librarian sensed something about it, for she curtly turned her head sideways when speaking of the Morgans as if she did not wish to answer.

Frustrated in her inquiry, Alice left and went back to her chores. One night in October of 1965, Alice was walking in the hall of the postulancy, that part of the building reserved for the new girls who were serving their apprenticeship prior to being admitted to the convent and to taking their final vows.

It was a cool night, and Alice had walked fairly briskly to the extreme end of the hall and then stopped for a moment to rest. As she turned around and faced toward the opposite end of the hall, whence she had just come, she noticed a girl standing there who had not been there before. She wore a long, black dress similar to the dresses the postulants wore and Alice took her to be her friend.

She noticed the figure enter the room at the end of the hall. This room was not a bedroom but used by the postulants for study purposes.

"It's Vera," Alice thought, and decided to join her and see what she was up to in that room.

Quickly, she walked towards the room and entered it.

The lights were off and Alice thought this peculiar. Was her friend perhaps playing games with her? The room at this hour was quite dark.

So she turned on the lights, and looked around. There was no one in the room now, and there was no way anyone could have left the room without her noticing it, Alice reasoned. She examined the windows and found them tightly closed. Not that she expected her friend to exit the room by that way, but she wanted to be sure the person— whoever she might have been—could not have left that way. This was on the third floor and anyone trying to leave by the windows would have had to jump, or have a ladder outside.

Suddenly it hit Alice that she had not heard anything at all. All the time she had seen the figure walk into the room, there had been no footsteps, no noise of a door opening, nothing at all. Morgan Hall's doors open with a considerable amount of squeaking and none of that was audible when she had seen the figure before.

Alice quickly left and hurried to her own room to figure this out quietly.

On recollection, she visualized the figure again and it occurred to her at once that there was something very odd about the girl. For one thing, the long gown the postulants wear moves when they walk. But the figure she had seen was stiff and seemed to glide along the floor rather than actually walk on it. The corridor was properly lit and she had seen the figure quite clearly. What she had not seen were her ankles and socks, something she would have observed had it been one of her friends.

Although the door was not closed, the room was actually a corner room that could be entered in only one way, from the front door. Alice was sure she had not seen the figure emerge from it again. There was no place to hide in the room, had this been her friend playing a joke on her. Alice had quickly examined the closet, desk, and beds— and no one was hiding anywhere in that room.

Eventually, she gathered up enough courage to seek out her friend Vera and discuss the matter with her. She found that there was a "joke" going around the convent that Alice Morgan's ghost was roaming the corridors, but that the whole matter was to be treated strictly as a gag. Yet she also discovered that there was one part of the Hall that was off limits to anyone *alone.* In what the girls called the catacombs, at ground level, was the laundry room. The third section, way back, was never to be entered by any of them at night, and in the daytime only if in pairs. Yet, the area was well lit. Alice could not get any information for the reasons for this strange and forbidding order. In a convent, speaking to anyone but one's own group is extremely difficult without "proper permission" and this was not a fitting sub-ject to discuss.

The novices, whom she approached next, suddenly became serious and told her to forget it: there were things going on in the building that could not be explained. She was not to pay attention, and pray hard instead.

Alice wondered about this attitude, and perhaps it was then that her first doubts concerning her ecclesiastical future began to enter her mind.

Shortly after, she lay awake in bed at night, thinking of her future at the convent. The clock had just chimed eleven and she was still wide awake. Night after night, she had heard the walking in the hall. After weeks of these manifestations, her nerves began to get edgy and she could not sleep as easily as she used to when she still lived in Brooklyn. Sure enough, there they were again, those incessant foot-steps. They seemed to her the steps of a medium-heavy person, more like a woman's than a man's, and they seemed to be bent on some definite business, scurrying along the hall as if in a hurry.

Suddenly the night was pierced by a shriek: it seemed directly outside her door, but below. Since she was on the top floor, the per-son would have to be on the second floor.

There was no mistaking it, this was the outcry of a woman in great pain, in the agony of being hurt by someone!

This time she was almost too scared to look, but she did open the door only to find the corridor abandoned and quiet now.

She ran in to speak to the other postulants, regulations or no regulations. She found them huddled in their beds in abject fear. All eight of them had heard the bloodcurdling scream!

By now Alice was convinced that something strange had taken place here and that a restless personality was stalking the corridors.

A few nights later, she and Vera were in their room, getting ready to retire. It was a cold night, but no wind was about. The windows were the French window type that locked with a heavy iron rod from top to bottom. No one could open the window from the outside, the only way it could be opened would be from the inside, by pushing the rod up.

"We don't have to lock the window tonight, do we?" Vera said. "It isn't windy."

But they decided to do it anyway as they did every night. They put their shoes on the window sill, something they were in the habit of doing frequently so that the small draft coming in below the windows would "air them out."

After the window was locked, they retired.

It was well into the night, when the girls awoke to a loud noise. The French window had broken open by itself and the shoes had been tossed inside the room as if by a strong storm!

They checked and found the air outside totally still. Whatever had burst their window open had not been the wind. But what was it?

The room was ice cold now. They shuddered and went back to bed.

There is only a small ledge, for pigeons to sit on outside the window, so no one could have opened the window from that vantage point. One could hardly expect pigeons to burst a window open, either.

The girls then realized that the novices who had been complaining about the windows in their room being constantly open had not been fibbing. Alice and Vera always kept their windows closed, yet some unseen force had apparently opened them from inside on a number of occasions. Now they had seen for themselves how it happened.

Alice realized that the window had been broken open as if by force from *inside,* not outside.

"Someone's trying to get out, not in," she said, and her roommate could only shudder.

There were other peculiar things she began to notice. Strange cold drafts upstairs and in the attic. Crosses nailed to the wall next to the entrance to the upstairs rooms. Only to those rooms, and to no others, and not inside the rooms, as one might expect in a convent, but just outside as if they had been placed there to keep something, or someone evil out!

In the main dining room, a door, when closed, could not be distinguished from the surrounding wall. A trick window near the head of the table was actually a mirror which allowed the man at the head of the table to see who was coming towards him from all sides.

Banker Morgan lived in considerable fear of his life, whether imagined or real, but certainly the house was built to his specifications. In fact, trick mirrors were so placed in various parts of the main house so that no one could approach from downstairs and surprise anyone upstairs, yet no one could see the one watching through them.

Shortly after Alice had moved into the convent, she began to have strange dreams in which a blond young girl named Alice played a prominent role.

In the dream, the girl's blond hair changed to curls, and she heard a voice say, "This is Alice Morgan, I want to introduce you to her."

But when she woke up Alice thought this was only due to her having discussed the matter with the novices. Alice Morgan was not the disturbed person there, her psychic sense told her.

To her, all ghostly activities centered around that attic. There were two steps that always squeaked peculiarly when someone stepped on them. Many times she would hear them squeak and look to see who was walking on them, only to find herself staring into nothingness. This was in the daytime. On other occasions, when she was at work cleaning garbage cans downstairs—postulants do a lot of ordinary kitchen work—she would feel herself observed closely by a pair of eyes staring down at her from the attic. Yet, no one was up there then.

The torture of the nightly footsteps together with her doubts about her own calling prompted her finally to seek release from the convent and return to the outside world, after three months as a postulant. After she had made this difficult decision, she felt almost as if all the burdens had lifted from the room that had been the center of the psychic manifestations.

She decided to make some final inquiries prior to leaving and since her superiors would not tell her, she looked the place over by herself, talked to those who were willing to talk and otherwise used her powers of observation. Surely, if the haunted area was upstairs, and she knew by now that it was, it could not be Alice Morgan who was the restless one.

But then who was?

The rooms on the third floor had originally been servant quarters as is customary in the mansions of the pre–World War I period. They were built to house the usually large staffs of the owners. In the case of the Morgans, that staff was even larger than most wealthy families.

Was "the restless one" one of the maids who had jumped out the window in a final burst for freedom, freedom from some horrible fate?

Then her thoughts turned to the Communist Russian occupancy of the building. Had they perhaps tortured someone up there in her room? The thought was melodramatically tempting, but she dismissed it immediately. The figure she had seen in the hall was dressed in the long dress of an earlier period. She belonged to the time when the Morgan Hall was a mansion.

No, she reasoned, it must have been a young girl who died there while the Morgans had the place and perhaps her death was hushed up and she wanted it known. Was it suicide, and did she feel in a kind of personal hell because of it, especially now that the place was a convent?

Somehow Alice felt that she had stumbled upon the right answers. That night, the last night she was to spend at the convent prior to going home, she slept soundly.

For the first time in three months, there were no footsteps outside her door.

For a while she waited, once the ten o'clock bell had sounded, but nothing happened. Whoever it was had stopped walking.

The Greenwich Village Townhouse

F RANK PARIS AND T. E. LEWIS were puppeteers. Frank Paris was the creator of Howdy Doody. Children came to admire the little theater the two puppeteers had set up in the high-ceilinged basement of their old house in Greenwich Village, that old section of New York going back to the 1700s. The house at number 12 Gay Street was a typical old townhouse, the kind New Yorkers built around 1800 when "the village" meant *far uptown*.

In 1924, a second section was added to the smallish house, covering the garden that used to grace the back of the house. This architectural graft created a kind of duplex, one apartment on top of another, with small rooms at the sides in the rear.

The ownership of the house in the early days is hazy. At one time a sculptor owned number 12, possibly before the 1930s. Evidently he was fond of bootleg liquor, for he built a trap door in the ground floor of the newer section of the house, probably over his hidden liquor cabinet. Before that, New York's Mayor Jimmy Walker owned the house, and used it *well*, although not *wisely*. One of his many loves is said to have been the tenant there. By a strange set of circumstances, the records of the house vanished like a ghost from the files of the Hall of Records around that time.

Later, real-estate broker Mary Ellen Strunsky lived in the house. In 1956, she sold it to the puppeteer team of Paris and Lewis, who had been there ever since, living in the upstairs apartment and using the lower portion as a workroom and studio for their little theater.

None of this, incidentally, was known to me until after the visit I paid the house in the company of my medium for the evening, Betty Ritter.

It all started when a reporter from the *New York World-Telegram*, Cindy Hughes, came to interview me, and casually dropped a hint that she knew of a haunted house. Faster than you can say *The Daily News*, I had her promise to lead me to this house. On a particularly warm night in May of 1963, we followed Miss Hughes down to Gay Street. Betty Ritter knew nothing at all about the case; she didn't even know the address where we were going.

We were greeted warmly by Frank Paris, who led us up the stairs into the upper apartment. The sight of the elaborately furnished, huge living room was surprising. Oriental figurines, heavy drapes, paintings, statuary, and antiques filed the room.

In two comfortable chairs we found awaiting us two friends of the owners: an intense looking man in his thirties, Richard X., who, I later discovered, was an editor by profession, and Alice May Hall, a charming lady of undetermined age.

I managed to get Betty out of earshot, so I could question these people without her getting impressions from our conversation.

"What is this about the house being haunted?" I asked Frank Paris.

He nodded gravely.

"I was working downstairs with some lacquer. It was late, around 3 A.M. Suddenly, I began to smell a strong odor of violets. My black spaniel here also smelled it, for he started to sniff rather strangely. And yet, Ted, my partner, in the same room with me, did not get the strange scent at all. But there is more. People waltz up and down the stairs at night, time and again."

"What do you mean, *waltz*?"

"I mean they go up and down, up and down, as if they had business here," Frank explained, and I thought, perhaps they had, perhaps they had.

"A weekend visitor also had a most peculiar experience here," Frank Paris continued. "He knew nothing about our haunted reputation, of course. We were away on a short trip, and when we got back, he greeted us with—'Say, who are all these people going up and down the stairs?' He had thought that the house next door was somehow connected to ours, and that what he heard were people from next door. But of course, there is no connection whatever."

"And did you ever investigate these mysterious footsteps?" I asked.

"Many times," Frank and Ted nodded simultaneously, "but there was never anyone there—anyone of flesh-and-blood, that is."

I thanked them, and wondered aloud if they weren't psychic, since they had experienced what can only be called psychic phenomena.

Frank Paris hesitated, then admitted that he thought both of them were to some extent.

"We had a little dog which we had to have put away one day. We loved the dog very much, but it was one of those things that had to be done. For over a year after the dog's death, both of us felt him poking us in the leg—a habit he had in life. This happened on many occasions to both of us."

I walked over to where Ms. Hall, the gray-haired little lady, sat.

"Oh, there is a ghost here all right," she volunteered. "It was in February of 1963, and I happened to be in the house, since the boys and I are good friends. I was sitting here in this very spot, relaxing and casually looking toward the entrance door through which you just came—the one that leads to the hallway and the stairs. There was a man there, wearing evening clothes, and an Inverness Cape—I saw him quite plainly. He had dark hair. It was dusk, and there was still some light outside."

"What did you do?"

"I turned my head to tell Frank Paris about the stranger, and that instant he was gone like a puff of smoke."

Paris broke in.

"I questioned her about this, since I didn't really believe it. But a week later, at dawn this time, I saw the ghost myself, exactly as Alice had described him—wearing evening clothes, a cape, hat, and his face somewhat obscured by the shadows of the hallway. Both Alice and I are sure he was a youngish man, and had sparkling eyes. What's more, our dog also saw the intruder. He went up to the ghost, friendly-like, as if to greet him."

Those were the facts of the case. A ghost in evening clothes, an old house where heaven knows what might have happened at one time or another, and a handful of psychic people.

I returned to Betty Ritter, and asked her to gather psychic impressions while walking about the house.

"A crime was committed here," the medium said, and described a terrible argument upstairs between an Asian man and a woman. She described a gambling den, opium smokers, and a language she could not understand. The man's name was Ming, she said. Ming is a very common Chinese word meaning, I believe, Sun.

Betty also told Frank Paris that someone close to him by the name of John had passed on and that he had something wrong with his right eye, which Paris acknowledged was correct. She told Ted Lewis that a Bernard L. was around him, not knowing, of course, that Lewis' father was named Bernham Lewis. She told Richard X. that he worked with books, and it was not until after the séance that I learned he was an editor by profession. I don't know about the Chinese man and the opium den, but they are possibilities in an area so far removed from the bright lights of the city as the Village once was.

We went downstairs and, in the almost total darkness, formed a circle. Betty fell into trance, her neck suddenly falling back as if she were being possessed by a woman whose neck had been hurt.

"Emil," she mumbled, and added the woman had been decapitated, and her bones were still about. She then came out of trance and we walked back up the stairs to the oldest part of the house. Still "seeing" clairvoyantly, Betty Ritter again mumbled "Emil," and said she saw documents with government seals on them. She also felt someone named Mary Ellen had lived here and earlier some "well-known government official named Wilkins or Wilkinson."

Betty, of course, knew nothing about real-estate broker Mary Ellen Strunsky or Jimmy Walker, the former New York Mayor, who had been in this house for so long.

It now remained for us to find those bones Betty had talked about. We returned to the downstairs portion of the house, but Betty refused to go farther. Her impression of tragedy was so strong she urged us to desist.

Thus it was that the Ghost of Gay Street, whoever he may be, would have to wait just a little longer until the bones could be properly sorted out. It wasn't half bad, considering that Frank Paris and Ted Lewis put on a pretty nice puppet show every so often, down there in the basement theater at number 12 Gay Street.

The Ghosts of
Barbery Lane

"**I** KNOW A HOUSE IN RYE, NEW YORK, with a ghost," painter
Mary Melikian said to me, and there was pleasure in her voice
at being the harbinger of good news. Mary knew how eager
I was to find a haunted house, preferably one that was still haunted.

"A ghost," Mary repeated and added, tantalizingly, "a ghost that
likes to slam doors."

I pumped Mary for details. One of her friends was the cel-
ebrated portrait painter Molly Guion, known in Rye as Mrs. John
Smythe. Molly and her husband, an architect, lived in a sprawling
mid-nineteenth-century house atop a bluff overlooking the old New
Haven Railroad bed, surrounded by houses built in later years. The
Smythes' house was the first one on the tract, the original Manor
House, built there around 1860 by one Jared B. Peck.

I arranged with Mrs. Smythe to visit the house the following
week, in August of 1963. I was met at the train by Mrs. Smythe,
whose husband also came along to welcome us. The drive to the
house (originally called "The Cedars" but now only known as a number on Barbery Lane) took less than five minutes, yet you might well
have entered another world—so serene and rural was the atmosphere
that greeted us that moonlit evening, when the station wagon pulled

up to the gleaming-white 100-year old house the Smythes had called home since the summer of 1957.

Rising to four floors, the structure reminded me of the stylized paintings of Victorian houses associated with another world. A wide porch went around it at the ground level, and shady trees protected it from view and intrusion.

The huge living room was tastefully furnished with fine antiques and all over the house we encountered the marvelously alive portraits painted by Molly Guion, which blended naturally into the decor of the house. This was a stately mansion, less than an hour from New York by train, but as quiet and removed from the city of subways as if it stood in the Deep South or Down East. We seated ourselves comfortably. Then I came right to the point.

"This ghost," I began. "What exactly does it do and when did you first notice anything unusual in the house?"

This is my standard opener. Molly Guion was more than happy to tell me everything. Her husband left for a while to tend to some chores.

"We arrived in this house on a hot summer day in 1957—in July," she recalled. "About a week later—I remember it was a particularly hot night—we heard a door slam. Both my husband and I heard it."

"Well?"

"But there was absolutely nobody in the house at the time except us," Molly said, significantly. "We heard it many times after that. Maybe six or seven separate instances. Once around ten o'clock at night I heard the front door open and close again with a characteristic squeak. Mother was living with us then and I was not feeling well, so that a nurse was staying with me. I called out 'Mother,' thinking she had come home a bit early, but there was no reply. Since then I've heard the front door open many times, but there is never anyone there."

"Is it the front door then?"

"No, not always. Sometimes it is the front door and sometimes it is this door on the second floor. Come, I'll show you."

Molly led us up the winding stairs to a second floor containing many small rooms, all exquisitely furnished with the solid furniture of the Victorian period. There was a tiny room on one side of the corridor leading to the rear of the house, and across from it, the door that was heard to slam. It was a heavy wooden door, leading to a narrow winding staircase which in turn led up another flight of stairs to the third floor. Here Molly Guion had built herself a magnificent studio, taking up most of the floor space.

"One day in January of 1962," she volunteered, "I was downstairs in the kitchen talking to an exterminator, when I heard a door slam hard—it seemed to me. Yet, there was no one in the house at the time, only we two downstairs."

"Outside of yourself and your husband, has anyone else heard these uncanny noises?"

Molly nodded quickly.

"There was this man that worked for me. He said, 'Mrs. Smythe, every time I'm alone in the house, I hear a door slam!'"

"Anyone else?"

"A Scottish cleaning woman, name of Roberta Gillan. She lives in Harrison, New York. She once came to me and said, 'Did you just slam a door?' Of course, I hadn't."

We were now seated in a small room off the second-floor corridor. The light was moody and the air dank. There was a quietness around the house so heavy I almost wished I could hear a door slam. Molly had more to reveal.

"Once, a little girl named Andree, age eleven, came to visit us and within seconds exclaimed 'Mamma, there is a ghost in this house!'"

Our hostess admitted to being somewhat psychic, with some times comical results. Years ago, when a boyfriend had failed to keep their date, she saw him clearly in a dream-vision with a certain blonde girl. He later explained his absence in a casual way, but she nailed him with a description of his blonde—and he confessed the truth.

Two years after she moved into the house, Molly developed a case of asthma, the kind very old people sometimes suffer from. Strangely, it bothered her only in certain rooms and not at all in others. It started like a kind of allergy, and gradually worsened until it became a fully grown asthmatic condition. Although two rooms were side by side, sleeping in one would aggravate the condition, but sleeping in the other made her completely free of it!

"Did you hear any other noises—I mean, outside of the door slamming?" I asked.

"Yes. Not so long ago we had a dinner party here, and among the guests was a John Gardner, a vice president of the Bankers Trust Company."

Suddenly she had heard someone rap at the window of the big room downstairs. They tried to ignore the noise, but Gardner heard it too.

"Is someone rapping at your window?" he inquired.

He was assured it was nothing. Later he took Molly aside and remonstrated with her. "I distinctly heard the raps," he said. Molly just smiled.

Finally the Smythes called on the American Society for Psychic Research to find an explanation for all these goings-on. But the Society was in no hurry to do anything about the case. They suggested Molly write them a letter, which she did, but they still took no action.

I thoroughly inspected the premises—walked up the narrow staircase into Molly Guion's studio where some of the best portrait oils hung. Her paintings of famous Britons had just toured as an exhibition and the house was full of those she owned (the greater part of her work was commissioned and scattered in collections, museums, and private homes).

There was a tiny bedroom next to the landing in back of the studio, evidently a servant's room, since the entire floor had originally been servants' quarters. The house had sixteen rooms in all.

By now Mr. Smythe had joined us and I explained my mission. Had he ever noticed anything unusual about the house?

"Oh yes," he volunteered, speaking slowly and deliberately. "There are all sorts of noises in this house and they're not ordinary noises—I mean, the kind you can *explain*."

"For instance?"

"I was sleeping up here one night in the little bedroom here," he said, pointing to the servant's room in back of the landing, "when I heard footsteps. They were the steps of an older person."

But there was no one about, he asserted.

Jared Peck, who built the house in 1860, died in 1895, and the house passed into the hands of his estate to be rented to various tenants. In 1910, Stuyvesant Wainwright bought the property. In the following year, his ex-wife, now Mrs. Catlin, bought it from him and lived in it until her death in the 1920s.

The former Mrs. Wainwright turned out to be a colorful person. Born wealthy, she had a very short temper and the servants never stayed long in her house.

"She certainly liked to slam doors," Mr. Smythe observed. "I mean she was the kind of person who would do that sort of thing."

"One day she became very ill and everybody thought she would die," Molly related. "There she was stretched out on this very couch and the doctor felt free to talk about her condition. 'She won't last much longer,' he said, and shrugged. Mrs. Wainwright sat up with a angry jolt and barked, 'I intend to!' And she did, for many more years of hot-tempered shenanigans."

In her later years Mrs. Wainwright moved to the former servants' quarters on the second floor—whether out of economy or for reasons of privacy no one knows for sure. The *slamming door* was right in the heart of her rooms and no doubt she traveled up those narrow stairs to the floor above many times.

The plumber, painter, and carpenter who had worked for Mrs. Wainwright were still living in Rye then and they all remembered her as a willful and headstrong woman who liked to have her own way. Her granddaughter, Mrs. Condit, recalled her vividly. The Smythes were pretty sure that Mrs. Wainwright slept up there on the second floor—they found a screen in storage marked "My bedroom window" that fit no other window in any of the rooms.

The Smythes acquired the handsome house from the next owner, one Arthur Flemming, who also used Mrs. Wainwright's old room. But he didn't experience anything unusual, or at any rate said nothing about it.

There was a big theft once in the house and Mrs. Wainwright may have been worried about it. Strongly attached to worldly possessions, she kept valuables in various trunks on the third floor, and ran up to look at them from time to time to make sure everything was still there.

Could the slamming of the door be a re-enactment of these frequent nervous expeditions up the stairs? Could the opening and closing of the entrance door be a fearful examination of the door to see if the lock was secure, or if there was anyone strange lurking about outside?

The very day after our visit to this haunted house, a young painter friend of Molly's named Helen Charleton, of Bronxville, New York, was alone in the studio that Molly let her use occasionally to do some painting of her own. She was quite alone in the big house when she clearly heard the front door open. Calling out, she received no answer. Thinking that the gardener might have a key, and that she might be in danger, she took hold of what heavy objects she could put her hands on and waited anxiously for the steps that were sure to resound any moment. No steps came. An hour later, the doorbell rang and she finally dashed down to the entrance door. *The door was tightly shut*, and no one was about. Yet she *had* heard the characteristic noise of the opening of the old-fashioned door!

The mailman's truck was just pulling away, so she assumed it was he who had rung the bell. Just then Molly returned.

"I've heard the door slam many times," Helen Charleton said to me, "and it always sounds so far away. I think it's on the first floor, but I can't be sure."

Was Mrs. Wainwright still walking the Victorian corridors of "The Cedars," guarding her treasures upstairs?

When I returned from Europe in the fall of 1964, Molly Guion had news for me. All was far from quiet in Rye. In the upstairs room where Molly's invalid mother was bedridden, a knob had flown off a table while Mrs. Guion stood next to it. In the presence of a nurse, the bathroom lights had gone on and off by themselves. More sinister, a heavy ashtray had taken off on its own to sail clear across the room. A door had opened by itself, and footsteps had been heard again.

A new nurse had come, and the number of witnesses who had heard or seen uncanny goings-on was now eight.

I decided it was time for a séance, and on January 6, 1965, medium Ethel Meyers, Mary Melikian and I took a New Haven train for Rye, where John Smythe picked us up in his station wagon.

While Ethel Meyers waited in the large sitting room downstairs, I checked on the house and got the latest word on the hauntings. Molly Guion took me to the kitchen to show me the spot where one of the most frightening incidents had taken place.

"Last Christmas, my mother, my husband, and I were here in the kitchen having lunch, and right near us on a small table next to the wall was a great big bread knife. Suddenly, to our amazement, *the knife took off into the air*, performed an arc in the air and landed about a yard away from the table. This was about noon, in good light."

"Was that the only time something like this happened?"

"The other day the same thing happened. We were down in the kitchen again at nighttime. My husband and I heard a terrific crash upstairs. It was in the area of the servants' quarters on the second floor, which is in the area where that door keeps slamming. I went up to investigate and found a heavy ashtray lying on the floor about a yard away from the table in my husband's den."

"And there was no one upstairs—flesh-and-blood, that is?"

"No. The object could not have just slipped off the table. It landed some distance away."

"Amazing," I conceded. "Was there more?"

"Last week I was standing in the upstairs sitting room with one of the nurses, when a piece of a chair that was lying in the center of a table took off and landed in the middle of the floor."

"Before your eyes?"

"Before our eyes."

"What would you say is the most frequent phenomenon here?" I asked.

"The opening of the front door downstairs. We and others have heard this characteristic noise any number of times, and there is never anyone there."

I turned to Mrs. Witty, the nurse currently on duty with Molly Guion's mother.

"How long have you been in this house?"

"Since October, 1964."

"Have you noticed anything unusual in these four months?"

"Well, Mrs. Smythe and I were in the patient's bedroom upstairs, when we heard the front door downstairs open. I remarked to Mrs. Smythe that she had a visitor, and went down to the front door, and looked. *The heavy chain was swinging loose, and the front door was slightly ajar!*"

"Did you see any visitor?"

"No. I opened the door, looked all around, but there was no one there."

"Anything else?"

"A couple of weeks later, the same thing happened. I was alone in the house with the patient, and the door was locked securely. An hour after I had myself locked it, I heard the door shut tightly, but the chain was again swinging by itself."

I next turned to Mr. Smythe to check up on his own experiences since we had last talked. Mr. Smythe was a naval architect and very cautious in his appraisal of the uncanny. He was still hearing the "measured steps" in the attic room where he sometimes slept, even when he was all alone in the house.

I returned to Ethel Meyers, the medium, who had seated herself in a large chair in the front sitting room downstairs.

"Anything happening?" I asked, for I noticed a peculiar expression on Ethel's face, as if she were observing something or someone.

"I picture a woman clairvoyantly," Ethel said. "She looks at me with a great deal of defiance."

"Why are you pointing across the room at that sofa?" I asked Mary.

"I saw a light from the corner of my eye and I thought it was a car, but no car has passed by," Mary said.

If a car *had* passed by, no reflection could have been seen at that spot, since no window faced in that direction.

While Ethel prepared for the trance sitting, I went outside the room to talk to Georgia Anne Warren, a young dancer who had modeled for some of Molly Guion's paintings. Her full-length nude study graced the studio upstairs, and there amid the Churchill portraits and faces of the famous or near-famous, it was like a shining beacon of beauty. But Miss Warren wasn't only posing for a painter, we discovered—she was also modeling for a ghost.

"I heard a thumping noise, as if someone were going upstairs. I was in the kitchen. The steps sounded as if they were coming from the dining room. There was no one coming in. The only people in the house at the time were Molly Guion and myself. No doubt about it."

I thanked the redheaded model and followed Ethel Meyers up the stairs, to which she seemed propelled by a sudden impulse. There, on the winding Victorian steps, Ethel made her first contact with the ghost.

"Make the body very cold. Don't put it in the ground when it's warm. Let it get very cold!" she mumbled, as if not quite herself.

"Let her speak through you," I suggested.

"She is," Ethel replied, and continued in a somewhat strange voice. "Ring around the rosies, a pocketful of posies . . ."

I turned toward the stairwell and asked the ghost to communicate with us, tell her tale, and find help through us. There was no further answer.

I led Mrs. Meyers back to her chair, and asked Molly Guion to dim the lights a little so we could all relax. Meanwhile, other witnesses had arrived. They included *New York Times* reporter N. Berkowitz, Benton & Bowles vice-president Gordon Webber, publicist Bill Ryan, and book critic John K. Hutchins. We formed a long oval around Ethel Meyers and waited for the ghost to make her appearance.

We did not have to wait long. With a sudden shriek, Ethel, deep in trance, leapt to her feet, and in the awkward posture of an old crone, walked toward the front door. Nothing I could do would hold her back. I followed her quickly, as the medium, now possessed by the ghost, made her way through the long room to the door.

As if a strong wind had swept into the sitting room, the rest of the guests were thrown back by the sheer drive of Ethel's advance. She flung herself against the heavy wooden door and started to alternately gnaw at it and pound against it in an unmistakable desire to open it and go through. Then she seized the brass chain—the one Mrs. Witty had twice seen swinging by itself—and pulled it with astonishing force. I had all I could do to keep the medium from falling as she threw her body against the door.

In one hand I held a microphone, which I pressed close to her lips to catch as much of the dialogue as possible. I kept the other hand ready to prevent Ethel's fall to the floor.

"Rotten," the entranced medium now mumbled, still clutching the chain.

I tried to coax her back to the chair, but the ghost evidently would have none of it.

"It stinks . . . Where is it?"

"Is this your house?" I asked.

Heavy breathing.

"Yes. Get out!"

"I've come to help you. What is your name?"

"Get out!" the microphone picked up.

"What is it that you want?" I asked.

"My body."

"You've passed on, don't you understand?"

"No . . . I want my body. Where is it?"

I explained again that this was no longer her house, but she kept calling for the return of "her body" in such anger and despair that I began to wonder if it had not been buried on the premises.

"They took it, my body. I saw them, I saw them!"

"You must let go of this house. It is no longer yours," I said.

"No, my house, my house. They took it. My body. I have nothing. Get it. I feel I have one."

I explained that we had lent her a body to speak through for the moment.

"Who are you?" *It* sounded quieter.

"A friend," I replied, "come to help you."

Instead of replying, the entranced medium grabbed the door again.

"Why do you want to open the door?" I asked. It took a moment for the answer to come through trembling lips.

"Go out," she finally said. "I don't know you. Let me go, let me go."

I continued to question the ghost.

"Who are you? Did you live in this house?"

"My house. They took it out. My body is out there!"

I explained about the passage of time.

"You were not well. You've died."

"No, no . . . I wasn't cold."

"You are free to go from this door. Your loved ones, your family, await you outside."

"They hate me."

"No, they have made up with you. Why should they hate you?"

"They took me out the door."

Then, suddenly the medium's expression changed. Had someone come to fetch her?

"Oh, Baba, darling . . . Oh, he loved me."

There was hysterical crying now.

"He's gone . . . My beloved . . ."

"What is his name?"

"*Wain* . . . Where is he . . . Let me go!"

The crying was now almost uncontrollable, so I sent the ghost on her way. At the same time I asked that Albert, Ethel's control on the etheric side of the veil, take over her physical body for the moment to speak to us.

It took a moment or two until Albert was in command. The medium's body visibly straightened out and all traces of a bent old crone vanished. Albert's crisp voice was heard.

"She's a former tenant here, who has not been too well beloved. She also seems to have been carried out before complete death. This has brought her back to try and rectify it and make contact with the physical body. But here is always unhappiness. I believe there was no love toward her as she was older."

"Can you get a name?" I asked.

"If she refuses, I cannot."

"How long ago was this?"

"During the Nineties. Between 1890 and 1900."

"Is this a woman?"

"Yes."

"Anything peculiar about her appearance?"

"Large eyes, and almost a harelip."

"Why is she concerned about her body?"

"There was no great funeral for her. She was put in a box and a few words were said over her grave. That is part of her problem, that she was thus rejected and neglected."

"Why does she run up to the attic?"

"This was her house, and it was denied to her later in life."

"By whom?"

"By those living here. Relatives to her."

"Her heirs?"

"Those who took it over when she could no longer function. She was still alive."

"Anything else we should know?"

"There is a great deal of hate for anyone in this house. Her last days were full of hate. Should she return, if she is spoken to kindly, she will leave. We will help her."

"Why is she so full of hate?"

"Her grief, her oppressions. She never left her tongue quiet when she was disrupted in her desire to go from her quarters to the rest of the house."

"What was her character?"

"As a young person she was indeed a lady. Later in life, a strong personality, going slightly toward dual personality. She was an autocrat. At the very end, not beloved."

"And her relationship with the servants?"

"Not too friendly. Tyrannical."

"What troubled her about her servants?"

"They knew too much."

"Of what?"

"Her downfall. Her pride was hurt."

"Before that, how was she?"

"A suspicious woman. She could not help but take things from others which she believed were hers by right."

"What did she think her servants were doing?"

"They pried on her secret life. She trusted no one toward the end of life."

"Before she was prevented, as you say, from freely going about the house—did she have any belongings in the attic?"

"Yes, hidden. She trusted no one."

I then suggested that the "instrument" be brought back to herself. A very surprised Ethel Meyers awakened to find herself leaning against the entrance door.

"What's the matter with my lip?" she asked when she was able to speak. After a moment, Ethel Meyers was her old self, and the excursion into Mrs. Wainwright's world had come to an end.

The following morning Molly Smythe called me on the phone. "Remember about Albert's remarks that Mrs. Wainwright was restrained within her own rooms?"

Of course I remembered.

"Well," Molly continued, "we've just made a thorough investigation of all the doors upstairs in the servants' quarters where she spent her last years. They all show evidence of locks having been on them, later removed. *Someone was locked up there for sure.*"

Ironically, death had not released Mrs. Wainwright from confinement. To her, freedom still lay beyond the heavy wooden door with its brass chain.

Now that her spirit self had been taken in hand, perhaps she would find her way out of the maze of her delusions to rejoin her first husband, for whom she had called.

The next time Molly Smythe hears the front door opening, it'll be just her husband coming home from the office. *Or so I thought.*

But the last week of April, 1965, Molly called me again. Footsteps had been heard *upstairs* this time, and the sound of a door somewhere being opened and closed, and of course, on inspection, there was no one *visible* about.

Before I could make arrangements to come out to Rye once again, something else happened. Mr. Smythe was in the bathtub, when a large tube of toothpaste, safely resting well back on a shelf, flew off the shelf by its own volition. No vibration or other *natural* cause could account for it. Also, a hypodermic needle belonging to one of the nurses attending Molly's invalid mother had somehow disappeared.

I promised to bring Sybil Leek to the house. The British medium knew nothing whatever of the earlier history of the case, and I was curious to see if she would make contact with the same or different conditions, as sometimes happens when two mediums are used in the same house. It's like tuning in on different radio wavelengths.

It was a cool, wet day in May when we seated ourselves in a circle upstairs in the "haunted room." Present in addition to the hosts, Sybil Leek, and myself, were Mrs. Betty Salter (Molly's sister); David Ellingson, a reporter from the Port Chester, N.Y. *Item;* Mr. and Mrs. Robert Bendick, neighbors and friends of the Smythes;

and Mary Melikian. Mr. Bendick was a television producer specializing in news programs.

Sybil went into hypnotic trance. It took several minutes before anything audible could be recorded.

"Who are you?" I asked.

A feeble voice answered:

"Marion . . . Marion Gernt . . ."

Before going into trance, Sybil had volunteered the information that the name "Grant," or something like it, had been on her mind ever since she set foot into the house.

"What year is this?" I asked.

"1706."

"Who built the house?"

"My father. . . Walden."

She then complained that people in the house were disturbing *her*, and that therefore she was *pulling it down.*

"My face is swollen," she added. "I'm sick . . . Blood."

Suddenly, something went wrong with my reliable tape recorder. In all my previous investigations it had worked perfectly. Now it wouldn't, and some parts of the conversation were not recorded. The wheels would turn and then stop, and then start again, as if someone were sticking their fingers into them at will!

I tried my camera, and to my amazement, I couldn't take any pictures. All of a sudden, the mechanism wouldn't function properly, and the shutter could not be un-cocked. I did not get any photographs. Bob Bendick, after the séance, took a good look at the camera. In a moment it was working fine again. After the séance, too, we tried to make the tape recorder work. It started and then stopped completely.

"The batteries have run out," I explained, confident that there was nothing more than that to it. So we put the machine on house current. Nothing happened. It wasn't the batteries. It was something else.

After we left the "haunted room" and went downstairs, I put the tape recorder into my traveling case. About ten minutes later, I heard a ghostly voice coming from my case. *My* voice. The tape recorder that I had left in a secure turn-off position had started up by itself . . . or . . . so it seemed.

But one can't be sure in haunted houses. The reporter David Ellingson and Mary Melikian were standing next to me when it happened. John Smythe was wondering if someone had turned on the radio or TV. So much for the instruments that didn't work— temporarily.

But, let us get back to Sybil and the ghost speaking through her. She claimed to have been burned all over in a fire. John Smythe confirmed later that there were traces of a fire in the house that have never been satisfactorily explained.

The ghost seemed confused about it. She was burned, on this spot, in what was then a little house. The place was called Rocher. Her named was spelled M-a-r-i-o-n G-e-r-n-t. She was born at Rodey, eight miles distant. She was not sure about her age. At first she said 29, then it was 57. The house was built by one Dion, of Rocher.

I then tried to explain, as I always do, that the house belonged to someone else and that she must not stay.

"Go away," the ghost mumbled, not at all pleased with the idea of moving. But I insisted. I told her of her husband who wanted her to join him "over there."

"I hate him!" she volunteered, then added—"I start moving things . . . I break things up . . . I want my chair."

"You must not stay here," I pleaded. "You're not wanted here."

"He said that," she replied in a sullen voice. "Alfred did. My husband."

"You must join him and your children."

"I'll stay."

I repeated the incantation for her to leave.

"I can't go. I'm burned. I can't move," she countered.

I explained that these were only memories.

Finally she relented, and said—"I'll need a lot of rags . . . to cover myself."

Gently now, she started to fade.

"I need my chair," she pleaded, and I told her she could have it. Then she was gone.

Sybil came back now. Still in trance, she responded quickly to my questions about what she saw and felt on the other side of the veil. This is a technique I find particularly effective when used prior to bringing the medium out of trance or from under hypnosis.

"An old lady," Sybil said. "She is quite small. I think she is Dutch. Shriveled. She is very difficult. Can't move. Very unpleasant. Throws things because she can't walk. This is her house. She lived here about three hundred years ago. She wants everything *as it was.* She has marks on her face. She was in a fire."

"Did she die in it?" I asked.

"No. She died near here. Doesn't communicate well."

"There is a box with two hearts, two shields," Sybil said. "It means something to this woman."

"Were there any others around?" I asked.

"Lots, like shadows," Sybil explained, "but this little woman was the one causing the commotion."

"She likes to throw things," Sybil added, and I couldn't help thinking that she had never been briefed on all the objects the ghost had been throwing.

"She doesn't know where any doors are, so she just goes on. The door worries her a lot, because she doesn't know where it is. The front and rear have been changed around."

Sybil, of course, knew nothing of the noises centering around the main door, nor the fact that the rear of the house was once the front.

I told Sybil to send her away, and in a quiet voice, Sybil did so.

The seance was over, at least for the time being.

A little later, we went up to the top floor, where both Molly and Sybil suddenly sensed a strong odor of perfume. I joined them, and I smelled it, too. It was as if *someone were following us about the house!*

But it was time to return to New York. Our hosts offered to drive us to the city.

"Too bad," I said in parting, "that nobody has seen an apparition here. Only sounds seem to have been noticed."

Betty Salter, Mrs. Smythe's perky sister, shook her head.

"Not true," she said. "I was here not so long ago when I saw a black figure downstairs in the dining room. I thought it was Molly, but on checking found that I was quite alone downstairs . . . That is, except for her."

Mrs. Wainwright, of course, was of Dutch ancestry, and the description of the character, appearance, and general impression of the ghost Sybil gave did rather fit Mrs. Wainwright.

Was the 1706 lady an ancestor or just someone who happened to be on the spot when only a small farm house occupied the site?

The Smythes really didn't care whether they have two ghosts or one ghost. They preferred to have none.

The Girl Ghost on Riverside Drive

O NE DAY IN JANUARY OF 1965, a gentleman named H. D. Settel called me on the phone to report a ghost in his Victorian apartment on Riverside Drive in New York City. Since I also lived on the Drive, it seemed the neighborly thing to do to go have a look. Mr. Settel, who was in his late twenties or early thirties, had lived in the fourth floor walk-up apartment of what was once a small townhouse for some time. He got married and his wife joined him there in October of 1964.

Since moving in, his normally cheerful wife had gone into fits of despondency for which there seemed to be no rational explanation. Spending a lot of time at home, she felt a great anxiety at times, as if something momentous were about to happen. Gradually, the sensation changed to one of dissociation, a desire to leave her physical body. Fighting this tendency, she reported the strange sensations to her husband, who was sympathetic, and suggested she stop fighting the "take-over." When she followed his advice, she found herself crying for no apparent reason.

This was followed by most unusual behavior on her part. In the middle of the night, she sat up in bed and started to talk in a most irritated fashion. Unfortunately, neither of the Settels remembered the substance of her outbreak.

About mid-January, Mrs. Settel was on the threshold of sleep when she heard a curious tapping sound on the dresser. Quickly she turned on the light and the tapping stopped, but she had the fleeting impression that there was someone else in the apartment, and the strange, floating sensation came back.

Her husband also had an unusual experience. He awoke one night toward five in the morning, and asked his wife whether she had screamed. She assured him that she hadn't. Trying to get hold of himself, Settel explained that he had just heard a young girl scream. He had seen a girl dressed in a maid's uniform standing in the doorway of the two-room apartment, looking into the bedroom, and holding a large white dog on a leash. *Her look was one of pure evil.*

Somehow he had the impression that her name was Eudrice, and he felt himself compelled to write down the words "Eudrice was a girl of young looks." Neither phrasing nor handwriting was his own. The Settels had never heard of anyone named Eudrice, so they called the public library and were told that it was a Colombian form of the Greek name Eurydice.

I asked whether either of them had had psychic experiences before coming to the house on Riverside Drive.

On their honeymoon, Mr. Settel saw a very old lady during the night, and described the vision in great detail to his wife the next morning. From the details of appearance, dress, brooch, room, and chair in which he saw her sitting, Mrs. Settel realized that her husband had seen her long-dead grandmother, with whom she had lived as a child. Her husband had never seen a picture of her. Mr. Settel was in the textile business, and Mrs. Settel had been a radio and television broadcaster.

I offered to visit the house, and did so the last week of February, 1965. The apartment on the fourth floor was done in modern style, and the Settels had made the most of the small area. There was a curious closet that suggested there had once been a door near the entrance to the bedroom. In the old days, the servants' quarters usually were located on the top floors, and this apartment undoubtedly was once just that.

I questioned Mr. Settel about the ghostly maid. Was there any light in the room at the time?

"Well, the sun was just coming up, and I could distinguish her outline quite clearly. She was a girl in her middle twenties, I'd say," he replied. "She was completely solid and real, not transparent or wavering. She had very long black hair, extremely white skin. I was terrified, stared at her for about thirty seconds, just lying there. Next thing, she was gone. We turned on the light, but, of course, there was nobody but us two in the apartment."

"What else have you observed here?" I asked.

"There was, and is, an oppressive heaviness in the atmosphere of this place, and a constant feeling of a presence other than our own," Mr. Settel replied. "Usually at night, between 9 and 3 A.M."

I turned again to Mrs. Settel.

"I almost committed suicide here once, something I would not normally think of," she confided. "Sometimes I seem to be almost possessed—I have the feeling if I allowed myself to leave my physical body, I would not be able to return."

The house had been built in 1897, and bought in 1910 from the builder by a Mrs. Gillen from Detroit. Before the house was built, the area had just been woods. From the time Mrs. Gillen bought the house, around 1910, Wall Streeters and such notables as Thomas Dewey had lived in the house. It had been a townhouse, subdivided by Mrs. Gillen into plush apartments.

There were five floors. The Settels had the fourth floor. A man named Alleyn had come to the house in 1925. From Panama, and married to a West Indian woman, he died in the house in 1956—he dropped dead, it seems, on the second floor.

For twenty years, the Settel apartment had been owned by a retired Army colonel named Villaflora and his wife. He was from Panama and she was Polish.

The Settels were able to get a lot of information about the building from one of the older tenants, a Mrs. Morgan. The superintendent's wife had committed suicide in the apartment downstairs.

The information thus obtained left a gap between 1897 when the house was built, and 1910 when it was sold to Mrs. Gillen. Thirteen years of mystery. Many interesting tenants coming and going!

I encouraged the Settels to use a Ouija board to see if their combined psychic acumen would obtain anything evidential.

"Did you get anything worthwhile?" I asked. Ouija boards often aren't reliable. It all depends on what checks out, of course.

"Yes indeed," Mr. Settel replied. "We got so much we stopped—in a hurry. The communicator identified herself as Eudrice Fish. She claimed to have come from Germany, and to have died in 1957 by suicide. Much of it was garbled."

I took some photographs of the apartment, but none of them showed anything unusual. I had decided there was nothing more I could do in this case, when I received an urgent call from Mrs. Settel.

"Three nights after your visit, Mr. Holzer," she said, "I was lying in bed. It was about 4 A.M., and I was not asleep, having just turned out the lights. Suddenly, the bedsheet was pulled down from around my neck to below my chest. I did not move or attempt to awaken my husband, who was asleep beside me. A few minutes later, the corner of the pillow beneath my head moved *as though it were being tugged,* and I began to sense a presence. The air seemed heavy and expectant, and briefly I felt myself floating again. To my surprise, nothing further occurred, and I fell asleep in about five minutes after that.

"The night before—it was a Thursday; you were here on Tuesday—I went into the bathroom to find the water running in the sink. Neither of us had left it on. We are quite neat about such things. The bathroom also houses our cat, who seems to behave strangely at times lately. Last Christmas we went out and left the bathroom door open for her to go to her sandbox. On our return it was firmly closed—something the cat could not have done!"

I promised to come again, and this time bring Sybil Leek with me to see if contact with the ghost could be made.

Before I came, Mrs. Settel had a strange dream. She saw a male figure, and received the impression that she was very fond of this unknown man. She believed in him, but he was really quite evil. He seemed to be trying to talk her into something, and sway her. She was wondering if the ghost was trying to tell her something about her own life.

When I brought Sybil Leek to the apartment, a change took place in Sybil's face almost as soon as she set foot inside the door. The Victorian staircase and appointments outside had pleased my antique-loving friend, but when she had settled herself into the easy chair in the larger of the two rooms, she said immediately:

"It's not very pleasant here. I feel a person here who died very badly. It's a man. Something affecting his back. There is a younger person with him. They are dark, curly head, the man has a beard. European, Polish. About 1900. Something was lost here."

We adjourned to the bedroom, and Sybil went into trance. Soon she would be deeply "under."

A heavy male voice announced his presence.

"Oscar."

"Do you live here?" I asked.

"Yes."

"Your second name."

"Tratt. Oscar Tratt."

"Where are you from?"

"Efla. Near Cracow."

"What is your profession?"

"Make shoes. Out of wood. Wood shoes."

"Who lives here with you?"

"Mella. Woman. My *Gnaedige Frau.* My wife."

"Whom do you pay rent to?"

"Flynn. Sammy Flynn."

"What year is this?"

"1902."

"How old are you now?"

"Sixty-three."

"Are you well?"

"No. I'm waiting for Ernst to come back."

"Who is Ernst?"

"Mella's boy."

"Your son?"

"Who knows?"

"Why do you want him to come back?"

"Burn him."

"Why?"

"Took too much money from me." The ghost's voice rose in anger. "She let him take it!"

It wasn't clear whether he worked for Mella or whether she was his wife or both.

I continued the questioning.

"Did you get hurt here?"

"Yes, I broke my back. Ernst . . . his door by the steps, on this floor." Now the ghost broke into tears.

"I'm lost . . . find Ernst."

"Is there anyone else here? A woman perhaps?"

You could imagine the ghost shrugging, if ghosts can shrug.

"Common girl. They come and go. Looking for Ernst. Bad. Takes anybody's money . . . my back . . . bad boy."

"What is his family name?"

"Tratt . . . my son."

Schratt or Tratt—I couldn't be quite sure.

The son was about 35 and single, the ghost claimed. He belonged to the Jewish faith, and was somehow connected with a synagogue on Ninety-sixth Street. He also went to school on Ninety-sixth Street.

The ghostly voice began to falter and Oscar complained that he could not remember some things, and that his back hurt him.

"Did you go to the hospital?" I asked.

"No. Stayed here till they come for me."

"Why are you troubled?"

"Lost a lot of money here. Want to make some more shoes."

I began to send him away, gently, but firmly. After he had slipped out of Sybil's body, the medium's own personality reappeared, called back by me.

I asked Sybil, still entranced, to look around and report to me what she observed.

"There are lots of people at the top of the stairs . . . two men and two women. A man is falling down the stairs . . . and a little girl is crying."

"How old is the little girl?"

"Very pretty, like a little foreign girl. She's a servant. Perhaps 20 years old. She has a gray dress with a high neck. She's very unhappy because of what happened. She was upstairs, then she came down and hid in the cupboard . . . here. She was frightened of the young man that he might hurt her."

"Did she know him well?"

"Very well. He liked her."

"Was there anything between her and the young man?"

"Yes. She liked him, but she liked the old people, too. She used to listen to them quarrel."

"What were her duties in this house?"

"She had to look after a lot of gentlemen who lived in this house, but not really after these two here."

"What was her name?"

"Irene . . . Eurine . . . Erundite . . . Eireene." Sybil's voice expressed uncertainty.

"Why is she here?"

"No place to go."

"How did she die?"

"Very sick in her throat . . . died here. She never told anyone about the old man. My throat's bad . . ." Sybil was taking on the "passing symptoms" of the spectral maid.

"How long ago did she die?"

"1912."

Suddenly another person was speaking to us. A very agitated voice calling for "Mella!" Evidently, the servant girl had taken over. The throat seemed to hurt her still. Eventually she calmed down.

"What is your name?" I asked.

"Erundite." It could have been Erundice, or something like that.

"Where were you born?"

"Here . . . 27 London Place . . . down by the river."

I asked her to repeat her name. It now sounded like "Irene Dyke."

Her mother's name, she said, was Martha, and her father's Mostin Dyke. Or it could have been Austin Dyke. The voice was faint.

She did not know where her father came from. Only that it was far away where there were ships.

"What was your work here?"

"Servant. Laundry maid."

"Were there any pets in the house?"

"There was always something to fall over. Parrot. Ten cats."

"Any dogs in the house?"

"Oh, there was this big old monster . . . he was gray."

"Did you take him out?"

"He followed me."

"What sort of clothes did you wear when you served here?"

"Gray dress, and black apron . . . there is no water in the house, you know. Got to get some across the road. Dog fell into the river."

"What year is this?"

"1907–1908."

"Did you have an affair with Ernst?"

"I'm not going to say."

"Did you see him hurt his father?"

"Yes."

"What did you do after that?"

"I came in with Mella and I waited in the cupboard. I cried. Somebody came, that's why I stayed in the cupboard."

"Was Oscar gone then?"

"Think so. Never saw him again."

Everybody, it would seem, accused Ernst. He came back, and she saw him, but then her throat started to bother her.

"Why are you still here?"

"Mella said wait here in the cupboard."

She thought it was 1913. I coaxed her to leave the closet, and to forget about her bad throat.

"1913 I had my worst bad throat. It was very cold by the river. I went back to the cupboard."

"You're free now," I said. "You may leave this cupboard . . . this house . . . and join your loved ones."

Gradually, the tense body of the medium slackened as the servant girl left.

Soon, Sybil Leek was back to her old self.

"I feel fine," she said, and looked around. She remembered nothing of Oscar or the servant girl.

And there it is. How do you trace the name of a servant girl, even so unusual a name as Eurydice, or Irene Dyke, or whatever it was, in a rooming house in 1913? You can't. Telephones were still rare then, and the directories were far from complete.

Needless to say, Sybil knew nothing whatever about "Eurydice" or that a servant girl had been seen here by Mr. Settel. I had kept all that to myself.

Apparently, Oscar has made his peace with Ernst, and the pale young servant girl is forever out of the cupboard. The spot where Mr. Settel had seen her apparition was indeed where an old cupboard had been made into a walk-in closet. As for the big dog, why, there may be a place for him, too, on the other side. At any rate, the Settels have heard, seen, and felt nothing since Sybil's visit.

The Roommate
Problem

I T ALL STARTED WITH MY APPEARANCE on a program called "To Tell the Truth," which, to tell the truth, frequently doesn't— in the interest of good showmanship, of course.

The program, as most Americans remember, consisted of a panel of three or four so-called celebrities, who fired questions at three guests, and tried to determine, by their answers, which one was the real McCoy, and which two were imposters.

I appeared as one of three alleged ghost hunters, two of whom were frauds. One of my imposters, incidentally, was later involved in a real fraud, but my ESP wasn't working well at the time of my meeting with him, or I would have objected to his presence.

I played it cool, appearing neither too knowing nor exactly stupid. Nevertheless, the majority of the panel knew which of us was the Ghost Hunter and I was unmasked. Panelist Phyllis Newman thought I was pale enough to be one of my own ghosts, and comedian Milton Kamen wondered about the love life of my ghosts, to which I deadpanned, "I never invade the private lives of my clients." Artie Shaw wanted to know if I had read a certain book, but of course I had to inform him that I usually read only *The Ghost Hunter*.

Actually, I almost became a ghost myself on this program, for the lights so blinded me I nearly fell off the high stage used to highlight the three guests at the start of the show.

Shortly after my appearance on the show, I received a note from the receptionist of the program, who had apparently read *The Ghost Hunter* and had something of special interest to tell me.

Alice Hille is a young lady of considerable charm, as I later found, whose family was originally from Louisiana, and who had always had an interest in ghost stories and the like.

The experience she was about to report to me concerned a staffer at Goodson-Todman, Frank R., a television producer, and about as levelheaded a man as you'd want to find.

It was he who had had the uncanny experience, but Alice thought I ought to know about it and, if possible, meet him. She wrote me:

It seems that there was a black man named John Gray. He was a personal friend of Frank's. Mr. Gray, who was from the segregated South, had renounced his race and had proceeded to live in the "white world," dressing with only the finest of taste. He died of cancer after a long illness, and his family provided him with a real old-fashioned black Southern funeral. Mr. Gray would have been appalled at the way he was being laid to rest, as he had once said, should he die, he wanted to be cremated, and his ashes spread over the areas of Manhattan where he would not have been allowed to live, had he been known as a black.

Alice then proceeded to tell me of Frank's uncanny experience, and gave me the address of the apartment where it happened.

It took me three or four months to get hold of Frank R. and get the story firsthand. Finally, over a drink at Manhattan's fashionable Sheraton-East Hotel, I was able to pin him down on details.

Frank had met John Gray through his roommate, Bob Blackburn, and they had a genuine friendship even though Frank R. is white and the other two men were black. They, like so many intelligent people, evaluate a man's character rather than the color of his skin.

At the time Bob and Frank lived not far from what was now the haunted apartment, and when they heard that John Gray was ill, they went to see him in the hospital. This was the year 1961. Gray, only thirty-three, knew he was dying. To the last he complained that his friends did not come to visit him often enough. He had odd working hours which often brought him home to his apartment in the middle of the afternoon.

Three months after John Gray's death, the two friends took over his vacated apartment. Not long after, Frank R. found himself alone in the apartment, resting in bed, with a book. It was the middle of the afternoon.

Suddenly, he clearly heard the front door open and close. This was followed by a man's footsteps which could be heard clearly on the bare floor.

"Who is it?" Frank called out, wondering. Only his roommate Bob had a key, and he certainly was not due at that time. There was no reply. The footsteps continued slowly to the bedroom door, which lies to the right of the large living-room area of the small apartment.

He heard the characteristic noise of the bedroom door opening, then closing, and footsteps continuing on through the room towards the bed. There they abruptly stopped.

Frank was terrified, for he could not see anything in the way of a human being. It was 3 P.M., and quite light in the apartment. Sweat started to form on his forehead as he lay still, waiting.

After a moment, he could hear the unseen visitor's footsteps turn around, slowly walk out again, and the noise of the door opening and closing was repeated in the same way as a few moments before. Yet despite the noise, the door did not actually open!

At first Frank thought he was ill, but a quick check showed that he did not suffer from a fever or other unusual state. He decided to put the whole incident out of his mind and within a day or so he had ascribed it to an overactive imagination. What, however, had brought on just this particular imaginary incident, he was never able to say.

He also thought better of telling Bob about it, lest he be branded superstitious or worse. There the matter stood until about six weeks later, when Bob Blackburn had the same experience. Alone in bed, he heard the steps, the doors open and close, but he did not panic. Somehow an incipient psychic sense within him guided him, and he *knew* it was his departed friend, John Gray, paying his former abode a visit.

The atmosphere had taken on a tense, unreal tinge, electrically loaded and somehow different from what it had been only a moment before.

Without thinking twice, Bob Blackburn leaned forward in bed and said in a low, but clear voice, "May your soul rest in peace, John."

With that, the unseen feet moved on, and the footsteps went out the way they had come in. Somehow, after this the two roommates got to discussing their psychic experiences. They compared them and found they had met John Gray's ghost under exactly the same conditions.

They left the apartment for a number of reasons, and it was not until about three years later that the matter became of interest again to Frank R.

At a party in the same neighborhood—Thirty-fourth Street and Third Avenue, New York—one of the guests talked about his friend Vern who had just moved out of a haunted apartment because he could not stand it any longer.

Frank R., listening politely, suddenly realized, by the description, that Minor was talking about John Gray's old apartment.

"People are walking all over the place," Vern was quoted as saying, and he had moved out, a complete nervous wreck.

The apartment remained empty for a while, even though the rent was unusually low. The building passed into the hands of the owners of a fish restaurant downstairs. Most of the tenants in the five-story walkup were quiet artists or business people. The building was well kept and the narrow staircase revealed a number of smallish, but cozy flatls, of which Manhattan never has enough to satisfy the needs of the younger white-collar workers and artists.

John Gray must have been quite comfortable in these surroundings and the apartment on Third Avenue probably was a haven and refuge to him from the not-so-friendly world in which he had lived.

"Very interesting," I said, thanking Frank R. for his story. I asked if he himself had had other psychic experiences.

"Well, I'm Irish," he said, and smiled knowingly, "and I'm sort of intuitive a lot of times. When I was very young, I once warned my mother not to go to the beach on a certain day, or she would drown. I was only fourteen years old at the time. Mother went, and did have an accident. Almost drowned, but she was pulled out just in time."

"That explains it," I said. "You must be psychic in order to experience the footsteps. Those who have uncanny experiences are mediumistic to begin with, otherwise they would not have heard or seen the Uncanny."

Frank R. nodded. He quite understood and, moreover, was willing to attend a seance I was going to try to arrange if I could talk to the present occupants of the haunted apartment. On this note we parted company, and Frank promised to make inquiries of the landlord as to whether the apartment was still vacant.

Apartment 5A was far from empty. A young and attractive couple by the name of Noren had occupied it for the past six months.

When I called and identified myself, they were puzzled about the nature of my business.

"Do you by any chance hear footsteps where no one is walking, or do you experience anything unusual in your apartment?" I asked innocently.

It was like a bombshell. There was a moment of stunned silence, then Mrs. Noren answered, "Why, yes, as a matter of fact, we do. Can you help us?"

The following day I went to visit them at the haunted apartment. Mr. Noren, a film editor for one of the networks, had not had any unusual experiences up to that time. But his wife had. Two or three months before my visit, when she was in the shower one evening, she suddenly and distinctly heard footsteps in the living room. Thinking it was her husband and that something was wrong, she rushed out only to find him still fast asleep in the bedroom. They decided it must have been he, walking in his sleep!

But a few weeks later, she heard the footsteps again. This time there was no doubt in her mind—they had a ghost.

I arranged for a seance on July 22, 1964, to make contact with the ghost.

My medium was Ethel Johnson Meyers, who was, of course, totally unaware of the story or purpose of our visit.

Among those present were three or four friends of the Norens, Frank R., Bob Blackburn, Alice Hille, an editor, Mrs. Harrington, a student of psychic science, the Norens, my wife, Catherine, myself— and two tiny black kittens who, in complete defiance of all tradition laid down for familiars and black cats in general, paid absolutely no attention to the ghost. Possibly they had not yet been told how to behave.

In a brief moment of clairvoyance, Ethel Meyers described two men who were attached to the place: one a white-haired gentleman whom Bob Blackburn later acknowledged as his late father, and a "dark-complexioned man," not old, not terribly young.

"He is looking at you and you," she said, not knowing the names of the two men. Frank and Bob tensed up in expectation. "He looks at you with one eye, sort of," she added. She then complained of breathing difficulties and I remembered that John Gray had spent his last hours in an oxygen tent.

Suddenly, the ghost took over. With a shriek, Mrs. Meyers fell to the floor and, on her knees, struggled over to where Bob Blackburn and Frank sat. Picking out these two contacts from among the many present was a sure sign of accuracy, I thought. Naturally, Mrs. Meyers knew nothing of their connection with the case of the ghost.

She grabbed Bob Blackburn's hand amid heavy sobs, and the voice emanating now from her throat was a deep masculine voice, with a trace of a Southern accent. "It's a dream," he mumbled, then began to complain that Bob had not come to visit him!

Soothing words from Bob Blackburn and myself calmed the excited spirit.

When I tried to tell him that he was "dead," however, I was given a violent argument.

"He's mad," the ghost said, and sought solace from his erstwhile friend.

"No, John, he's right," Bob said.

"You too?" the ghost replied and hesitated.

This moment was what I had hoped for. I proceeded to explain what had happened to him. Gradually, he understood, but refused to go.

"Where can I go?" he said. "This is my house."

I told him to think of his parents, and join them in this manner.

"They're dead," he replied.

"So are you," I said.

Finally I requested the assistance of Ethel's control, Albert, who came and gently led the struggling soul of John Gray over to the "Other Side" of life.

"He isn't all there in the head," he commented, as he placed the medium back into her chair quickly. "Narcotics before passing have made him less than rational."

Was there any unsettled personal business? I wanted to know.

"Personal wishes, yes. Not all they should have been."

Albert explained that he had brought John's parents to take his arm and help him across, away from the apartment which had, in earth life, been the only refuge where he could really be "off guard."

An hour after trance had set on Mrs. Meyers, she was back in full command of her own body, remembering absolutely nothing of either the trance experience with John Gray, or her fall to the floor.

It was a steaming hot July night as we descended the four flights of stairs to Third Avenue, but I felt elated at the thought of having John Gray roam no more where he was not wanted.

The Specter in
the Hallway

PORT WASHINGTON IS A BUSY LITTLE TOWN on Long Island, about forty-five minutes from New York City. A lot of people who live there commute daily to their jobs downtown or midtown, and the flavor of the town is perhaps less rustic than other places further out on Long Island. Still, there are a few back roads and quiet lanes that are as quiet and removed from the pace of Main Street as any small town might boast. Such a street is Carlton, and a house in about the middle of the block not far from the waterfront fits the description of a country home to a tee. It is a two-story wooden structure about fifty years old, well-preserved and obviously redecorated from time to time. The house sits back from the street on a plot of land, and all in all, one could easily overlook it if one were not directly searching for it. There is nothing spectacular about this house on Carlton, and to this day the neighbors think of it only as a nice, old house usually owned by nice, respectable people whose lives are no different from theirs and whose problems are never of the kind that make headlines.

But the house behind the nice, old trees has not always been so pleasant looking. When Mr. and Mrs. F. first saw it, it was nothing more than a dilapidated shell of its former splendor, yet it was imbued with a certain nobility that translated itself, in their minds, into the hope of being capable of restoration, provided someone lavished enough care and money on the place. Mr. F. was not wealthy, but he had a going business and could afford a good-sized house.

Mrs. F.'s own father had been involved in the building of the house on Carlton though she did not realize it at the time she first saw it. He had been in the building trade in this town, and Mrs. F. had grown up here. It seemed the natural thing to her to settle in a town she was familiar with, now that their two girls were of school age, and she had to think of the future. The house was for sale and as they walked through it they realized that it had been neglected for some time. The real estate man was properly vague about previous owners, and would say only that it had been built by respectable people fifty-three years ago, and they could have it very reasonably. Real estate agents are not historians, they are not even concerned with the present, but only the near future: tomorrow's sale and commission. If the F.'s did not want to buy the old house, sooner or later someone else would, or perhaps the house could be torn down and another one built here. The land was almost more valuable than the house itself. Suburbia was stretching further and further and Port Washington was a most convenient location.

But the F.'s did buy the house in 1961 and even though the place was a shambles, they managed to move in right away and live in it while they were restoring and redecorating it. There were twelve rooms in all, on two floors. A broad staircase with two landings led up to the second story. The second landing led directly into a hallway. To the left was the master bedroom, to the right a second bedroom they turned over to their two girls, aged thirteen and eight. The first few days were busy ones indeed, as the family tried to settle down in unfamiliar surroundings. Mr. F. worked in the city, and the girls were in school mornings, so Mrs. F. was alone in the house a good part of the day. The master bedroom in particular was an eyesore, dark and forbidding as it was, and wholly depressing to her.

She decided to start work immediately on the bedroom, and had it painted white. That caused some problems in the mornings when one wanted to sleep late, for they had morning sun, and the white walls made the room even brighter. But this occasional inconvenience was more than offset by the general cheerfulness the change in color gave the room. Mrs. F. felt optimistic about the house and was sure it would make a splendid home for them.

One day soon after their arrival, she was hanging curtains in the bedroom. Suddenly she felt a hostile glare in back of her and turned to see who had entered the room. There was no one to be seen. And yet, she was sure another person was next to her in the room, a person whose hatred she could literally feel!

Immediately, Mrs. F. put down the curtains and left the house. For a few hours, she went shopping in town. As it became time to return home, she dismissed the whole incident as imagination. She had no interest in the occult even though over the years she had shown a marked degree of ESP powers. Whenever someone close to her, or even a mere acquaintance, was involved in a tragedy, she knew it beforehand. Often she would anticipate what someone was about to say to her, but she had learned to play down this peculiar talent lest people in the community might think her an oddball. If anything, she hated being "different," or causing her husband dismay for leanings that did not sit well with his employers or the people they socialized with.

Shortly after this incident, she was in bed asleep when she awoke to the incessant ringing of the telephone. The telephone was downstairs, so she got up and started on her way down the stairs to answer it. Who would call them at that hour? Theirs was an unlisted number.

She was fully awake as she reached the stairs. The phone was still demanding her attention. As she put one foot onto the top step, she felt herself pushed by unseen hands and fell down to the first landing. As soon as she fell, the telephone stopped ringing. As a consequence of this "accident," she was crippled for several months. Her husband ascribed the fall to her drowsiness, but she knew better. She had felt a hard push in the back: she had not slipped on the stairs. They patiently went over the entire list of those who had their unlisted phone number. None of them had called.

From this moment on, her optimistic outlook about the house changed. She longed for the time she could be outside the house, have the choice of running away from it when she felt like it. But her legs were still bruised and the time passed slowly.

Then one evening, while her husband was out, she sat quietly in the living room downstairs, reading a book. For some unexplainable reason, she suddenly felt that someone was watching her. She lifted her eyes from the book, turned, and glanced up at the stairway. There, at the very spot where she had fallen, stood a man. His face was in the shadows, but he was tall and wearing dark clothes. She stared at the figure with amazement for several moments. When she was fully aware of it, the apparition vanished, as if it had only wanted to let her know of its presence.

Too horrified to move from the chair, Mrs. F. just sat there until her husband returned. She knew the man on the stairs wanted her to come up to him, but she could not bring herself to do it. Neither could she tell her husband what had happened.

Much later, when she confided in him, she found out that he did not think her mad, and his compassion only increased their deep affection for each other.

The larger incidents were accompanied by a continuing plethora of odd sounds, creaking noises on the stairs or in the master bedroom. Most of the latter noises she had heard downstairs in the living room, which was located directly underneath the master bedroom. Old houses make odd noises, she rationalized to herself, and probably the house was just settling. But to make sure, she decided to call in some termite specialists. They came and removed paneling from some of the basement walls in that part of the house and gave the place a thorough examination. As she watched, they inspected the beams and the foundation of the house. They found nothing. The house was neither settling nor shifting, the experts explained, thus removing the pat explanation Mrs. F. had given to herself for the odd noises. She wished she had never called in the termite experts, for now that she knew there were no natural causes for the disturbances, what was she to do?

So far neither her husband nor her children had noticed anything odd, or if they had, they had not said anything to her. Mrs. F. dreaded the thought of discussing such matters with her children. One night she busied herself in the living room after dinner. Her husband was out and the two girls were presumably in their own room upstairs. Suddenly there was a loud thumping and knocking overhead in the master bedroom.

"The girls are out of their beds," she thought, and called up to them to go back to bed immediately. There was no reply. When she went upstairs to check, she found both girls fast asleep in their room. She went back to continue her chores in the living room. Immediately, the noises started up again overhead. Despite her fears that he was up there waiting for her, Mrs. F. went up again. There were seven doors opening onto that hallway and yet she knew immediately which door he was lurking behind: her bedroom's. She turned around and grabbed the banister of the stairs firmly. This time he wasn't going to push her down again. Slowly, she descended the stairs. She knew in her heart the specter would not follow her down. His domain was the upstairs part of the house. She soon realized that the uncanny house guest had his limitations as far as movements were concerned and it gave her unsuspected strength:

she knew he could not follow her outside, or even into the living room; there she was safe from him. Often, when she was outside in the yard, she could *feel* him peering out at her, watching, always watching with slow-burning eyes. When she went out to the market and closed the door behind her, a wave of hatred hit her from inside the empty house. He resented being left alone. Had the ghostly presence developed an attachment toward her?

Psychic feelings had been a subject studiously avoided by Mrs. F. in her conversations, but when she mentioned her problem accidentally to her mother, she was surprised to find not a questioning gaze but an understanding acknowledgment.

"I too have always felt there is someone in the house," her mother admitted, "but I think it's friendly."

Mrs. F. shook her head. She knew better. Her mother then suggested that a portrait of Jesus be placed in the entrance foyer to ward off "evil influences." Mrs. F. was not religious, but under the circumstances, she was willing to try *anything*. So a portrait of Christ was duly placed in the foyer at the landing. It apparently made a difference, for the presence of the man in black faded away from the spot from that day. However, he was as strongly present as ever in the bedroom.

One night, the F.'s intimate relationship was literally interrupted by the ghostly presence, and it took them years to get over the shock. They could never be sure that they were truly "alone," and even if they moved to another room, Mrs. F. feared the jealous specter would follow them there.

During the day, she continuously felt a call to go up to the bedroom, but she never went when she was alone in the house. That was "his" domain and she had hers in the downstairs area of the house.

One evening, while her husband was taking a shower, she felt encouraged enough to venture alone into the bedroom. A thought ran through her mind, "Why, he isn't here after all!" Scarcely had she finished thinking this, when she clearly heard a voice shout into her ear: "I am here!" And as if to underscore his presence, a necktie rose off its clasp and placed itself on her shoulder!

Mrs. F. tried to behave as if that happened every day of her life. As if speaking to herself she said, aloud, "Oh, stupid tie, falling like that!" But she knew she was not fooling him, that he knew he had terribly frightened her with this performance. That was the straw that broke the camel's back.

The same evening, she and her husband had a quiet discussion about the house. They both loved it and they had spent considerable money and much time in fixing it up. It was most inconvenient to move after only four years. But what were they to do? Share it forever with a ghost?

She found that her husband had felt odd in the house for a long time also, and had thought of selling it. While he failed to see how a ghost could possibly harm them—having had plenty of chances to do so and not having done so, apart from the "accident" on the stairs he did not wish to subject his family to any form of terror.

They placed an ad in *The New York Times* and listed their telephone number for the first time. At least, Mrs. F. thought, if the phone rang now, it would be someone calling about the house, not a ghost trying to rouse her from deep sleep.

But houses do not always sell overnight, especially old ones. They wanted to sell the house, but they didn't want to lose money. Still, having made the decision to move eventually made things easier for Mrs. F. She was even able to muster some curiosity about their unbidden guest and made inquiries among neighbors, especially some old-timers who knew the area well. Nobody, however, could shed any light on the situation. Of course, Mrs. F. did not come right out and speak of her experiences in the house, but she did ask if any unusual events had ever occurred in it or what the history of the house had been. Still, the result was not encouraging and they realized they would leave the house without ever knowing who it was that had caused them to do so!

Then Mrs. F. discovered that she was, after all, a natural medium. She would simply sit back in her chair and rest and gradually her senses would become clouded and another person would speak to her directly. It felt as if that person was very close to her and she could take the message the way a telegraph operator takes down a telegram, word for word, and the more relaxed she was and the less fear she showed, the more clear the words were to her.

She fought this at first, but when she realized that it meant only more discomfort, she relaxed. Then, too, she knew the specter would not harm her—their relationship had somehow changed since the time he had pushed her down those stairs. She felt no fear of him, only compassion, and sensed he needed help badly and that she was willing to extend it to him.

While they were waiting for a buyer for the house, she would often lapse into semiconsciousness and commune with her tormentor, who had now become a kind of friend. Gradually she pieced together his story and began to understand his reasons for doing what he was doing to get her attention. As she listened to the ghost, his anger gave way to an eagerness to be heard and understood.

A young man of about seventeen and of small build, he had light hair, high cheekbones, and deep-set eyes. At that tender age he was lost at sea as a member of the Canadian Navy. A French Canadian, he desperately wanted her to deliver a message to someone, but she was unable to clearly get either the message or the name of the individual. Perhaps the very emotionalism of such an attempt caused its failure. But she did get the name of his ship, something that sounded to her like Tacoma. Whenever Mrs. F. awoke from her trance state, that word stood strongly in her mind. Finally she wrote to the United States Navy Department. Unfortunately, there had been four ships by that name! But her intuition told her to contact the Canadian Navy also. The boy had been lost during World War II, while on duty, and while she did not have his name, perhaps the name of the ship could be traced. No, the Canadians did not have a Tacoma, but they did have a mine sweeper named Transcona, and instantly she felt that was the right ship. It had been in war service from 1942 to 1945.

As her inquiries went on, she felt the atmosphere in the house change. It was no longer heavy with frustration, but the presence was still there. Twice during that month he was seen by the children. The thirteen-year-old girl wanted to know who was "the big boy walking back and forth in the hallway all night" and Mrs. F. told her she had dreamed it all, for there was no one in the hall that night.

Either unable or unwilling to question this explanation, the girl thought no further about it. The younger girl, however, reported another incident a few days later. She knew nothing of her older sister's experience. As she was bathing, a young man had opened the door and then turned and walked into her sister's room! Mrs. F. was hard put to explain that away, but eventually she managed to calm the little girl.

But despite Mrs. F.'s willingness to let him communicate with her in trance, the young man was unable to give either his name or that of the person whom he tried to reach. His own emotions were still pitched high from the sudden death he had suffered and he did not know how to cope with the situation.

In October of that year, after a wait of half a year, they sold the house. The new owner was a police officer in retirement with little sympathy for ghosts. Both he and his wife were devout Catholics and any suggestion at investigating the disturbances to free the unfortunate soul was simply not answered. The F.'s had moved out but stayed in town, so they could not help hearing some of the local gossip concerning the house.

If the police officer was bothered by the ghostly sailor, he certainly did not speak of it to anyone. But word of mouth was that the new owners were disappointed with their new home: it wasn't as happy a place to them as they had anticipated when they bought it. Lots of little things were going wrong seemingly for no apparent reasons. For example, no matter how often the bedroom door was opened, it would "close itself."

Mrs. F. smiled wryly, for she remembered that the ghostly sailor always liked that door open. She, too, had closed it to have privacy, only to find it opened by unseen hands. Finally, she understood that it wasn't curiosity or evil thoughts on his part, but simple loneliness, the desire not to be shut out from the world, and she left it open, the way he wanted it.

How long would it take the lieutenant to understand the lad? She mused and wondered if perhaps he could leave the house of his own free will, now that he had told her at least part of his story. Shortly after, the F.'s moved to Florida. They wondered if the power for the manifestations had come from their young daughters, who were at the time of "poltergeist" age. If so, the police lieutenant would have the same problem: he had children of his own.

When the Dead Stay On

NOTHING IS SO EXASPERATING as a dead person in a living household. I mean a ghost has a way of disturbing things far beyond the powers held by the wraith while still among the quick. Very few people realize that a ghost is not someone out to pester you for the sake of being an annoyance, or to attract attention for the sake of being difficult. Far from it. We know by now that ghosts are unhappy beings caught between two states and unable to adjust to either one.

Most people "pass over" without difficulty and are rarely heard from again, except when a spiritualist insists on raising them, or when an emergency occurs among the family that makes intervention by the departed a desired, or even necessary, matter.

They do their bit, and then go again, looking back at their handiwork with justified pride. *The dead are always among us*, make no mistake about that. They obey their own set of laws that forbids them to approach us or let us know their presence except when conditions require it. But they can do other things to let us feel them near, and these little things can mean a great deal when they are recognized as sure signs of a loved one's nearness.

Tragedies create ghosts through shock conditions, and nothing can send them out of the place where they found a sad end except the realization of their own emotional entanglement. This can be accomplished by allowing them to communicate through trance. But there are also cases in which the tragedy is not sudden, but gradual, and the unnatural attachment to physical life creates the ghost syndrome. The person who refuses to accept peacefully the transition called death, and holds on to material surroundings, becomes a ghost when these feelings of resistance and attachment become psychotic.

Such persons will then regard the houses they lived and died in as still theirs, and will look on later owners or tenants as merely unwanted intruders who must be forced out of the place by any means available. The natural way to accomplish this is to show themselves to the living as often as possible, to assert their continued ownership. If that won't do it, move objects, throw things, make noises—let them know whose house this is!

The reports of such happenings are many. Every week there were new cases from reliable and verified witnesses, and the pattern emerges pretty clearly.

A lady from Ridgewood, New York, wrote to me about a certain house on Division Avenue in Brooklyn, where she had lived as a child. A young grandmother, Mrs. Petre had a good education and an equally good memory. She remembered the name of her landlord while she was still a youngster, and even the names of all her teachers at Public School 19. The house her family had rented consisted of a basement, parlor floor, and a top floor where the bedrooms were located.

On a certain warm October day, she found herself in the basement, while her mother was upstairs. She knew there was no one else in the house. When she glanced at the glass door shutting off the stairs, with the glass pane acting almost like a mirror, she saw to her amazement a man peeking around the doorway. Moments before she had heard heavy footsteps coming down the stairs, and wondered if someone had gotten into the house while she and her mother had been out shopping. She screamed and ran out of the house, but did not tell her family about the stranger.

Sometime after, she sat facing the same stairs in the company of her brother and sister-in-law, when she heard the footsteps again and the stranger appeared. Only this time she got a good look at him and was able to describe his thin, very pale face, his black hair, and the black suit and fedora hat he wore.

Nobody believed the girl, of course, and even the landlady accused her of imagining all this. But after a year, her father became alarmed at his daughter's nervousness and decided to move. Finally, the landlady asked for details of the apparition, and listened as the girl described the ghost she had seen.

"My God," the landlady, a Mrs. Grimshaw, finally said. "I knew that man—he hanged himself on the top floor!"

Sometimes the dead will only stay on until things have been straightened out to their taste. Anna Arrington was a lady with the gift of mediumship who lived in New York State. In 1944, her mother-in-law, a woman of some wealth, passed on in Wilmington, North Carolina, and was buried there. There was some question about her will. Three days after her death, Mrs. Arrington was awakened from heavy sleep at 3 A.M. by a hand touching hers.

Her first thought was that one of her two children wanted something. On awakening, however, she saw her mother-in-law in a flowing white gown standing at the foot of her bed. While her husband continued to snore, the ghost put a finger to Mrs. Arrington's lips and asked her not to awaken her son, but to remember that the missing will was in the dining room of her house on top of the dish closet under a sugar bowl. Mrs. Arrington was roundly laughed at by her husband the next morning, but several days later his sister returned from Wilmington (the Arringtons lived in New York City at the time) and confirmed that the will had indeed been found where the ghost had indicated.

Back in the 1960s, I was approached by a gentleman named Paul Herring, who was born in Germany, and who lived in a small apartment on Manhattan's Eastside as well as in a country house in Westchester County, New York. He was in the restaurant business and not given to dreaming or speculation. He struck me as a simple, solid citizen. His aged mother, also German-born, lived with him, and a large German shepherd dog completed the household.

Mr. Herring was not married, and his mother was a widow. What caused them to reach me was the peculiar way in which footsteps were heard around their Westchester house when nobody was walking. On three separate occasions, Mrs. Herring saw an apparition in her living room.

"It was sort of blackish," she said, "but I recognized it instantly. It was my late husband."

The "black outline" of a man also appeared near light fixtures, and there were noises in the house that had no natural origins.

"The doors are forever opening and closing by themselves," the son added. "We're going crazy trying to keep up with that spook."

Their bedspreads were being pulled off at night. They were touched on the face by an unseen hand, especially after dark.

The September before, Mrs. Herring was approaching the swinging doors of the living room, when the door moved out by itself and met her! A table in the kitchen moved by its own volition in plain daylight.

Her other son, Max, who lived in Norfolk, Virginia, always left the house in a hurry because "he can't breathe" in it. Her dog, Noxy, was forever disturbed when they were out in the Westchester house.

"How long has this been going on, Mrs. Herring?" I asked.

"About four years at least," the spunky lady replied, "but my husband died ten years ago."

It then developed that he had divorced her and married another woman, and there were no surviving children from that union. Still, the "other woman" had kept all of Mr. Herring Sr.'s money—no valid will was ever found. Was the ghost protesting this injustice to his companion of so many years? Was he regretting his hasty step divorcing her and marrying another?

The Herrings weren't the only ones to hear the footsteps. A prospective tenant who came to rent the country house fled after hearing someone walk *through a closed door.*

Mrs. E. F. Newbold seemed to have been followed by ghosts since childhood as if she were carrying a lamp aloft to let the denizens of the nether world know she had the sixth sense.

"I'm haunted," she said. "I've been followed by a 'what's it' since I was quite young. It simply pulls the back of my skirt. No more than that, but when you're alone in the middle of a room, this can be awfully disconcerting."

Mrs. Newbold's family had psychic experiences also. Her little girl had felt a hand on her shoulder. It ran in the family.

"My husband's aunt died in Florida, while I was in New Jersey. We had been very close, and I said good-bye to her body here at the funeral at 10 A.M. At 9 P.M. I went into my kitchen and though I could not see her, I *knew* she was sitting at the table, staring at my back, and pleading with me."

"What about this skirt pulling?"

"It has followed me through a house, an apartment, a succession of rented rooms, two new houses, and two old houses. I've had a feeling of not being alone, and of sadness. I've also felt a hand on my shoulder, and heard pacing footsteps, always overhead.

"The next house we lived in was about 35 years old, had had only one owner, still alive, and no one had died there. It looked like a haunted house, but it was only from neglect. We modernized it, and *then* it started! Pulling at my skirt went on fairly often. One night when I was alone, that is, my husband was out of town and our three children were sound asleep—I checked them just before and just after—I was watching TV in the living room, when I heard the outside cellar door open. I looked out the window to see if someone was breaking in, since I had locked the door shortly before. While I was watching, I heard it close firmly. The door didn't move, however. This door had a distinctive sound so I couldn't have mistaken it.

"I went back to my seat and picked up my scissors, wishing for a gun. I was sure I heard a prowler. Now I heard slow footsteps come up from the cellar, through the laundry room, kitchen, into the living room, right past me, and up the stairs to the second floor. They stopped at the top of the stairs, and I never heard it again. Nor do I want to. Those steps went past me, no more than five feet away, and the room was empty. Unfortunately, I have no corroboration, but I was wide awake and perfectly sober!"

So much for the lady from Harrington Park, New Jersey.

Miss Margaret C. and her family lived in what surely was a haunted house, so that I won't give her full name. But here is her report.

"In December of 1955, just two days before Christmas, I traveled to Pennsylvania to spend the holidays with my sister and her husband. They lived on the second floor (the apartment I am now renting) of a spacious mid-Victorian-style home built around a hundred years ago.

"Due to the death of my sister's mother-in-law, who had resided on the first floor of the house, the occasion was not an entirely joyous one, but we came for the sake of my brother-in-law.

"We had come all the way from Schenectady, New York, and we retired between ten-thirty and eleven o'clock. The room I slept in was closest to the passage leading to the downstairs, and the two were separated only by a door.

"Once in bed, I found it rather difficult to sleep. As I lay there, I heard a piano playing. It sounded like a very old piano and it played church music. I thought it quite strange that my brother-in-law's father would be listening to his radio at that hour, but felt more annoyed than curious.

"The next morning, as we were having coffee, I mentioned this to my sister. She assured me that her father-in-law would *not* be listening to the radio at that hour and I assured *her* that I *had* heard piano music. It was then she mentioned the old piano her husband's mother had owned for many years and which sat in the downstairs front room.

"We decided to go and have a look at it. The dust that had settled on the keyboard was quite thick, and as definite as they could possibly be were the imprints of someone's fingers. Not normal fingers, but apparently quite thin and bony fingers. My sister's mother-in-law had been terribly thin and she loved to play her piano, especially church music. There was positively no one else in the house who even knew how to play the piano."

Another New Jersey lady named Louise B., whose full name and address I have in my files, told me of an experience she will never forget.

"I cannot explain why I am sending this on to you, merely that I feel compelled to do so, and after many years of following my compulsions, as I call them, must do so.

"My mother had a bachelor cousin who died and was buried around Valentine's Day, 1932. He had lived with two maiden aunts in Ridgewood, New Jersey, for most of his lifetime. He was a well-known architect in this area. He designed local monuments, one of which is standing in the Park in Ridgewood today. He was short of stature, with piercing eyes and a bushy gray full beard, and he smoked too many cigars. I was not quite 14 years old when he passed away.

"My parents decided to spare me the burial detail, and they left me at home on the way to the cemetery with instructions to stay at home until they returned. They planned on attending the burial, going back to the house with my great-aunts and then coming home before dinner, which in our house was 6 P.M.

"I have no recollection of what I did with my time in the afternoon, but remember that just before dusk I had gone indoors and at the time I was in our dining room, probably setting the table for dinner, as this was one of my chores.

"We had three rooms downstairs: the living room faced north and ran the full length of the house, while the kitchen and dining room faced southeast and southwest respectively, and a T-shaped partition divided the rooms. There was a large archway separating the dining and living rooms.

"I don't recall when I became aware of a 'presence.' I didn't see anything with my eyes, rather I felt what I 'saw,' or somehow sensed it and my sense 'saw.' This is not a good explanation, but about the closest I can come to what I felt.

"This presence was not in any one spot in the room, but something that was gradually surrounding me, like the air that I was breathing, and it was frightening and menacing and very evil and stronger, and somehow the word *denser* seemed to apply and I knew that it was 'Uncle' Oscar. I could feel him coming at me from every direction (like music that gets louder and louder), and my senses 'saw' him as he had been dressed in the casket, with a red ribbon draped across his chest, only he was alive and I was aware of some terrible determination on his part and suddenly I knew that somehow he was trying to 'get inside me' and I began to back away. I don't recall speaking, nor his speaking to me. I just knew what his intention was and who he was. I last remember screaming helplessly and uselessly at him to go away. I do not know how long this lasted. I only know that suddenly he was gone, and my parents came into the room. I was hysterical, they tell me, and it took some doing to quiet me."

Many years later Mrs. B. discovered that "Uncle" Oscar had died a raving maniac to the last.

Grace Rivers was a secretary by profession, a lady of good background, and not given to hallucinations or emotional outbursts. I had spoken with her several times and always found her most reluctant to discuss what to her seemed incredible.

It seemed that on weekends, Miss Rivers and another friend, by the name of Juliet, were the house guests of their employer, John Bergner, in Westbrook, Connecticut. Miss Rivers was also a good friend of this furniture manufacturer, a man in his middle fifties. She had joined the Bergner firm years before, about six years after John Bergner had become the owner of the Westbrook country house built in 1865.

Bergner liked to spend his weekends among his favorite employees, and sometimes asked some of the office workers to come up to Connecticut with him. All was most idyllic until the early 1950s, when John Bergner met an advertising man by the name of Philip Mervin. This business relationship soon broadened into a social friendship, and before long Mr. Mervin was a steady and often self-invited house guest in Westbrook.

At first, this did not disturb anyone very much, but when Mervin noticed the deep and growing friendship between Bergner and his right-hand girl, something akin to jealousy prompted him to interfere with this relationship at every turn. What made this triangle even more difficult for Mervin to bear was the apparent innocence with which Bergner treated Mervin's approaches. Naturally, a feeling of dislike grew into hatred between Miss Rivers and the intruder, but before it came to any open argument, the advertising man suddenly died of a heart attack at age 51.

But that did not seem to be the end of it by a long shot.

Soon after his demise, the Connecticut weekends were again interrupted, this time by strange noises no natural cause could account for. Most of the uncanny experiences were witnessed by both women as well as by some of the office men, who seemed frightened by it all. With the detachment of a good executive secretary, Miss Rivers lists the phenomena:

Objects moving in space.

Stones hurled at us inside and outside the house.

Clanging of tools in the garage at night (when nobody was there).

Washing machine starting up at 1 A.M., *by itself*.

Heavy footsteps, banging of doors, in the middle of the night.

Television sets turning themselves on and off at will.

A spoon constantly leaping out of a cutlery tray.

The feeling of a cold wind being swept over one.

And there was more, much more.

When a priest was brought to the house to exorcise the ghost, things only got worse. Evidently the deceased had little regard for holy men.

Juliet, another office worker, brought her fiancé along. One night in 1962, when Juliet's fiancé slept in what was once the advertising man's favorite guest room, he heard clearly a series of knocks, as if someone were hitting the top of the bureau. Important to mention, her fiancé had been alone in the room, and he did not do the knocking.

It became so bad that Grace Rivers no longer looked forward to those weekend invitations at her employer's country home. She feared them. It was then that she remembered, with terrifying suddenness, a remark the late Mr. Mervin had made to her fellow workers.

"If anything ever happens to me and I die, I'm going to walk after those two girls the rest of their lives!" he had said.

Miss Rivers realized that he was keeping his word.

Her only hope was that the ghost of Mr. Mervin would someday be distracted by an earlier specter that was sharing the house with him. On several occasions, an old woman in black had been seen emerging from a side door of the house. A local man, sitting in front of the house during the weekdays when it was unoccupied—Bergner came up only on weekends—was wondering aloud to Miss Rivers about the "old lady who claimed she occupied the back part of the house." He had encountered her on many occasions, always seeing her disappear into the house by that same, seldom-used, side door. One of the office workers invited by Tom Bergner also saw her around 1:30 A.M. on a Sunday morning, when he stood outside the house, unable to go to sleep. When she saw him she said hello, mentioned something about money, then disappeared into a field.

Grace Rivers looked into the background of the house and discovered that it had previously belonged to a very aged man who lived there with his mother. When she died, he found money buried in the house, but he claimed his mother had hidden more money that he had never been able to locate. Evidently the ghost of his mother felt the same way about it, and was still searching. For that's how it is with ghosts sometimes—they become forgetful about material things.

Do the Barrymores
Still Live Here?

PAULA DAVIDSON WAS A CHARMING, introspective young woman from Cleveland, Ohio, who decided that a career in the entertainment field could be best achieved by moving to Los Angeles. In 1969 she arrived in Beverly Hills and took a job with a major advertising agency. The job was fine, but there was something peculiar about the house into which she had moved. In the first place, it was far too large to be a one-family home, and yet she had been told that it once belonged to one family—the family of Lionel Barrymore. Perched high in the Hollywood Hills, the house gave a deceptive impression if one approached it from the street. From that side it presented only two stories, but the rear of the house looked down into a deep ravine, perhaps as much as five or six stories deep. There was even a private cable car, no longer in use. The once beautiful gardens had long since fallen into disrepair and presented a picture of sad neglect.

On the whole, the house was the kind of palatial mansion a Barrymore would have felt at home in. Although the gardens had been neglected for years, the house itself was still bright, having been painted recently, and its Spanish décor added to the mystique of its background. When Paula Davidson took up residence there, the owner had been forced to sublet part of the house in order to hold on to the house itself. One of the rooms in what used to be the former servants' quarters was rented to Heidi, a composer who wrote musical scores for films. She was in the habit of practicing her music in the music room on the first level. Since the house was quiet during the daytime, everyone having gone off to work, Heidi liked to practice during that part of the day. In the stillness of the empty house she would frequently hear footsteps approaching as if someone unseen were listening to her playing. On one occasion she clearly heard a baby cry when there was no baby in the house.

I promised Paula to look into the matter, and on May 31, 1969, she picked me up at the Continental Hotel to take me to the Barrymore mansion. With us was another friend named Jill Taggart. Jill had worked with me before. A writer and sometime model, Jill had displayed ESP talents at an early age and shown amazing abilities with clairvoyance and psychometry. It occurred to me that taking her to a place she knew nothing about, without telling her where we were going and why, might yield some interesting results. Consequently I avoided discussing anything connected with the purpose of our visit.

When we arrived at the mansion, the owner of the house greeted us cordially. Paula, Heidi, the owner and I started out following Jill around the house as my psychic friend tried to get her bearings. Unfortunately, however, we had picked an evening when some of the other tenants in the house were having a party. What greeted us on our arrival was not the serene stillness of a night in the Hollywood Hills but the overly loud blaring of a jukebox and the stamping of many feet in one of the basement rooms.

I had never worked under worse conditions. Under the circumstances, however, we had no choice but to try to get whatever we could. Even before we entered the house Jill remarked that she felt two people, a man and a woman, hanging on in the atmosphere, and she had the feeling that someone was watching us. Then she added, "She died a long time after he did." I questioned her further about the entities she felt present. "She's old; he's young. He must have been in his thirties; she is considerably older. I get the feeling of him as a memory. Perhaps only her memory of him, but whichever one of the entities is here, it is madder than hell at the moment." With the noise of the music going on downstairs I couldn't rightly blame the ghost for being mad. Jill then pointed at a corner of the house and said, "I keep seeing the corner of the house up there."

I later discovered that the top room was a kind of ballroom with a balcony. In it Heidi frequently heard a telephone all times of the day, and there was never anyone up there.

Jill was passing by us now. "I picked up a name," she said. "Grace—and then there is something that sounds like Hugen." I looked at the owner of the house. Jill was out of earshot again. "The party who had the house before us was Arty Erin," the owner said, shrugging.

"Did anyone ever die of violence in this house?" I asked.

"I've heard rumors, something having to do with the cable car, but I don't know for sure."

We all walked over to the cable car, covered with rust and dirt and long out of commission. Jill placed her hands on it to see if she could get any psychometric impression from it. "This cable car has been much loved, I should say, and much enjoyed." Then her facial expression changed to one of absolute horror. Quickly she took her hands off the cable car.

"What is it, Jill?" I asked.

"Someone came down violently, down the hill in the cable car. Later he wound up here near the pulley."

We walked down to the bottom of the ravine, where there was a magnificent swimming pool. The pool itself was still in operating condition, and there was a pool house on the other side of it. Down here the sound of the music was largely muted, and one could hear one's voice again. Jill obviously had strong impressions now, and I asked her what she felt about the place.

"I feel that a very vicious man lived here once, but I don't think he is connected with the name Grace I got before. This may have been at a different time. Oh, he had some dogs, kind of like mastiffs. I think there were two and possibly three. They were vicious dogs, trained to be vicious."

"What did this man do?"

"I see him as a sportsman, quick with words. There were also two young people connected with this man, a boy and a girl. I see them laughing and romping about and having a wonderful time here as teenagers. He seems not to like it at all but is tolerating it. But the dogs seemed to have played a very big part in his life. Nobody would dare enter his property without his permission because of those dogs. Permission, I feel, was rarely given except with a purpose in mind. He has exerted the strongest influence on this house, but I don't think he was the first owner."

"Do you feel that anyone well-known was connected with this house?"

"Yes. More than one well-known person, in fact." I asked Jill to describe the personality that she felt was strongest in the atmosphere of the house.

"I see this man with a small moustache, dark thinning hair, exceedingly vain, with a hawklike nose. He has brownish eyes; they have dark circles under them. He doesn't look dissipated by an excess of drink or food, but he does look dissipated through his own excesses. That is, his own mind's excesses. He prides himself on having the eye of the eagle and so affects an eagle-eyed look. I also suspect that he is nearsighted. I see him wearing a lot of smoking jackets. One in particular of maroon color."

The description sounded more and more fascinating. What profession did she think the man followed?

"I see him with a microphone in his hand, also a cigarette and a glass. He might be an actor or he might be a director."

I asked Jill whether this man owned the house or was merely a visitor.

The question seemed to puzzle her. "He might be a visitor, but I see him down here so much he might be staying here. The young people I described before might belong to the owner of the house."

I wondered if the man in the maroon jacket was one of the disturbing entities in the house.

Jill nodded. "I think this man is as well aware now of what he does as when he was alive. *I think he is still here.*"

"Can you get an indication of his name?"

"I get the letter *S*, but that's because he reminds me so much of Salvador Dalí."

"Anything else?"

"Yes, there is an *L* connected with him. The *L* stands for a name like Lay or Lee or Leigh, something like that. Oh, and there is something else. A Royal typewriter is important. I don't know if it's important to him because he writes letters or what, but *Royal* is important."

I was about to turn to the owner of the house when Jill's arm shot up, pointing to the balcony. "That woman up there—she acts very much the owner of the house. I imagine it's Grace." Since none of us could see the woman, I asked Jill for description of what she saw.

"She's a woman in her sixties, with gray or white hair. And it's very neat. She is very statuesque—slender and tall—and she wears a long flowing dress that has pleats all over. She seems to be raising her hand always, very dramatically, like an actress."

I thanked Jill for her work and turned to Marie, the owner of the house. How did all this information stack up with the knowledge she had of the background of her house—for instance, the business of telephones ringing incessantly when there were no telephones about?

"At one time this house was owned by a group of gamblers. They had telephones all over the house. This goes back several years."

"What about this Grace?"

"The name rings a bell with me, but I can't place it."

"And the baby Heidi keeps hearing?"

"Well, of course, the house used to belong to actor Lionel Barrymore. He and his wife had two babies who died in a fire, although it was not in this house."

Apparently Lionel Barrymore had owned this house, while his brother John lived not far away on Tower Road. Thus John was in a very good position to visit the house frequently. Jill had spoken of a man she saw clairvoyantly as reminding her of Salvador Dalí. That, we all agreed, was a pretty good description of the late John Barrymore. Jill had also mentioned the name Lee or Leigh or something like it. Perhaps she was reaching for Lionel.

The mention of the word *Royal* I found particularly fascinating. On the one hand, the Barrymores were often referred to as the royal family of the theater. On the other hand, if a typewriter was meant, one must keep in mind that John Barrymore had been hard at work on his autobiography in his later years, though he had never completed it. Yet the matter of finishing it had been very much on his mind. As for the teenagers Jill felt around the premises, the two children, Diana and John, Jr., had been at the house a great deal when they were teenagers. John Barrymore, however, didn't like children at all; he merely tolerated them.

I asked Marie (who had been here for more than a year prior to our visit) if she had ever seen or heard anything uncanny.

"No, but I can feel a presence."

The house has twelve rooms altogether, but according to local tradition, the three bottom rooms were added on somewhat later. "Has anything tragic ever occurred in this house, to your knowledge?"

"A man fell down those stairs head first and was killed. But it was an accident."

Obviously the house had been lived in for many years both before and after the Barrymore tenancy. It seems only natural that other emotional events would leave their mark in the atmosphere of the old house. Despite all this, Jill was able to pick up the personalities of both John and Lionel Barrymore and perhaps even of sister Ethel, if she was the lady in the gray robe. We left the house with a firm promise to dig into the Hall of Records for further verification.

Two weeks later I received a letter from Paula Davidson. She was having lunch with a friend of hers, director William Beaudine, Sr., who had been well acquainted with both John and Lionel Barrymore. Paula mentioned her experience at the house with Jill and me and the description given by Jill of the entity she had felt present in the house. When she mentioned the vicious dogs, Mr. Beaudine remarked that he remembered only too well that John had kept some Great Danes. They might very well have been the vicious dogs described by Jill.

Since that time Paula Davidson moved away from the house on Summit Ridge. Others moved in, but no further reports came to me about the goings-on at the house. If the noisy party we witnessed during our visit was any indication of the mood of the house, it is most unlikely that the Barrymores will put in an appearance. For if there was one thing the royal family of the theatre disliked, it was noisy competition.

The Ghost
in the Closet

I N 1964, I WAS LECTURING FOR the American Society for Psychic Research in Los Angeles, and a good many people came forward to tell of their own psychic experiences, especially those involving ghosts and apparitions. In fact, so many people attended this lecture, and so many more got in touch with me afterwards about their own experiences, that the Society got worried about it, and I haven't spoken for them since. Small wonder, for I never mince words and I don't send my audience home wondering if the speaker really believes what he is telling his public. My cases are well documented and I call a spade a spade—er, a ghost a ghost!

One of the people who could not get to hear me speak was a lady named Verna Kunze. She had seen a ghost and I asked her to make a written statement about her experience. A practical and factual woman, Mrs. Kunze did not hesitate to do so.

"I had purchased an apartment building in San Bernardino, California, on G Street, which had formerly been a nun's home on E Street closer in town. Undoubtedly it had been a single dwelling mansion at one time.

"The upper right hand apartment was most suited to my needs and the one I was occupying during the time—September 1957 to October 1960.

"After I had lived there for some months I came in from a shopping trip and, going to the closet in the front bedroom, opened the door to hang up my coat. There I saw very clearly, standing inside the closet in front of the door, a man of medium height (about 5' 8"), round face, fair complexion, dressed in clothing about the style of the early 1900s, pink and white striped shirt, no coat, high stiff turned-over collar, sailor straw hat on his head, nondescript tan trousers and button shoes—I think they were brown with white trim. Garters to hold up his sleeves were on his arms.

"At first I was so startled (not scared) that I couldn't say anything but while I was staring at him, the picture faded from sight.

"I saw him again in the same position, same clothing, in exactly the same manner on three other occasions.

"Being rather psychic but not a medium, I asked the Supreme Deity for protection and thought nothing of it. After about the third appearance, I asked that he depart, asked God's blessing on him and saw him no more. However, on the last impression, it seemed to me that he might have been murdered and stood in the closet to be hidden—or had committed a murder and was hiding in the closet. He was as clear in picture as though he were real. I told a medium friend about it who visited me a short time later but no one else.

"Later I sold the apartment and returned to Santa Ana to live. I do not know who owns the apartment building now as it has changed hands since."

I was traveling a great deal and it wasn't until the fall of 1966 that I finally got around to the ghost in San Bernardino. I got in touch with Mrs. Kunze to see if anything had happened, or at any rate if she could arrange for us to visit her old apartment.

Mrs. Kunze went to see the current owners of the house and found them somewhat hesitant about the whole business. They had not received any complaints from anyone about ghosts and would just as well let sleeping ghosts lie. But Mrs. Kunze is a persuasive person, having spent many years working for the immigration service. She promised not to divulge the exact address of the house or the name of the current owners, and finally an appointment was made for us to have a look at the house in October 1966. Fortunately, the tenant of the corner apartment we were interested in had just vacated and the new owner had not yet moved in—so we would find an empty flat.

In return for so much spade work, I promised Mrs. Kunze to address the Psynetics Foundation in nearby Santa Ana, a group in which she was active. The visit to their headquarters was a most pleasurable experience.

After we arrived in Los Angeles, I phoned Mrs. Kunze again to make sure we had access to the apartment, for the drive to San Bernardino takes two hours and it was one of the periodic hot spells the area suffers—so I wanted to be sure we were welcome. All was in readiness, and we arrived at the house on schedule, at four in the afternoon on a hot October day.

The house sat back from the street, a modest yellow stucco building of two stories which belied its age, which was, I later discovered, considerable for this part of the world.

A dark-haired lady received me at the door, while Catherine and Sybil Leek remained in the car, out of earshot. Mrs. Kunze also came out to greet me. I then fetched the others, and without saying anything pertaining to the house, we left the dark-haired lady, who was the landlady, downstairs and walked up to the second floor where we followed Sybil into the "right" apartment. She knew just where to go.

Mrs. Kunze sat down in one of the chairs, Sybil stretched out on the bed and we waited for what might happen now. We did not have to wait long, for Sybil instantly got the scent of things.

"Death and destruction," she said, "comparatively recent. This is an absolutely horrible place."

She shivered, though the temperature outside was above 90 degrees. I, too, felt a chill and it wasn't the power of suggestion, either.

"I think death has hung over this place for some time,"

Sybil elaborated now. "If there was anyone in it I would warn them not to be here."

"Is any entity present?" I asked casually, for I already knew the place was haunted. What I did not know of course was the story behind the haunting or anything more than what Mrs. Kunze had originally written me. And Sybil had no knowledge of that, either.

"I seem to be attracted to the bathroom and that little door there," Sybil commented. "The bathroom has some significance in this. Stomach feels irritated."

"What about any structural changes ?" I interjected.

"I haven't paid attention to that, for the overwhelming influence is of terribly brooding, resentful . . . death. Like having my head in a piece of *black velvet*. Something hanging right over me."

"Does it involve violent death ?"

"Yes. Suffocation. But then again, I have this sickness of the stomach, but that may be associated with someone here. . . ."

"Is it murder, suicide, or accidental death?"

"*Two people* are involved. A murder, because of the resentfulness. Connection with the door. Not clear yet. An usurper, a person who should not be here."

"How far back do we go here?"

"It could be now . . . it seems very close. Recent."

"Describe the person you feel present here."

"A slightly round-faced lady . . . funny, I keep getting another house!"

Sybil interrupted herself. She knew nothing of the fact that this house had been moved to its present site from another place.

"Where is the other house?" I asked.

"The person who is here was involved with *another* house. Tall, thin trees nearby. Two houses . . . the other is a pleasant house . . . light colored car. . . ."

I asked Sybil to look at the woman again, if she could.

"Hair short in neck. . . ." Sybil said, gradually becoming more and more in trance, "I can't find the body, though . . . one part of her is here and one part of her is there . . ."

"Is she present now?"

"I follow her. . . ."

"Is she in this room?"

"Yes . . . and then she goes . . . Don . . ."

"What is her occupation?"

"The voice . . . voice . . . she runs away . . . somebody mustn't know, she says . . . she is very vain . . ."

"How is she dressed?"

"Black head," Sybil said. It struck me suddenly that Sybil might be describing a nun's habit.

"Why is the black head here?" Sybil now demanded to know.

But Sybil was speaking of a black *face*.

"Light car, black face," she mumbled.

"Why is she here?" I wanted to know.

"Waiting for . . . this isn't her home. Waiting for relief. Somebody came to take her away from here. A woman. Because she did not live here."

"How did she get here then?"

"She needed to stay here to wait for things . . . to come to her."

"Whose place is this?"

"Don't know . . . knew someone here. The little car, light car. D-o-n."

"What happened to her here?"

"She—was—suffocating—sick to stomach—head and neck—"

"Did she commit suicide?"

"No."

"Was she murdered?"

"Don't say that!"

"Was she killed?"

"Yes . . ."

"By whom?"

"Don."

"Why did he kill her?"

"From the house . . . somebody made her come here . . ."

I explained, via Sybil, that she must not stay on here. But it did not go down well with the elusive ghost.

"Wants to be alone here," Sybil reported.

"What is troubling her?"

"Mistaken identity. She was . . . misjudged . . . the *other house*. . . ."

Had someone accused this woman of something she did not do? Was she a nun?

"Verraco," Sybil said, clearly. It did not ring a bell with Mrs. Kunze, who was observing the proceedings closely. Nor, of course, with me.

"I don't know what it means . . . Verraco," Sybil said.

"Does she realize she is dead?"

"No, she thinks she is sick."

"Can she hear you?"

"She understands, but then she goes away again. I have to go after her."

I asked Sybil to instruct the ghost about her true status.

"Man . . . doesn't trust him," Sybil reported. Had the ghost woman been hurt by a man and did she therefore not trust any other man?

Sybil nodded, that was it. But it was of no avail.

"Go away, she says," Sybil continued, "people upset her, nobody understands what she feels like. Very unhappy woman."

There was a moment of interruption, when I changed tapes. Meanwhile, Sybil startled us with an expression that did not seem to fit in.

"Sing to me," she said, in a drowsy tone, "she was singing . . . she likes music . . . she was misjudged . . . two people, two lives . . . *she was two people . . .*"

I kept coaxing her to confess.

"Suppose he comes back again. . . ." There was terror in Sybil's voice now.

I promised to protect her. She remained doubtful. How did I know?

"I have the power to send him away," I assured her.

"What is the truth about her?"

"The truth is that she did nothing to hurt the woman; that was a misunderstanding."

"Who is the other woman?"

"E.K."

"Where does she live?"

"Verracho." It had been "Verraco" before.

"And Don?"

"Man with light car and dark face."

"Does he know the woman, E.K.?"

"Yes."

"Did she send him here?"

"She knew."

"Was she behind it?"

"She organized it . . . to destroy."

"What is her name . . . the one who is here?"

With ghosts, if you don't succeed at first, try again.

"A.D.," Sybil said softly.

"What year are we in?" I asked.

"Today . . . September . . . 16 . . . '63 . . . lot of people round the house, strange people . . . just looking around . . . she is here watching . . . body in the bathroom. . . ."

Was the ghost re-living the discovery of her body?

"Tell her the world knows that she is innocent," I intoned.

Sybil, still under the spell of the entity, reacted almost violently. "She *is* innocent!"

I kept reassuring her. Finally, Sybil said: "She will sing . . . A.D. . . . Must not return here ever . . . She is gone now. . . ."

Deeply breathing now, Sybil was completely "out" for a few moments, prior to taking over her own body once again.

I then brought Sybil quickly to herself, but for some time after, she kept feeling quite uncomfortable and sighed with relief when we left the place.

Mrs. Kunze, who had witnessed all this, had nodded several times during the hour. I now wanted to find out if there was anything she could add to the brief testimony she had given me originally.

"Did this apparition you told me about ever look at you?" I inquired. The man with "the German face" in the straw hat must have been quite a sight greeting her from the open closet door—very dead.

"No, he did not," Mrs. Kunze replied. "I immediately got the impression that he was dead. His eyes did not move. A minute later he was gone and I hung up my coat."

A month later, when he reappeared to her, he did not stay as long, she explained, but the view was the same.

The third time she started to pray for him, and instead of fading away as on the previous occasions, he disappeared like a flash.

"Weren't you curious about the apartment? I mean, didn't you make some inquiries about its previous occupants?"

"I did not. I knew when I bought the place that it had been the home of nuns, and the house had been moved here after some years from another location—where the Junior High School now stands. The building is at least sixty years old. There may have been two or three other owners before I purchased it. It was remodeled around 1953 or '54. Until then it belonged to the nuns."

Again I questioned her about the appearance of the ghost. She stuck to her story. The man was more 1903 than 1953.

"At that time there were certainly nuns here," she commented.

Had she had other uncanny experiences in this haunted apartment?

"Only this," Mrs. Kunze replied. "In my inspirational work, I found I could not work here. My guides told me this was an evil house. But I haven't heard anything."

"How long have you yourself been psychic?"

"When I was about thirteen, I was invited to a Sunday school party, and I was a stranger in the neighborhood, not knowing anyone there. That was in Columbus, Ohio. About a week before the party I told my mother that I had dreamt of and had seen this party, the girls there and even the pictures on the wall—in great detail. A week later I went and recognized it all."

"Have you had any other premonitions?"

"A number of them. I do automatic writing, and a lot of predictions have thus been dictated to me by what I call my masters, my spiritual guides."

I decided we should leave metaphysics alone, and turn to the business at hand.

"About the material obtained just now through Sybil Leek," I said, "does any of it ring a bell with you?"

"Well, she certainly got the business with the two houses," Mrs. Kunze commented. "This house was in two locations, as you know."

"What about the trees surrounding the house?" In this part of California, trees are not common and would naturally be a landmark.

"Probably so," Mrs. Kunze said, "and she mentioned a face covered with black velvet—could that not be a nun covered with a coif?"

"Could be," I agreed. "It seems strange, though, that you haven't felt a female influence here, or have you?"

"Not at all," Mrs. Kunze confirmed, "but I felt from the looks of the *man* that he had either committed a murder or done something very wrong. I just felt it as I saw him there in the closet. I suppose he had jumped in there to avoid detection."

Evidently Mrs. Kunze had seen the ghost of the murderer while Sybil found the ghost of the victim. Now if Mrs. Kunze's prayer had indeed freed the ghost from the spot where his crime had been committed, then it was only natural that Sybil did not feel him any longer there.

At the same time, if Mrs. Kunze felt the overpowering tragedy of the murderer tied to the spot of the crime, it would have blotted out the comparatively weaker presence of the victim, who after all, was not guilty of *anything!*

I discovered that the building in its original site faced a Catholic school. Thus a convent would not have been out of place here.

On November 5, 1960, Mrs. Kunze moved out of the haunted apartment to a new house in nearby Santa Ana. The ghost, of course, did not move along with her, for the new apartment was free from any and all psychic influences, pleasant, in fact, in every sense of the word.

While she lived at the San Bernardino address, the evil atmosphere of the place seemed to have taken its toll of her day-to-day life. Everything she seemed to touch went wrong; her personal life was a shambles—apparently for no logical reason. The moment she moved away from the apartment, all went well. Suggestion? Not really. The facts were quite solid.

As for the empty apartment in San Bernardino, it is all ready for the new tenant to move in.

"I wouldn't take this place for nothing," Sybil mumbled, as she rushed past me down the stairs and into the street.

Considering the fact that Sybil had been apartment-shopping with a vengeance at the time, the victim of the ghost in the closet must have made quite an impression on her.

At any rate, the restless nun doesn't live there any more.

The Ghostly Eviction

SOMETIMES THE GHOSTLY DENIZENS drive the living out—only to find themselves without a home in the end. Such was the strange case of a house in Paso Robles owned by the Adams family. I heard about their predicament when I appeared on the "Art Linkletter Show."

Mrs. Adams had three children, aged 11, 10, and 9. Their problem: the house they bought used to be a "red light house," as she put it. Before they bought it, two ladies lived there with an old man as a kind of chaperon. After the police forced the girls out of business, the old man remained behind until his death.

Shortly after moving in, the Adams family noticed that all was not well with their home. The husband worked nights, and at the time he went to work between the hours of midnight and 3 A.M., strange noises were heard outside the house, such as banging on the wall—only nobody human was doing it. This was in December of 1957. Gradually, the noises changed from a slight rattle to a big, loud bang on the walls. Occasionally it sounded as if someone were ripping the window screens off the house.

Mrs. Adams called the police repeatedly, but they could not find anything or anyone causing the disturbances. Her husband, who worked in a bakery, also heard the noises one night when he stayed home. Always around the same time, in the early morning hours.

Soon Mrs. Adams also distinguished footsteps and human voices when nobody was walking or talking. On one occasion she clearly heard two men talking, one saying he would try to get into the house. Then there were knocks on the walls as if someone were trying to communicate.

It got so bad that the Adamses started to make inquiries about the past of their property, and it was then, two years after they had moved in, that they finally learned the truth about the house and its former use.

They decided to let the ghosts have the house and moved out, to another house which had always been free from any disturbances. The haunted red light house they rented out to people not particular about ghosts. But they did not do too well at that. Nobody liked to stay in the house for long.

That was in 1964. When I checked up on Mrs. Adams a few years later, things had changed quite a lot.

"They tore it up repeatedly," Mrs. Adams explained, and since it was an old house, the owners did not feel like putting a lot of money into it to fix the damage done by the nightly "party."

It got to be under standard and the city council stepped in. Thus it was that the ghost house of Paso Robles was torn down by official order. The Adams family now owned an empty lot on which they couldn't afford to build a new house. And the ghosts? They had no place to go to, either. Serves them right!

The Restless Dead

NOT ONLY HOUSES CAN BE haunted, but people as well. There are literally thousands of cases where people have seen or heard the ghost of a dead person, usually a person with unfinished business on his mind at the time death overtook him.

Let me set down my criteria for such experience, so that we understand what we are dealing with. When a person dreams of a dead relative this may or may not have significance. When the dream includes specific details unknown to the dreamer at the time and later found correct, then the dreamer is getting a psychic message in the dream state when his unconscious is free from the conscious mind and thus easier to reach.

I have examined hundreds upon hundreds of cases and carefully eliminated the doubtful or hallucinatory. What remains is hardcore evidence.

California, land of sunshine and pleasant living, has a great many such incidents, perhaps because death here is something alien, something that does not quite fit with the warmth and serenity of climate and outlook.

Take the case of Mrs. A., in Santa Susana, for instance. Mrs. A. was not a person given to belief in the supernatural. In fact, her total disbelief that the events that shook her up in 1958 were in any way psychic caused her to contact me. Somehow the "rational" explanation—grief over the passing of her husband—did not satisfy her eager mind and ultimately she wanted to know.

Her husband and Mrs. A. were working on their boat in the backyard on a warm California day. Suddenly, she heard him cry out "Honey!" as if in pain. He had been working with an electric sander at the time. Alarmed, Mrs. A. turned around in time to see him clutching the sander to his chest. He had been accidentally electrocuted. Quickly she pulled the electric plug out and tried to hold him up, all the while screaming for help; but it was too late.

The ironical part was that A. had had nightmares and waking fears about just such an accident—death from electrocution.

Two months went by and Mrs. A. tried to adjust to her widowhood. One night she was roused from deep sleep by "something" in the room. As soon as she was fully awake she perceived an apparition of her late husband, suspended in the air of their room!

He did not make any sound or say anything. Strangely enough, the apparition wore no shirt; he was bare-chested, as he would not have been in life.

In a moment he was gone, and Mrs. A. went back to sleep. In the morning she convinced herself that it was just a case of nerves. The day wore on. It was 4:30 in the afternoon and Mrs. A. was seated on her living room couch, relaxing and waiting for a telephone call from her mother. All of a sudden, she heard her car drive up to the door. She realized at once that this could not be the case, since she was not driving it, but it struck her also that this was the precise time her husband always drove up to the door, every afternoon!

Before she could fully gather her wits, he was there in the room with her. He looked as he had always looked, not transparent or anything as ethereal as that. Mrs. A. was literally frozen with fear. Her late husband knelt before her seemingly in great emotion, exclaiming, "Honey, what's wrong ?"

At this point, Mrs. A. found her tongue again and quietly, as quietly as she was able to, told her late husband what had happened to him.

"There has been an accident, and you were killed."

When she had said those words, he uttered the same sound he did at the time of the accident—"Honey!" as if remembering it—and instantly he vanished.

Mrs. A. never felt him around her again since. Evidently, her husband adjusted to his new state.

Ralph Madison was a man who lived life and enjoyed every moment of it. He was a great-grandfather four times over and not a young man, but he was still working in 1965, when I heard his strange story, as a part-time security guard in the museum at Stanford University.

He made his home in Palo Alto, and had been married to the same woman since 1916. Not boasting much formal education, Madison considered himself a self-made man. Perhaps the only thing unusual about him was a penchant to send people tape recordings instead of letters. But perhaps Madison was only being practical. And, the time may come when we may all correspond in a way other than letters.

I would not be interested in Mr. Madison if it weren't for one particular incident in his life, an incident that made him wonder about his sanity—and, after having reassured himself about it—about the meaning of such psychic experiences.

It happened in 1928 in Palo Alto, on Emerson Street. Ralph Madison was minding his own business, walking in the vicinity of the five-hundred block, when he noticed a man he knew slightly, by the name of Knight. Mr. Knight operated a cleaning establishment nearby. The two men stopped to talk and Madison shook hands with his acquaintance.

It struck him as peculiar, however, that the man's voice seemed unusually wispy. Moreover, Knight's hands were clammy and cold!

They exchanged some words of no particular significance, and then they parted. Madison started out again and then quickly glanced around at his friend. The man he had just shaken hands with had disappeared into thin air. At this moment it came to him with shocking suddenness that Mr. Knight had been dead and buried for five years.

In a high state of excitement, Madison ran into a real estate office operated nearby by a Mr. Vandervoort whom he knew well. Quickly relating what had happened to him, Madison was assured that Knight had indeed been dead for five years and that he, Madison, was seeing things.

But Ralph Madison knew in his heart he shook hands with a dead man on a street corner in Palo Alto, in plain daylight.

A strange case came to my attention, strange among strange experiences in that it involves a kind of possession against which orthodox medicine seems to be powerless.

At least Mrs. B. of Burlingame went to six doctors for help, took countless nerve tonics and calming agents—but to no avail. When she heard of my work in ESP, she contacted me with a cry for help. This was in March of 1966 and I finally talked to her in October of the same year. Her voice was firm and there was no sign of panic in it. Still, what had happened to her would cause a lot of stronger people to throw in the towel in a struggle against insanity.

Now a widow, Mrs. B. originally came from the Middle West where her father had been a physician, as were his father and grandfather before him. Her mother had been a high school teacher and she was the daughter of a Senator.

Mrs. B. taught school also and later took up nursing as a profession. She was married from 1949 to 1960 and considered her marriage a most happy one. No emotional turmoils followed her widowhood, since Mrs. B. was an avid reader and musician and had surrounded herself with congenial friends. One could safely say that her life was serene and well ordered.

But it took her three letters, before she could commit to paper the shocking experiences that had suddenly entered her life. I always insisted on written statements from those reporting seemingly paranormal cases, and Mrs. B. reluctantly complied. It was her feeling of shame that prompted me to omit her full name from this account.

It started with a presence in the room with her, when she knew that she was quite alone. Before long, she felt the intimacies of another person on her body a person she could not see!

She thought she was ill and consulted every conceivable specialist, but got a clean bill of health. Yet, the attacks continued. Was she imagining the unspeakable? She began to question her own sanity. The physicians she consulted knew no answer except to reassure her that she had no physical ailment to account for the strange sensations.

Now I had heard similar stories about "attacks" by sex-minded ghosts before and sometimes they are the imagination of a frustrated person. Thus it was with extreme caution that I accepted the testimony of this lady. I wanted to be sure the case was psychic, not psychiatric.

I questioned her along ESP lines. Had she ever had psychic experiences—other than the very graphically described invasions of her privacy—in the house she lived in, or elsewhere?

Apparently, the answer was affirmative. Some months before her contacting me, she was doing housework on a Sunday, when she heard a voice speak to her, apparently out of thin air, a voice she did not recognize but which sounded rather low and was speaking in a whisper.

"The G.'s are coming today." Now the G.'s were friends of Mrs. B.'s living at some distance. She had not seen or heard from them for months, thus was not expecting their visit in any way. Consequently, Mrs. B. refused to believe the strange "voice." But the voice insisted, repeating the sentence once more!

Mrs. B. continued with her work, when around 1 P.M. she decided to take a rest. At 2 o'clock, the doorbell rang. Since she was not expecting any visitors, she was slow in answering it. It was the G.'s, just as the voice had said!

After that experience, the ghostly voice was heard by Mrs. B. many times, always announcing someone's coming. The voice never erred. The name, day and sometimes even the exact hour were given and each time it came to pass.

The presence of an unseen person continued to trouble Mrs. B. but in addition she heard a voice speak two words, "my wife," several times, and on another occasion, "her husband," as if someone were trying to tell her something she should know.

Mrs. B., of course, rejected the idea that it might be her own late husband who was haunting her, for he never believed in anything psychic while in the flesh. Shortly after this line of thought, she clearly heard the voice say, "She just does not understand."

When I was ready to see Mrs. B. in Burlingame, which is near San Francisco, she had already moved to another house in Santa Monica. It was there that I finally talked to her.

The situation was much the same, it appeared, ruling out any possibility that the ghost or invader was somehow tied up with the house in Burlingame.

The voice, which she still did not recognize, was very insistent now.

"Her husband . . . she just does not understand" was followed on another occasion by a statement, "I would do anything in the world . . . I wonder what she would do if she knew."

Then the words "sweetheart" and "my wife" were added and repeated on many occasions. All this happened to Mrs. B. in a house in which she was quite alone at the time.

Still, Mrs. B. refused to face the possibility that her husband, skeptic though he might had been in the physical state, had learned the truth about psychic communications and was now trying to reach her—in the way *a husband might!*

Sometimes the tragedies that make people of flesh and blood into non-physical ghosts were less horrifying than the ghosts that continue a kind of forlorn existence in the world in between—or rather I should say the ghosts were not the comparatively benign apparitions of people as we knew them, but something far more terrible, far more sinister.

Wayne Barber was a young ambulance driver who used to run the service out of Baker, California, one of the worst stretches of road because of the many automobile accidents that have happened on it. Now it is my personal opinion that half the people driving cars should not, and, furthermore, that licenses should be renewed only after annual examinations of those who qualify for them. What happened to Mr. Barber was only one case in point.

Aged 29 years, six feet tall and married, Wayne Barber was a rough and tough man who, as he put it, "can eat a ham sandwich in complete comfort with dead bodies all over the highway." It was part of his business and he wasn't the least bit sentimental about it.

Until February 1966 he had absolutely no belief in anything resembling the human soul, anything beyond death. But then something pretty terrible happened.

On Washington's Birthday there was a wreck about five miles east of Baker, California, in which seven people died. A group of three drunks was heading down the freeway in the wrong direction and had a head-on collision with a carload of people going to Las

Vegas. In this car a mother and father were taking their daughter and her fiancé to be married!

The car headed in the wrong direction burned before the bodies could be removed. The others, mother and father, were pinned in their car and the two children that were to be married were thrown clear. All seven were dead.

"Any wreck involving the living is worse than handling the dead," Barber explained, "and this was not the worst wreck my attendant and I had ever handled. I am mentioning this so you don't think we had a case of nerves."

After making certain there were no survivors, they cleared the bodies off the highway and started to check them for identification. Removing the bodies was part of an ambulance crew's work, and Barber and his aide did just that—or what was left of the bodies—in order to clear the road for traffic.

A day later a sandstorm came up, and five women travelers in the area could not proceed because of poor visibility on the road. They appealed to Barber to put them up overnight at the ambulance station, and he readily agreed. He then went to the rear of the building to put together five cots for them from his supplies of standby equipment.

It was around 10:30 P.M. and the yard lights failed to work. He could see only about five feet, but he carried a small flashlight. As he busied himself on the standby rig near the corner of the building, he suddenly felt himself *watched*. Who would be standing there watching him in the driving storm?

He spun around and faced something he had never faced before.

There at arm's length was what he later described as "a thing," a terribly mutilated figure of a human being, a boy, with legs hanging crookedly, just as they had been compounded in the accident, the body twisted at the waist and the head hanging at a weird angle, indicating a broken neck. But the eyes were watching him, looking straight into his—living, human eyes!

Barber was frozen to the spot long enough to observe every detail of the horrible apparition.

"There was a sad longing in the eyes, and gratitude," Barber said afterwards. "In those eyes there was no intention to harm me."

Suddenly, his reactions returned and he tore into the ghost with his flashlight as if it were a knife. But he was thrashing thin air, and nothing but sand hit his face!

At this point his German shepherd, a very rugged animal, came out of the darkness howling, out of his senses with fear. Barber continued on back to the house with the stretchers for the cots. It was then that he saw what he calls "the other thing." This one was a girl. He did not see as many details of this ghost as he had observed of the male apparition, but he saw her outline clearly. It was enough for him to take a day off immediately.

But the dog was not the same for weeks, becoming a complete nervous wreck until he had to be given away to a sympathetic lady. Soon after, he was run over and killed.

Barber married after this experience and he had no intention of ever talking about it to his new bride. But the dog he had acquired to take the place of the shepherd soon behaved in the most extraordinary fashion also, precisely the same as the shepherd. What was the dog seeing around the place? Barber then told his wife about the two ghosts.

The second dog had to be given away, too, when he became unmanageable in the place. But, Barber had a pug dog who seemed to be able to tolerate the influences that still pervaded the spot a little better than his two predecessors.

"Something here is protecting me," Wayne Barber explained, and he and his wife refer to the ghosts somewhat bravely as "the little people."

Had the spirits of those two who never lived out their normal lives attached themselves to their rescuer?

Mrs. Daphne R. lived in Malibu, California, with her husband and children. Her second husband was a Navy man and they had moved frequently. Originally English, Mrs. R. had had a number of psychic experiences and was unquestionably mediumistic. But the incident I found most fascinating had to do with a ghost her little daughter encountered. It interested me because not all the restless dead are hopeless, pathetic human beings in trouble, unable to help themselves. This ghost even helped another person. It happened in 1952.

"I was working in Heidelberg as a secretary, and I had a little three-year-old daughter from a broken marriage, who lived with my parents in England. I got awfully lonely, and increasingly sure that I ought to bring her over to Germany to live with me. So one day I flew over to England, and rode the train down to Folkestone, collected the child and her belongings and took her back to London. I had to wait a few days for her papers, so I stayed at the private home of a friend, a rather well-known photographer.

"He was most kind, and offered to put my daughter and me up for the time we had to spend in London. He was a widower. I hardly saw him, as he was out all the time on assignments. He had a small boy of around four or five, and an English nanny. They lived in a rather posh narrow house.

"One night I wanted to go to the theatre, and asked the nanny if she would baby-sit for me and keep an eye on my little girl. I should add here that the child was in a terrible emotional state about leaving my parents (I was almost like a stranger to her), and she wept all the time, and seemed calmer with the nanny than with me.

"Anyway, I went out, and left the little girl in the double bed we were sharing, and the nanny promised to pop in and out of the bedroom to watch her, as the little boy had also gone to bed nearby. I wore a black suit—which is an item of importance. When I got back around 11 P.M., the nanny was in the kitchen, and she said Kitty had cried quite a bit (not for me, but for my parents, whom she missed), and that suddenly she had been quiet, so the nanny had run up to take a peek at her, and she was fast asleep and smiling in her sleep. The next morning I awakened, and the child was in a very happy mood, so much so that I said to her that I was so happy to see her smiling for the first time in about two days, and that perhaps she was a bit happier about going to live with Mummy in Germany. She replied that yes, she was very happy. Then she said, 'I was unhappy last night, and I cried, because I wanted my Nana (she referred to my mother), but then the LADY came over to my bed and stroked my head and told me you were out and would be back soon, and that she would stay with me until you got back.' I merely thought she was referring to the 'nanny' in the house, and said 'Yes, nanny is a nice lady,' and my daughter said, 'Oh no, it wasn't the nanny, it was a pretty lady with long red hair, and she was beautiful.' Then she went on to prattle about how the 'Lady' had told her how much Mummy loved her, and how unhappy it made Mummy to see the child cry, and that really it was much better for her to be with her mother than with her grandparents, and the child ended up saying 'I realized she is right, Mummy.'

"Later that day, I asked the nanny if she had had a guest, and when she said no, I told her about the above incident, and she was quite aghast, and related to me that her master's late wife had long red hair, and was a beautiful woman, but had been very unhappy, and I suppose nowadays we would think she was mentally unbalanced; apparently she threw herself from the balcony of the room in which my daughter and I had been sleeping. She was so interested in this— the nanny, I mean—that she asked my daughter what the 'lovely lady' had been wearing, and Kitty, my daughter, said, 'A lovely long blue satin nightie,' and later the nanny said that the late lady of the house had committed suicide in a blue satin evening house-gown."

Maureen B. was a San Francisco housewife when I met her, but in 1959, when her first brush with the uncanny took place, she was attending college summer school and living by herself in the old house her parents, Mr. and Mrs. John F., had bought recently on Toravel Street.

Records showed the house dated back to 1907, which was pretty old for the area. The parents had gone away on vacation and Maureen should have had the place to herself—but she didn't.

Sometimes she would stay awake all night because she had the feeling of not being alone in the house. There was *something* or *someone* staring at her—someone she could not see!

The tension made her ill, but nothing further happened until the summer of 1960 when she found herself studying late one night in the breakfast room downstairs.

Although physically tired, she was mentally quite alert. The door leading to the back porch, where the pantry was situated, was locked from the inside, and the key was in the lock. The door leading from this back porch into the yard outside was double-locked and the key was hidden away. None of the windows in the old house would open.

Nevertheless Maureen suddenly heard, in the still of the night, a swishing sound from the other side of the door, followed by footsteps and the clinking of a chain. Her heart pounded with fear as she sat there frozen, staring at the door. The key in it was turning and a voice outside the door was moaning.

For a couple of moments Maureen sat still. Then she gathered up her wits and ran up the stairs and roused her father. Quickly he came down and unlocked the door, and searched the back porch and the yard. There was nobody to be seen.

The next day the family decided that Maureen "must have heard" streetcar noises from the street. As for the key turning in the lock, why, that was just her overtired eyes playing tricks on her.

Maureen knew differently, for she had lived with the noises of streetcars for a long time and the moan she had heard outside the door was no streetcar. And the key moved back and forth in the lock before her eyes. It did not make a clicking sound, however, as it does when it engages the lock to unlock the door. Since the rest of the family had not experienced anything out of the ordinary in the house and did not accept the possibility of the psychic, Maureen found it convenient to let the matter drop, even though she found out a few things about the house her folks had acquired back in 1957.

It had been an antique shop previously, and prior to that an old invalid had lived there. His bed was near the front window giving onto the street, so that he could watch the goings-on outside in the way old people often want to—it gives them a feeling of not being shut-ins, but still part of the active world. By the time he died, the house was in deplorable condition and a real estate firm bought it and fixed it up.

For many years the old man had called this house his home, gradually becoming more and more invalided until death had taken him away from it. But had it?

When I appeared on a special television program with Regis Philbin in Los Angeles in the fall of 1966, on which we discussed ghosts and psychic experiences and illustrated them with some of the evidential photographs I had taken of such apparitions, many people wrote or called with psychic adventures of their own or houses they wanted me to investigate.

One of the most interesting cases involved a man not particularly friendly toward the possibility of personal survival or mediumship who had been forced by his experiences to re-evaluate his views.

Earle Burney was an ex-Marine who lived in San Diego. He was discharged from the Marine Corps in June 1945 and went to work for the Navy as a guard at a Navy Electronics Laboratory installed in an old mansion at Loma Portal, California. The work was highly classified, and security at the place was pretty strict as a consequence.

At first Burney's job was to guard the mansion during the night, coming in at 11:15 P.M. He knew nothing about the place, and the man he relieved, for some strange reason, never talked to him about the work—seconds after Burney got there, his predecessor was out the door, as if he could not get away fast enough to suit himself.

Burney then inspected the place from top to bottom, which was part of his routine. He locked the door he had come through and put a pot of coffee or the fire in the kitchen. The house had retained much of its ancient glory, with mahogany paneling and a big, winding stairway leading up to the second story. He was puzzled, though, by a bullet hole someone had put in one of the wall ventilators.

One morning not long after he had started his job, he was sitting at his watchman's desk drinking coffee, when he heard footsteps upstairs. It was just two o'clock and there was no one in the building besides himself.

Naturally, Burney jumped up immediately. The footsteps were heavy and were coming down the hallway toward the head of the stairs. Burney started up the stairs, but when he reached the top, the footsteps had stopped dead and there was nobody within sight.

He searched every inch of the house but could not find any human being who could had caused the footsteps.

After that, he heard the steps again a few more times, but by now he was not so excited over it. He decided to ascribe it to "the house settling or cooling off," although he could not really explain how such a noise could sound like human footsteps.

Then another phenomenon puzzled him even more. He would be sitting by his desk with only a small light burning, and the rest of the house as dark as could be. Still, he would hear music. The first time this happened, he thought that perhaps someone had left a radio on somewhere. But he found no radio anywhere. Then he discovered, as he searched the dark recesses of the old mansion, that the music was heard everywhere exactly the same way—no louder, no softer. It was faint, but then it would stop, and Burney realized he had not imagined it but had really heard "something."

Burney decided to take his little spaniel dog Amber with him for company. The dog was friendly and fun-loving, about as normal as a dog can be.

That night, he took her with him and made her lie down by his desk. No sooner had he done so than he noticed a strange change in the behavior of the animal. Suddenly very nervous, the dog would not go near the stairs, and just lay there near the desk, whining.

At two A.M. the ghostly footsteps came. The dog let out a blood-curdling scream and headed for the door. Burney let her out and she shot out into the dark, hitting an iron statue across the yard. Although not physically hurt, the dog was never the same after this incident. The slightest noise would frighten her and her fun-loving nature had given way to a pitiful existence full of neurotic fears.

Burney was very much puzzled by all this and decided to ask some questions at last.

He discovered that others had heard those nighttime footsteps too. In fact, there was a big turnover of guards at the mansion and the reason he, an ex-Marine, had been hired was primarily because of the strange events. They figured he would not be scared of a ghost. He wasn't, but the job was hard on him, nevertheless. Especially after he found out about the bullet hole in the wall ventilator. A frightened guard had put it there. But, of course, bullets don't stop ghosts.

The Restless Dead walk on, walk on. Some of them are lucky because someone cares and brings a medium to the house or calls a psychic to help. But for every restless one who gets help, there are a thousand who don't. I have come to the conclusion that there are literally thousands and thousands of houses where someone died unhappily in one way or another—not necessarily violently, but not peacefully—and still walks the floors. I wish I could help them all.